Terry H. White

from

Mom & Dad White

REQUIEM FOR A KINGFISH

REQUIEM

FOR A

KINGFISH

By Ed Reed

AWARD PUBLICATIONS/ED REED ORGANIZATION
Baton Rouge, Louisiana 1986

Jacket design by Andy Smith, Baton Rouge, Louisiana

First Printing October 1986
Second Printing November 1986

Composition by Lunar Graphics, Baton Rouge, Louisiana

The author gratefully acknowledges the assistance given by Charles East, Baton Rouge; Mmes. Harriett Callahan, Blanche Cretini and Pat Leeper of the Louisiana State Library; and Marshall Stone Miller, Jr., Head of the Manuscripts and Archives Office of Louisiana State University.

Acknolwedgement is made to Wilbur E. Meneray, Head of Rare Books and Manuscripts, Tulane University; G. Rollie Adams, Director, Louisiana State Museum; D. Clive Hardy, Archivist, University of New Orleans and Patricia Meador, LSU-Shreveport Archives for permission to reprint many of the excellent photographs in this volume.

0-9617384-0-5

Library of Congress Catalog Number: 86-71787

Printed and bound in Canada by John Deyell Company

To the women in my life, Lorraine, Michele, Colleen and Hope.

"And it is here under this oak where Evangeline waited for her lover, Gabriel. This oak is immortal but Evangeline is not the only one who waited here in disappointment. Where are the schools, the roads and highways, the institutions for the disabled you sent your money to build? Evangeline's tears lasted through one lifetime— yours through generations. Give me the chance to dry the eyes of those who still weep here."

Campaign speech by Huey Long, 1927
Restated by his son, U.S. Senator Russell B. Long on the Senate floor, September 10, 1985, the 50th anniversary of his father's death

"Mr. President, I am not undertaking to answer the charge that I am ignorant. It is true. I am an ignorant man. I have had no college education. I have not even had a high school education. But the thing that takes me far in politics is that I do not have to color what comes into my mind and into my heart. I say it unvarnished. I say it without veneer. I have not the learning to do otherwise and therefore my ignorance is often not detected. I know the hearts of people because I have not colored my own...I have one language. Ignorant as it is, it is a universal language within the sphere in which I operate. Its simplicity gains pardon for my lack of letters and education."

Spoken by Huey Long in the U.S. Senate
March 5, 1935

Table Of Contents

Preface

One of my earliest recollections about Huey Long has to do with a bloody nose that was visited upon me at the age of 10 by a neighbor boy of the same age. In New Orleans, on Bienville Street, it was common for neighbors to sit outside on their "stoops," small porch-like structures at the front of the shotgun houses that abounded in New Orleans at that time and still do. It was the summer of 1934 and a hot one at that.

My mother, one of my two sisters and my brothers were all outside.

I got into an argument with a boy, about my age, who lived next door. As I remember, we called him "Ikey," which was short for "Aloysius." I know this doesn't make a lot of sense but at the age of ten, who wants to be sensible?

My father and mother were both strongly pro-Huey Long. My father supported the man because of his pledges to redistribute the wealth. My mother seemed to feel that she had a personal friend in Washington and Baton Rouge as long as Huey Long was around. Since my father was a disabled Spanish-American War veteran and his pension was all we had to live on, we frequently had cash shortfalls. On occasion, the utility company would turn off the lights and when that happened (or when anything else unpleasant occurred) my mother would grit her teeth and threaten, "I'm going to talk to Mr. Long about this."

With this rearing, it should be no surprise that I was, at the time, strongly in favor of Huey Long and whatever he did. At the time, what Huey Long was doing was declaring martial law and taking over the registrar of voters office in New Orleans. Ikey's father was employed by the Old Regulars in New Orleans and he was pronouncedly anti-Long, as were all the Old Regulars. He charged that Long was having truckloads of soldiers drive along the streets shooting civilians. He knew this, he claimed, because one of his relatives who worked at City Hall had told him.

i

Without any real knowledge of the situation, I couldn't mount a defense and I remember weakly assuring Ikey that if Huey Long was having people shot down in the streets he must have had a very good reason for doing so. One word led to another and we started punching each other. Being asthmatic and underweight, I wasn't much of an opponent for Ikey and I quit when the blood started coursing from my nose.

Such were the strong feelings roused by Huey Long in the citizens of Louisiana, even those in the pre-teen years. There was no middle ground. You were for him or against him.

All my life I have been fascinated by and drawn to this man. My life seems to have been constantly interwoven with his presence. I went to Baton Rouge following his funeral and was intrigued by the peddlers selling poems, songs and leaflets about him.

During my short abortive try at higher education at Tulane, I attended a seance which I located to gratify a professor who doubted that the dead could communicate with the living. Huey Long was one of the spirits who conversed with us.

When I became active in politics and moved to Baton Rouge, I worked for the state of Louisiana's Department of Commerce of Industry on the 24th floor of the state capitol, which was Huey's aerie before it became part of the public domain and was used for the routine functions of government after his death.

About nine years ago, I received a contract to do public relations for the Capitol House, a hotel in Baton Rouge that succeeded the old Heidelberg, where Huey stayed when he was in Baton Rouge. I was instrumental in tracing much of his comings and goings in the hotel and today there are monuments to the areas where Huey Long slept, where he ate, where he collaborated in composing "Every Man a King" and even where he once dropped a plate of fried oysters on the floor of the restaurant because they were improperly cooked.

I have ambivalent feelings about Huey Long.

Without Huey Long, Louisiana would have entered the 20th century many years later than it did. Without Huey Long, Louisiana would never have had the generous public assistance, educational and road systems it has. Many say that other states have these benefits and they have not witnessed the totalitarianism that struck Louisiana and they may have a point. But my point is that these benefits would have been slower in coming in Louisiana had not the opposition power structure been dismantled by Huey Long at the time that it was.

There were also many unsavory things about Huey Long. I do not attempt to judge him in this manuscript. I have tried to tell the truth as I see it. I do not say this is any kind of final or definitive work on Long's shooting and death but I modestly believe it is a slim ray of light in an area that has been shrouded in darkness for more than 50 years.

Perhaps those who come after and use any parts of this work will help in reaching a truthful conclusion, if it is not reached in these pages.

I had a great deal of support in writing this book. At times I almost decided to shuck the whole thing. But there were enough people who encouraged me and this gave me the strength to write what you are now reading.

I owe more to Dr. Tom Weiss, brother of Carl Weiss, than I can ever pay. He was free and candid when I interviewed him. He made it possible for me to talk with the Pavy family, the in-laws of Carl Weiss, the so-called assassin. He allowed me to submit the medical portions of the manuscript to physicians who practiced in the 1930s to give me what amounts to an expert critique of an area about which I know nothing.

I expect that Tom will have serious reservations about what I have written. While it exonerates his brother, to a degree, nevertheless it is not the complete, final "not guilty" verdict that Tom would like to see and I apologize if I cannot espouse this belief.

Ernie Gremillion, an ex-IRS investigator, helped me in understanding the nature of ballistics and firearms and he also gave me valuable counsel in interpreting the movements of the FBI and other federal agencies.

When I initially tried to get the hospital records from Our Lady of the Lake Medical Center I was turned down flatly. It was Dr. Hypolite Landry, coroner of East Baton Rouge Parish, who was able to obtain these records for me and I will forever be in his debt. I did not ask him how he succeeded in getting records that were denied to me on several occasions but I do not believe I should look a gift doctor in the mouth.

A longtime friend, Chris Faser, helped me launch this project some nine years ago and gave me encouragement and support at a time when I needed it most. Another friend, Gene Cretini, has read and reread this manuscript and it is better as a result.

Another friend, Elaine Ventress Johnson, made it possible for me to obtain the first interview I had with a doctor who was at the hospital. Up until that time, everyone had stonewalled it. Kathy Coon, a school psychologist, put me in touch with an agent in New York City who helped me along but, in the final analysis, believed the book was not ready for publication. I believed otherwise but I appreciate what Kathy did for me.

One of those who read the manuscript in its very early beginnings was Angela deGravelles, public relations consultant whom I would recommend to anyone needing a sharp and savvy public relations consultant in Baton Rouge or, for that matter, anywhere on the planet.

I composed the manuscript on a $199 computer, viewed it on a $59 monitor, with a $350 disk drive and a $399 daisywheel printer. I never could have done it without the help of the people at Software Solutions in Baton

Rouge, namely, Brad and Bruce.

My wife, Lorraine, put up with the early morning sounds of a computer printout, corrected my spelling, read proofs and saved me from myself. My daughter Colleen checked copy and cleaned up the manuscript for me.

There are others who cheered me on and I may have left them out. I apologize. I hope they will understand the pressures of doing something like this.

—Ed Reed
Baton Rouge
October, 1986

INTRODUCTION

On Friday, September 21, 1984, at the Tulane Medical School in New Orleans, there occurred a remarkable event. It coincided with the 150th anniversary of the founding of the medical school and consisted of a symposium by four learned men who were graduates of Tulane. Three had finished as medical doctors; the fourth finished in law.

All four men had distinguished themselves, not only in their chosen careers, but also by contributions to publishing, politics and government. In addition to these common characteristics, all were a vital part of a chapter of Louisiana history that represents the greatest enigma in the history of a state where the mystical and the dramatic are routine.

They were all involved in the strange and, as yet, unexplained death of Huey P. Long.

Long was shot on the night of Sunday, September 8, 1935, as he left the governor's office on the first floor of Louisiana's new skyscraper state capitol, a legacy to the state by Long himself. He was surrounded by a dozen bodyguards, part of a hundred or so (some reckoned several hundred) that had been summoned to the capitol that night to prevent just such an occurrence. He died some 30 hours later of causes that are still not clearly defined.

Long left other legacies. He left a name that possessed great magic. The citizens were willing, for many years, to elect his followers to public office strictly on their connection with him.

Those fortunate enough to bear the name of "Long," or to have been a part of his machinery, held—and still hold—elective posts in local, state and national governments. In fairness to these officeholders, most had above average talent and ability, although it is not certain that they would have been as successful with the talent and ability alone.

1

After Huey, there were five Longs elected to the Congress from Louisiana.

Huey's brother Earl was twice elected governor. He first acceded to the office from that of lieutenant governor when the incumbent governor resigned from office prior to being shipped off to prison. Earl died in 1960 after having been elected to Congress, climaxing a brilliant but turbulent career that established him as one of the truly great governors of Louisiana, his contributions rivaling, in many areas, those of his exalted older brother.

Other Long descendants have been elected to the legislature and to other offices in the state.

Virtually everything that is modern in Louisiana's government had its beginnings with Huey Long. Before him, the state was little more than an ill-educated, poverty-stricken enclave that was an embarrassment to the nation. As a territory, Louisiana had been exploited and drained by one conquering foreign power after another. When the territory became a state and elected its own leaders, succeeding administrations did little to better the lot of the natives.

After Long, the state had a tax base swollen by levy upon levy. Some pointed to this increased taxation as proof of his failure and that of his programs. But many citizens felt that, for the first time, they had been given a return on their tax money. They were satisfied.

With Long, Louisiana entered the 20th century. There is no doubt that this renaissance would never have occurred at the time it did had he not appeared.

Another legacy, not a happy one, was the aristocracy—a type of pirates' plutocracy—spawned from those around Long who pillaged state lands and treasury for personal gain, enriching themselves at the expense of a bewitched, subservient and gullible citizenry.

So there were entries on both sides of the ledger. Most were good. Some were bad.

Much has happened in the more than 50 years since Long's life was snuffed out in one of the most celebrated assassinations in American history. But during this time there has persisted a nagging and unsolved riddle: Who really did kill Huey Long?

Few in Louisiana believe the "official" theory, advanced by those around Long, that a 29-year-old ear, nose and throat specialist, Dr. Carl Austin Weiss, gunned him down. The Long administrationists tied Weiss to a plot supposedly hatched by political enemies. They used the concoction four months after Long's death to generate sweeping mandates for his political heirs in the next elections for governor and other state and local offices. There was a conspiracy of enemies and Weiss was the agent of that conspiracy. So the story went.

But a continuing doubt caused the sponsors of Tulane University's sesquicentennial observance to offer a panel featuring the learned gentlemen referred to earlier.

Dr. Edgar Hull, a physician who attended Long during the 30 hours between injury and death, was the first speaker on the panel.

Hull, weakened, in failing health and confined to a wheelchair (he died a little more than a month later from cancer), nevertheless was strong and resolute in his recollections when he took the audience, composed mostly of physicians, back to those hours in 1935 when more than a score of doctors watched powerless while the life drained from Long's body. His tone was positive, his memories clear and his conclusions unequivocal.

Hull said that Huey Long died of peritonitis, an infection of the abdominal cavity that invariably occurs following penetrating wounds of that part of the body. "There was no negligence in surgery on Huey," Hull insisted. He quoted the specialist who inserted a hypodermic syringe into the areas surrounding both kidneys as diagnosing, "You can forget about bleeding from the kidneys!"

"The surgery was not bungled!" the aging physician stated to his colleagues. The surgeon in charge was a good surgeon who may have been out of practice, Dr. Hull conceded, but his first assistant had no peer in the treatment of gunshot wounds of the abdomen.

It was peritonitis, and that was that.

Following Hull was Dr. Frank Loria. Loria had studied 478 cases of penetrating wounds of the abdomen over a 15-year period and offered his findings in one of the most definitive treatments of this type of wound ever published.

Loria, crippled by the effects of a stroke which caused him to speak in labored tones, is, as Dr. Hull was, an octogenarian. He drew the ire of Hull when he rejected the latter's contention that peritonitis was the cause of death of Long. It was an internal hemorrhage that did it. According to Loria:

> "They put the catheter in his bladder and drew out almost pure blood. Then they knew they had a kidney injury. And the same was true, about 3:30 in the morning, or 1:30, Dr. T. Jorda Kahle, a wonderful urologist in New Orleans, came in and he aspirated the region of the injury in the back and drew out almost pure blood." (Dr. Kahle was the selfsame specialist who, according to Dr. Hull, said, "You can forget about bleeding from the kidneys!")

Loria was rudely interrupted by Hull, who, in a strained and angry voice, asked incredulously, "What?"

Loria repeated, "He drew almost pure blood."

"No sir!" snapped Hull.

"Yes, sir!" argued Loria, raising his voice and slapping the table with his opened palm for emphasis. "He told me he drew out pure blood."

Hull shot back, "I was there! He drew out no blood!"

It was a dramatic moment and its import was not lost on the physicians in attendance. It was a case of two experts disagreeing, with no prospect of compromise. Implicit in Loria's remarks was the charge that the surgery was indeed bungled, contrary to what Hull contended and that failure to examine the kidneys and the structures around them doomed Long to death.

(Following the panel, Hull, ashen and trembling, refused to leave the stage until he was allowed to confront Loria and restate his interpretation of the events involved in Long's death.)

Both physicians agreed that it was Dr. Carl Austin Weiss who fired the shot that resulted in Long's death. Hull, however, ruled out the possibility that Weiss acted in concert with others, taking issue with the "official" theory offered by many Long supporters.

The next speaker was Dr. Thomas E. Weiss, younger brother of the alleged assassin. He recalled the years of anguish that dogged the family as a result of the charge that his brother assassinated Long. In a moving recital of his motives in trying to keep the matter alive, he said, "Dad and Mother died in torment because of what had occurred on that night of September 8, 1935 and their subsequent hurt and sorrow for both the Long and Weiss families was very deep."

Weiss was the youngest of the panelists. He had been a teenager, enrolled in LSU and prepared to follow in the footsteps of his older brother, Carl, when the tragedy struck in 1935.

He relived for the assembled physicians the events of that Sunday in September. His presentation was more elaborate than those of the other speakers. On occasion he would ask that the lights be dimmed so that slides projected on a screen above his head could be seen clearly.

The first slide carried a single word, "Truth," accompanied by the following commentary from the physician:

> "Some of my friends have asked me why on God's green earth I would want to get involved in this. First, why would Tulane want to put on a program such as this? I think we have the obvious answer.
>
> "...I've been involved with this because of family connections for almost 50 years and there's one big word there: 'Truth.' We have lived with this for almost 50 years. If Carl was, in any way, directly responsible for walking into the capitol and inflicting a mortal wound, he was

wrong. We all agree to this: that one does not take a life.

"But we feel that there are so many circumstances that came forth and it's obvious from this discussion right here that we, as physicians, who always seek truth, sometimes can't find truth, even when there's a great tragedy."

Following some historical background about his family, Weiss traced the events of that Sunday, describing the actions of his brother, which seemed in no way to reflect any anxiety or aberration that might cause him to commit the act with which he was later charged. According to his brother, Carl was simply a normal American father, spending time in the bosom of his family—wife, child and parents.

Thomas Weiss' commentary was in no way medical. It was instead historical, dealing with the chronology of the day, the investigation into the shooting of Long and the inconsistencies of witnesses who testified that Carl Weiss was the assassin.

Doctors Hull and Loria both believed that Carl had shot Long, although Hull rejected any prospect of there having been a conspiracy. He felt Carl Weiss had acted alone. However, Carl's brother, Tom, discarded both hypotheses, hinting strongly that Long was a victim of those charged with protecting him—his bodyguards. He speculated that there could easily have been intrigues of such proportion that Carl may have been set up for the killing.

"Times have told us that dirty tricks did not end with Brutus," he said.

Weiss concluded on a bitter note. With anger and frustration showing, he charged that the "official" version of the assassination was false. He incriminated those Long followers who, "...knowledgeable of the whole truth, are totally responsible for this smeared and distorted page of American history and for supplying false and incomplete information that has placed guilt where it should not be."

Following Dr. Weiss was the final panelist, a surprise to the audience. He had not been advertised as a participant. He was Cecil Morgan, jurist, legislator and corporate counsel who had served in the Louisiana legislature during the tumultuous days when Long was governor of the state. He had read of the planned symposium and decided that he would attend as a spectator. When his presence became known, sponsors insisted that he become a participant.

Morgan had served in the Louisiana House of Representatives as well as the Senate and was a member of what was called the "Dynamite Squad," a group of legislators that formed the core of Long's political opposition. He was later elected district judge from the upstate Shreveport area and eventually became chief legal counsel for Standard Oil of New Jersey.

Judge Morgan is not satisfied with the way history has, of late, recorded the actions of Huey Long. He deplores published accounts that failed to reflect the tenor of the times—the tension and fear that gripped many in the state because of the climate of intimidation fostered by Long.

At the Tulane meeting, Morgan described how he learned of the shooting:

"I went on a summer vacation with my family in a Model A Ford to visit her (his wife's) relatives in California and we came back in time for the opening of court in September. As we got into town and spoke to some of our relatives, they told us something had happened in Baton Rouge and we hurried to our little cottage, turned on our little old-fashioned, Gothic-shaped radio and heard that Huey Long had been shot.

"It scared my wife to death. She said, 'There's going to be something like a pogrom and everybody who's not for the administration is going to be purged!'"

But if there was fear among those who opposed Long, there was also rancor of monumental proportions. Morgan recalls, "...When Huey was undergoing his dying ordeal, there were literally thousands of people...we heard it all over the state—groups were praying for his death."

Morgan also rejected the theory that Carl Weiss acted as the agent of a group who planned Long's death. Nor was he convinced that Weiss did, in fact, even shoot Long. He said, "When I have been asked, 'Who killed Huey Long?' my answer has consistently been, 'I do not know!' And I have a lot of good reasons for not knowing who actually did it."

Morgan suspects the testimony of one of the principal witnesses to the shooting, Louisiana Supreme Court Justice John Fournet. Judge Fournet testified that the assassin pressed a pistol against Long's heart. It was Fournet who supposedly swiped at the pistol and forced it away from the heart, so that the wound was to the abdomen and not through the heart. He is generally credited (or blamed, in some quarters) for saving Long from instant death.

Fournet had died some months before the symposium and Morgan took note of this. He ended his remarks on a somewhat cryptic note:

"...I believe it's probably true that we'll never know all the truth...until a lot of people have died and Fournet just died the other day.

"I am told that..."(he named a retired reporter) "was the last person to interview him (Fournet). And I have also been told...that in the interview he refused to answer some pertinent

questions there, in that respect. So, I don't know
what the truth is yet."
What do we have here?

We have four men who have achieved prominence in their lifetimes and who have intimate knowledge of an event that shaped the course of Louisiana and United States history. They disagree on key points. Three disbelieve key elements of the "record," while the fourth seems noncommittal. Two have cast serious doubts about any part of the official theory, exhibiting grave questions about the reliability of witnesses.

And we have the "record" itself, a record written by passengers and patrons aboard a political juggernaut that has been labeled the "Louisiana Hayride" and memorialized as "The American Rehearsal for Dictatorship." It is a story of venality and corruption that is unequalled in the annals of American government. Perhaps the so-called "record," written by them, is a tale written by the fox and passed off as a true and accurate account of his excursion into the henhouse.

To inquire into the shooting and subsequent death of Huey Long is to enter the Twilight Zone.

For example, although both Baton Rouge city police and Louisiana state police investigated the shooting and death of Long, there are no records of the investigation in the files of either law enforcement agency.

The coroner of East Baton Rouge Parish held inquests to determine the cause of death of both Long and Weiss. The Weiss inquest was a peremptory and ceremonial thing. Noting the 63 bullet holes in the body, the panel had little choice except to label the killing as death by gunshot wounds.

The Long inquest was more elaborate. A number of witnesses was called. However, until 50 years after the event, the only records available to the public were contained in the clippings of the newspapers that covered the proceedings. On the 50th anniversary of the death of his father, U.S. Senator Russell Long inserted what he represented as a transcript of the coroner's inquest into the Congressional Record. There is no record of this transcript in the files of state or local governments. The coroner's office has a single document: the death certificate of Huey Long. This is all that remains of one of the most memorable happenings in Louisiana history.

Hospital records are sealed. My initial attempts to obtain these records were rebuffed. I finally managed to obtain them but it was by a rather devious route. Further, physicians known to have participated in the operation to save Long's life refused to talk while they were living. Now all are dead. Most of their survivors are silent.

It is as if the event never happened, although its consequences were felt, not only in Louisiana, but throughout the United States. And even today—almost 50 years after the fact—those who lived during those times and those who have studied it as history disagree about basic facts.

But it did happen, although the way it happened has only been whispered and hinted at. There are many persons, inside and outside Louisiana, who reject the "official" explanation of the shooting and death of Huey Long.

I am one of these. In the following pages, I offer what I consider to be an acceptable, plausible and truthful explanation of Huey Long's shooting and death.

CHAPTER ONE

A Unique Assassination

There has never been an assassination quite like that of Huey P. Long.

At the time, Long's killing was considered second in importance only to the assassination of President Abraham Lincoln. And, although there have been other celebrated assassinations since then, the Long murder occupies a special and unique place in the history of political killings in our nation or—for that matter—throughout the world.

Long was the first and, for more than 30 years following his death, the only United States senator ever to be assassinated.

As of the end of the year 1967, 1,199 persons had been elected to the U.S. Senate since the founding of the Republic. Two senators died violently, although one, California Senator David C. Broderick, was killed in a duel and not assassinated in the classic sense of the word.

Eight Presidents were targets of assassination attempts which resulted in four deaths. Seven congressmen were marked for assassination and, of these, three were killed.[1]

This premier ranking among senatorial assassinations of the Long slaying is enough, in itself, to qualify the event as an important slice of history. However, there are other aspects of the assassination which lend to it a special historical flavor.

The shooting of Huey Long was a departure from the traditional American pattern of assassination.

The publication *The Nation* termed Long's killing "a deliberate political act, one of the very few in its category of American experience."[2]

There has always been symbolism involved in our native assassinations. The targeted official has invariably been selected principally because of the office held. There has never been any personal relationship between the

9

killer and victim. The position occupied by the target has always been the primary reason for the attack. To a great extent, the killer has seemed to be acting as the agent for a class, rather than as an individual harboring a personal grievance.

President Lincoln was killed because he was President, as was President Kennedy; Senator Robert Kennedy was killed because he was a U.S. senator, not because he was Robert Kennedy; Martin Luther King was assassinated because of his leadership role in the civil rights movement. But Huey Long was killed because he was Huey Long. The killing is considered to have resulted as much from personal causes as political.

The authors of *The Politics of Assassination,* published in 1970, held the Long murder to be "the most dramatic and probably the most significant American political killing since the assassination of President Abraham Lincoln." It notes the high national status achieved by Long, remarking that the Southern figure "had achieved a position in national politics that far surpassed his nominal status as a backbench member of the United States Senate. Within the state of Louisiana he possessed political power exceeding that exercised by any other state political leader in American history..."[3]

And if Huey Long was an unlikely victim, the man alleged to be his assassin is altogether without parallel among those who have used murder to solve political questions. He has no counterpart in American history.

If one subscribes to the premise that within all of us is contained the potential for violent actions, even murder, just awaiting the proper blend of opportunity and provocation to combine, then there can be no such thing as a "typical" assassin. Each of us is capable of it. There are as many types of assassins as there are types of people.

But if, on the other hand, we remember that there are more non-murderers and that there are more people who resist the urge to liquidate the prominent and powerful than those who succumb to its perverse allure, then we are justified in attempting to categorize and compartmentalize those individuals who, motivated by revenge, personal reward or a desire for political change, take the life of a public figure.

Students of the phenomenon of assassination have isolated the character traits of assassins and generally agree that a "typical" assassin is a loser. He is a flop, a failure, a square peg in a round hole for whom society has no useful role. He is forced to become a vigilante to accomplish his ends. He is pushed farther and farther outside the system, finally attracting the attention of those inside it by precipitous action. He thus gains a place in a recital of history which otherwise would never even have noted his existence.

None of the profiles of likely assassin types tilts toward Carl Weiss. None of the descriptions based on historical experience resembles Weiss.

Lauran Paine, in his *Assassins' World,* refers to the National Commission on the Causes and Prevention of Violence's guidelines for identifying potential future assassins. An assassin would probably be

> "...short and slight of build, foreign born and from a broken family—most probably with the father either absent or unresponsive to the child. He would be a loner, unmarried, with no steady female friends and have a history of good work terminated one to three years before the assassination attempt by a seeming listlessness and irascibility. He would identify with a political or religious movement, with the assassination triggered by a specific issue which relates to the principles of the cause or movement. Although identifying with a cause, the assassin would not in fact be part of or able to contribute to the movement."[4]

Following the unsuccessful attempt on the life of President Ronald Reagan by John Warmock Hinckley, United Press International interviewed psychiatrists to determine a pattern of prospective assassins. They concluded:

> "...They walk unnoticed through their formative years and drift through early adulthood never completing anything they start. They run away from their problems and responsibilities, blaming failure on perfidious friends or unseen demons. Finally, they can bear failure no longer and decide to shoot someone of unquestionable success."[5]

This description fits many of the noted assassins of history, notably Guiteau, Czolgosz and Zangara, responsible for the deaths of Presidents McKinley and Garfield and Chicago Mayor Anton Cermak. Cermak was fatally wounded by a bullet intended for President-elect Franklin Roosevelt in Miami on February 15, 1933. It would probably also have application to the other assassins in American history.

But not to Carl Weiss.

Most assassins seem to have troubled personal histories that make their actions understandable, if not predictable. Certainly such figures as John Wilkes Booth, Sirhan Sirhan, Lee Harvey Oswald, "Squeaky" Fromme and John Hinckley were not normal people and some were certifiably insane. It would seem to go without saying that an attempt to assassinate could be considered prima facie evidence of insanity.

Try to use these guidelines to determine if Carl Weiss was the killer of Huey Long and very clearly the available evidence makes it doubtful that Weiss was capable of assassination.

He was a second generation American born into a professional family. While not wealthy, the family was blessed with a measure of middle class comfort.

He had none of the queerness that seems to flow from the personality of assassins, recognizable by some even upon casual contact. He was stable and balanced and, while not really gregarious, had a circle of friends and acquaintances who held him in high esteem. He was a Kiwanian, a member of the Baton Rouge Young Men's Business Club, a practicing Catholic, a member of the Medical Society and the father of a three-month-old son.

Some historians have noted the differences in character and background between Long and Weiss and have commented upon the obvious role reversal of the classic assassination protagonists: Long representing the "have-nots," Weiss the "haves." Usually the "haves" are the victims and those who lack are the perpetrators.

The two were opposite in other ways: redneck and citified cosmopolite; Baptist and Catholic; politician and physician and, perhaps most meaningful, a dictator and one who had observed fascism up close and feared it.

There is one final significant difference between Carl Weiss as an assassin and others who have fallen into this category.

Assassination is an ugly crime, evoking little sympathy from those who are not involved. However, Carl Weiss was glorified by many who considered him to be Long's killer. Letters, telegrams, tributes and even a medal found their way to the Weiss family as outpourings from citizens around the nation who believed that he had served as some kind of avenging angel.

His funeral was attended by virtually the entire membership of the medical society of East Baton Rouge Parish, who stood in ankle-deep rain to attend his funeral services. The respect and admiration accorded Weiss surely stand alone in the annals of assassinations.

The failure to fit Carl Weiss into the mold of the assassin is simply one element of an event in history that is still one great enigma. Doubts are generated at every step of the way when all the facts of the assassination are reviewed.

Most notable among the evidence offered by those who maintain the innocence of Weiss is the behavior of the physician during the last days of his life. His final hours were spent among family members in idyllic happiness. The days before saw him making preparations for home improvements and relocation of his office that seemed to point to long, productive and satisfying years ahead.

Also adding to the disbelief in Weiss' role as assassin is the lack of a clearcut motive for his deed. Many motives have been offered but none of these are based on actual fact.

There was no attempt made by Long's supporters or survivors (who controlled the machinery of government and had at their disposal investigative powers beyond measure) to establish a motive. In addition, although an inquest of sorts was held, no one interviewed the Weiss family or friends of the doctor to determine if, during the days prior to the assassination, there had been any unusual behavior on Weiss' part.

Following Long's shooting, many of his supporters claimed that he had been the victim of a conspiracy that included many of his political enemies. Proof would be forthcoming, they said. Yet none of these "enemies" were investigated and all attemps to link Weiss to known foes of the Kingfish failed. In this respect, it is significant to note that Weiss has never been tied to any organized Long opposition. In fact, most of those who could have been considered to be likely assassins—those with a history of militant anti-Long activity—had never even met Weiss.

The inquest—a meandering probe conducted by the coroner of East Baton Rouge Parish—has now been elevated to the status and dignity of an investigation and is oftentimes referred to as the "official" investigation.

This inquiry was no such thing. At best it was an inconclusive hearing; at worst it was a whitewash which did not quite succeed.

Neither Long's supporters nor his enemies really wanted to push too strongly to uncover evidence of a plot or conspiracy to kill Long, each for his own reasons. Too many anti-Long people had threatened Long's life to risk delving too deeply into the intrigues surrounding the killing and many probably were actually involved in plots.

On the Long side, there was sufficient concern that it was not the bullet of Carl Weiss that did Long in and that conceivably—nay, probably—the fatal wound could have been inflicted by one of those charged with his protection.

All of the witnesses to the shooting, according to the testimony, were Long partisans—his bodyguards or those who had depended upon him for political favors. None of those who actually saw the shooting appeared at the inquest when it was officially convened the following day. The previous night, before he underwent surgery, Long ordered his men to remain silent. It was not until eight days after the shooting that they chose to appear at the hearing.

The meeting was convened in a climate of intimidation. The local officials participating, District Attorney John Fred Odom and Coroner Thomas Bird, were at disadvantages. Odom had been placed at a meeting the previous month at a hotel in New Orleans which the Long machine termed an assassination conference, called to arrange Long's death. This placed him under a cloud and one witness refused to testify because of this. Both Odom and Bird were on tight leashes, operating by the grace of the Long administration, which could have taken over the inquest at any time.

Armed partisans from the Long camp were confronted by anti-Long observers when a point was made by either side.[6]

Witnesses contradicted each other. On occasion, a witness gave testimony that contradicted earlier testimony by the same witness.

Every aspect of the Huey Long assassination invites suspicion and doubt. After he was gunned down by Long's bodyguards, Carl Weiss lay on the blood-spattered floor of the capitol. Over him, armed with a submachine gun, was a bodyguard. The head of the Criminal Bureau of Investigation, Louis Guerre, gave his men orders to shoot to kill any photographers attempting to take pictures in the building or at the hospital where Long lay.

The actual details of the operation on Long are shrouded in mystery. Large segments of the hospital records have disappeared. Attending physicians bickered among themselves. No autopsy was performed. To discourage any meddling or inquiry, armed guards surrounded the funeral parlor and, later, the casket in the state capitol where Long lay in state.

Repeated requests were made of the Federal Bureau of Investigation to investigate the shooting of Long, but Director J. Edgar Hoover turned them all down, insisting that no federal law was violated and therefore no federal investigation was warranted.

In Louisiana, too, there was resistance to going beyond the kangaroo court that masqueraded as an inquest. A resolution appropriating funds to study Long's death was killed by Governor Richard Leche, whom Long's machine supported in the gubernatorial election following Long's death. In 1936, newly-inaugurated Governor Leche would convene the Louisiana legislature in Texas to hear Franklin Roosevelt, mortal enemy of Long, in a campaign swing for reelection throughout the Southwest. For his part, Roosevelt would have his Attorney General drop charges against some of Long's henchmen in a swapout that some would call "The Second Louisiana Purchase."

When Long was shot on September 8, 1935, the news that Carl Weiss was the assassin was greeted with disbelief. It is a feeling that persists to this day.

During the time I researched this manuscript, I failed to encounter a single individual, other than those with solid connections to the Long organization, who believed that Carl Weiss actually killed Huey Long.

According to the supervisor of the guides who escort hundreds of thousands of visitors throughout the Louisiana state capitol every year, many doubt that Weiss was Long's assassin.[7]

Even some of those closest to Long were not entirely convinced that the shooting happened as the "official" report maintained.

Long's widow, Rose, did not rule out the possibility that her husband was cut down by his bodyguards. An attorney named Charles Rivet handled the succession of Long and recognized the impact that a determination of accidental death (as opposed to homicide) would have on the settlement by insurance companies for proceeds of Long's life insurance policies. He explained to Mrs. Long that the policies would pay only the face value in case Carl Weiss had murdered her husband, but the double indemnity clause would provide for twice that amount if Long was shown to be the victim of accidental stray bullets from his bodyguards. He asked the widow if he should pursue the latter hypothesis. She authorized him to do so.

The first person Rivet questioned was John Fournet, longtime Long follower, whose loyalty had paid off in his election to the state supreme court. Fournet told Rivet that his testimony had been that it was Weiss who fired the fatal shot and he would stick to it. Rivet reportedly abandoned the effort.[8]

But startling evidence uncovered 50 years after Long's death would seem to indicate that Rivet was on the right track.

Prompted by publicity generated by the 50th anniversary of Long's shooting and death in 1985, The Mutual Life Insurance Company of New York (now acronymized to "MONY") revealed that it had hired an investigator to study the circumstances surrounding Long's death.

The company had paid the $20,000 death claim and decided to retain one K.B. Ponder to determine "the real circumstances of the death in this case."

Ponder did so and rendered his opinion that "Long's bodyguards rushed Weiss and he attempted to draw a pistol. The bodyguards started firing their pistols and Long was killed by a bullet fired by one of his own bodyguards."

The significance of this evidence is self-apparent. It is understandable that the family and friends of Carl Weiss might rush to conclude that Long was killed by bodyguards. It is equally understandable that Long supporters would lay the blame on Weiss. But conflicting political ideologies and loyalties attempting to explain how Long was shot smack of the self-serving, while a decision by MONY to fork over an additional $10,000 voluntarily is quite another matter.[9]

Even among those members of the Long faction who accept the verdict that Carl Weiss was the assassin, there are many who believe that the physician did not act alone and that there were others involved in a plot.

Notable among these is Long's own son, Russell, who followed in his father's footsteps and is now a United States senator from Louisiana. A newsman reported that Russell asked him to investigate that possibility, hinted at in a transcript of a conference of Long opponents a month before Long's killing. Long's death was supposedly plotted and Weiss was named in the transcript as having been in attendance.[10]

Russell holds this belief to this day. He was guest of honor for an observance held in Louisiana on September 8, 1985, commemorating the 50th anniversary of his father's shooting. He expressed the belief that his father was murdered as the result of a conspiracy among racists who nourished grievances against Huey for having repealed the poll tax in 1934, offering the voting franchise to Negroes.

This quaint theory joins the mountain of unsupported speculation about motives for Huey Long's death. In all the research I have undertaken I never came across this theory.[11]

Long supporter Robert Brothers, identified by some as a trusted Long lieutenant and by others as a low-level "go-fer," charged that some in Washington had advance knowledge of Long's shooting. According to Brothers, Weiss died at 9:26 p.m., after having been cut down by the bodyguards surrounding Long. He was not identified, according to Brothers, until 9:49 p.m. However, Brothers maintained, a Washington newsman telephoned to Baton Rouge before Weiss was identified to confirm the assassin's full name and identity.[12]

The insistence that Weiss was part of a conspiracy of Long's enemies became a battle cry of Long's political survivors and was established as the theme of the Louisiana election of January, 1936, which chose Long's successor in the Senate and which elected all state and many local officials. Anti-Long candidates for state office were labeled the "Assassination Ticket" and were decisively beaten.

However, there was never any serious effort on the part of the Long forces in Louisiana to link anyone with Weiss in the shooting.

The national press of that time and since has been consistent in its refusal to admit that the circumstances of the shooting were as advertised, that is, that Carl Weiss encountered Long in the corridor outside the governor's office that fateful night and cold-bloodedly shot him—which is the version given by all of the Long-associated witnesses. Many believe that Weiss did not shoot Long at all. Others believe Weiss was provoked by remarks made by Long and this caused him to shoot.

Prominent among the news media is *Life* which, in 1939, called for an investigation of Long's shooting. It editorialized:

> "...after four years, rumors are stirring in Washington which indicate that others may try to solve as yet unexplained angles....Why have neither friends nor foes of Huey Long seemed anxious to clear up the mystery once and for all?"[13]

(Illustrating the *Life* editorial is a painting of the assassination scene by John McCrady which vividly depicts the vengeance of the bodyguards as they cut down Carl Weiss. Their faces twisted in anger, they poured bullets through his tortured body as he slowly sank beneath their withering fire. It was this painting from which Weiss' son, Carl, Jr., learned the truth about the circumstances of his father's death. Previously he had been told by his mother that his father had died in a "firearms mishap" and that he was in the wrong place at the wrong time. At the age of 15, Carl, Jr. was looking through old copies of the magazine and came across the illustration.)

Recently there have been several treatments that seem to support this theory, but the verdicts are not without reservations.

There have been three books of relatively recent vintage. Published in 1963 was the *Huey Long Murder Case* by veteran New Orleans reporter Hermann Deutsch. His account is important because Deutsch, while not present for the assassination, covered Huey Long for most of his political career. Deutsch's excellent reporting has provided source material for many who wrote following him, including this writer.

Deutsch firmly believes that the "official" theory of "one man, one gun, one bullet" is the key to Long's death. In his book he attempts to refute the charge that Long was killed by his own bodyguards, a theory he scorns as a "legend." However, he complains that continued repetition of this version made it "difficult to overestimate the fashion in which all this tended to perpetuate what began as a campaign legend." He points to the memoirs of Elmer Irey, section chief of the IRS:

> "Weiss had a .22 calibre pistol in his hand when Long's bodyguards mowed him down. Long died as the result of a single bullet wound made by a .45 calibre slug. Nobody has explained that yet."[14]

A second author, David H. Zinman, former Associated Press writer, published *The Day Huey Long Was Shot* in 1963, the same year as Deutsch's work. Zinman's conclusion is that Weiss approached Long, an argument ensued and Long was struck by Weiss. Reacting, the bodyguards opened fire. In the cannonade, Long was hit.

A third book was written by now-deceased Dr. T. Harry Williams, one of this nation's most respected historians. Dr. Williams' biography, titled simply *Huey Long,* is the definitive work on Huey Long's life. It is, however, a sympathetic biography, and critics have claimed, with some justification, that it is unduly influenced by the wishes of the Long family, who approved and authorized the biography and even contributed financially to its publication. The work needs no endorsement from me. It stands on its own merits as a monumental effort and as one of the most remarkable examples of the chronicling of oral history today.

I mean no disservice to Dr. Williams when I point out that the treatment of Huey Long's wounding and death in his remarkable work is largely superficial. The Alfred M. Knopf edition of Dr. Williams' work contains 876 pages, not counting preface and bibliographic essay, which increase the total to almost 1000 pages. Of this number, a scant 15 pages are devoted to the events of September 8 and the following days until Long died on September 10.

The treatment is abrupt. Williams borrows liberally from Hermann

Deutsch. For the most part, Williams leans heavily on Deutsch's conclusions and offers little that is new.

He alludes to a meeting among Carl Weiss and four members of an organization named the "Minute Men," where participants drew straws to see who would kill Long. It was Weiss who drew the short straw, to the dismay of his fellow conspirators, who believed that Weiss might fail in his mission. Thus believing, they laid plans for another assassination attempt the following week.

Although Williams' source is identified as "confidential communication," I spoke to a friend and confidant who assisted Dr. Williams in his work. The confidant offered to tell me the identities of the other conspirators if I could name at least one. I did name several and he was as good as his word, divulging the names of the others.[15]

I asked the son of one of the conspirators alleged to have been at the meeting if this could have happened and he told me his father had never met Carl Weiss.

I do not believe the meeting ever happened.[16]

Dr. Williams dismissed the prospect that Weiss was not guilty of Long's shooting as "a myth and a folklore," much as Deutsch did. He concludes dogmatically, "It is wrong."[17]

However, Dr. Williams was not always as emphatic in his beliefs about the circumstances of Long's shooting. He was a relatively recent convert to the "official" theory and at one time had doubts about this version. In the Summer, 1965 issue of the *Journal of the Louisiana Historical Association* he reviewed both Deutsch's and Zinman's books and judged:

> "I would hesitate to put forward a dogmatic claim. On the basis of present knowledge, I would cast a vote for the Deutsch thesis—" however, he adds cautiously, "but with the qualification that it might have happened another way."[18]

And indeed it did happen in an altogether different way. And that "other way" is documented in the following pages.

CHAPTER TWO

The Shooting

On the night of Sunday, September 8, 1935, the Louisiana legislature was in special session, as it had been on six other occasions during the preceding 13 months. Each succeeding session had grown in intensity and vindictiveness, extending the power of Huey Pierce Long, stripping public employees and citizens alike of basic civil rights.

Long had no official position in state government. He had served the state as governor from 1928 until 1932, when he resigned the office and took his seat in the United States Senate. Nevertheless, he still had almost absolute control of Louisiana. The legal, although nominal, governor of the state was Oscar Kelly Allen ("O.K." to friends), who presided over the affairs of Louisiana, but it was generally understood that Long told Allen what to do.

Long was given to seating himself in Allen's chair when he visited the capitol. He summoned Allen as one would call for a lackey. On one occasion, Long called for "his Governor" and Allen, embarrassed by the tone of Long's voice when friends were visiting and within earshot, pretended not to hear. Allen was blistered and soon responded when Long screamed, "Godddamn you, Oscar, don't you stall around with me! I made you and I can break you. Get those goddamned bills and get 'em quick!"

So it didn't matter who was governor and who was senator. Huey Long was in charge.

If you were a teacher, you had to be approved by a special board created by the legislature; if you were a deputy sheriff, you had to be approved by another board, also created by the legislature; even if you didn't work for the state, but owned real property, this was assessed by a board created by the legislature. If you had none of the above involvements and simply desired to vote in elections, you were still at the mercy of boards that ruled on your qualifications, also created by the legislature.

And Huey was in charge of the legislature.

Every citizen watched with interest when the legislature came to town.

For many it was a lot of laughs. What happened in the way of lawmaking was purely a byproduct. The real spectacle, the crowd pleaser, was Long. When the word was passed that Long would be on hand for a legislative session, seats would be at a premium in the state capitol.

He was "the Kingfish," his own nickname for himself, borrowed from a character on the blackface "Amos 'n' Andy" radio series. Originally an inside joke among members of the Long political organization, the nickname became public currency at a meeting of the State Highway Commission. Long was so heavy handed in dictating to the commission that one of the prospective bidders on the bonds up for sale questioned the governor's right to participate, since the law specified that it was the commission, and not the governor, that was charged with selling the bonds.

Long dismissed the rebuke. "I am participating here anyway, gentlemen. For the present, you can just call me the Kingfish!"[1]

The Kingfish was riding high in 1935.

Next to President Roosevelt, he was the most photographed, most caricatured and most publicized individual in the nation. His mail was estimated to average 50,000 letters weekly, delivered by the Post Office in sackfulls. The two national radio networks of the era made free public service time available to him whenever he asked. Other senators might get an hour a year, but Long was given eight broadcasts in the first seven months of 1935.[2]

The audiences for his radio broadcasts approached the saturation point. Not content with the listeners who tuned him in at the start of his program, he enlisted them as couriers to add their friends to his listenership. He would urge his followers:

> "Hello, friends, this is Huey Long speaking and I have some important things to tell you.
>
> "Before I begin I want you to do me a favor. I am going to talk along for about four or five minutes, just to keep things going. While I'm doing it I want you to go to the telephone and call up five of your friends and tell them Huey Long is on the air."[3]

None of his fellow senators approached his recognition factor. For the eight months in 1935 before his death, the *New York Times* carried a full six and a half news columns concerning him. The closest competitor for space in the journal was the Senate's most distinguished member, Borah of Idaho, who was able to muster only four columns for the entire year.

By September, 1935, Long had brought the Roosevelt administration to its knees. Much of his opposition to the President and his New Deal was personal. Long contemptuously referred to Roosevelt as "that fucker in the White House" and proceeded to sabotage many of the President's programs.[4]

One New Deal official called Long "the greatest individual challenge to Franklin Delano Roosevelt and to his New Deal politics." Democratic party head James Farley called him "the New Deal's number one problem child." Roosevelt himself labeled him one of the two most dangerous men in the country.[5]

Huey was the cock of the walk. He controlled Louisiana, including the legislature that convened in the state capitol that warm September night.

But on occasion it required brute force to maintain that control.

Twice in the previous 13 months, Long had called out the militia. National Guard troops had occupied the Registrar of Voters office in New Orleans the summer before, barely escaping an armed confrontation with the city's constabulary and causing the Roosevelt administration to cast worried looks toward Louisiana and even to consider military intervention.

In January of 1935, the capital city itself had been declared "First Military District" and placed under martial law. The occupation was lifted only a month before Long was killed.

It was into this setting that Huey summoned his legislature. The two houses convened Saturday, September 7. No one really knew what the agenda held until the bills were introduced that night, because Louisiana law required no advance notice of special sessions. It would be the following morning when most of Louisiana's citizens would read their newspapers and learn what was in the offing.

A total of 42 bills were introduced Saturday night. Two of the bills were sure to provoke controversy.

One bill provided a mandatory fine and jail sentence for any person who violated the Tenth Amendment to the U.S. Constitution. This amendment provides that all powers not specifically granted the federal government by the states remain the exclusive right of the states. Long's legislation was clearly aimed at the Roosevelt administration, which was using federal patronage to sustain the Long opposition in Louisiana.

This was the continuation of a feud between Long and Harold Ickes, Secretary of the Interior and a New Deal stalwart. Passage of the legislation would hold out the prospect of wholesale arrests and jailing of federal officials if they dared to implement New Deal programs opposed by the Kingfish. If the legislation were passed and implemented, it would certainly bring about the long-awaited confrontation between the national government and Long.

The second bill proposed to unseat one of Long's bitterest enemies, Judge Benjamin Henry Pavy, district judge in the southwest Louisiana parish of St. Landry and father-in-law of Baton Rouge physician Carl Austin Weiss, who would later be identified as the man who shot Long in the passageway of the state capitol. Pavy had served in his office for 28 years and was outspokenly anti-Long. The legislation proposed by Long at the session would redistrict Pavy's area, placing him in a new district with a heavy Long majority, making it virtually impossible for him to be re-elected.

The Long forces were jittery. Word had been passed that an assassination attempt would be made upon the life of the Kingfish.

According to one writer, Long had been warned on September 7, the day before he was shot, that a plot had been concocted to murder him and the deed would be done before adjournment of the legislative session. Harvey Fields, a former law partner of Long, travelled all night from Shreveport, more than 200 miles away, to warn Long.[6]

It was common knowledge within the Long camp that there would be an attempt on Long's life.

Every available highway patrolman and law enforcement agent in the state who could be spared from duty was reassigned to the state capitol.

Whereas the crowd of spectators who attended the opening session on Saturday night was free to roam throughout the House and Senate chambers, on Sunday night they were forbidden access to the floor and instead were relegated to the balcony.

Long went nowhere by himself. He carried with him a retinue of bodyguards whose only assignment was to protect the Kingfish. The methods they used to carry out this single assignment were crude and did not rule out violence. Anyone pestering the Kingfish, reporters included, was shoved or beaten by these goons.

Guarding the Kingfish was not an easy task. He walked faster than many men run. He was given to sudden starts and stops. Once underway, it was not easy to overtake him. He would leave a restaurant with no warning to his traveling companions, leaving them scurrying to catch up with him and to decide among themselves such niceties as who paid the check.

That night he was in top form.

Louisiana's capitol is a 34-story skyscraper tower built at Huey's direction in 1930. The tower itself rests on a five-story base whose first floor wings house the Senate and the House of Representatives. Dominating the floor and separating the two houses is a magnificent four-story high rotunda, or Memorial Hall. It is possible to go from one chamber to the other through Memorial Hall, but an alternate route is through a side hallway which passes the governor's office.

Sunday night the Senate was in adjournment. All bills had been introduced in the House of Representatives. The upper house had nothing to do until the legislation was reported out of the House and was ready for Senate consideration. If the Senate had been in session, no doubt Long would have crossed the rotunda many times, commuting between the two houses. However, with the Senate dark, his only stops were the governor's office and the House. Hence he used the side hallway.

It was on one of these trips along the hallway to the governor's office that the unthinkable happened! An armed intruder penetrated the security! The Kingfish was shot!

We have only the testimony of those who were in Long's entourage as to what actually happened. All witnesses generally agreed that it happened this way:

Shortly after 9:15 p.m., the House was in the process of completing its labors. The package of bills that had been introduced the previous night had been heard by the Ways and Means Committee Sunday morning and reported favorably. The House could take no action on the bills, since state law required that they lie over for a day. They would be voted on the following morning and then sent to the Senate.

A reporter who doubled as Long's Louisiana press agent was in Governor Allen's office, using the telephone to talk to his editor. The editor asked the reporter to solicit a quote from Long about the drowning of some young men, part of the New Deal's Civilian Conservation Corps, who were trapped in the Florida Keys during a hurricane.

The reporter availed himself of the second telephone in Allen's office to call Long, keeping the circuit open to his editor on the other telephone. Long told the newsman that yes, indeed, he would want to comment on Roosevelt's callousness in exposing Depression-age youngsters to the elements. Long advised that he was leaving the speaker's rostrum and would be arriving at the governor's office directly.

Long then abruptly left the speaker's rostrum, darted down the aisle and through the chamber, making a right turn into the corridor that led to the governor's office. He had outstripped his bodyguards and was making his way virtually alone down the 11-foot wide corridor. He turned into the governor's office and, moments later, emerged.

By this time, his entourage had caught up with him and he was once again enveloped by them. A thin young man in a white suit, in the company of several others and holding a white hat in front of him, approached Long. All witnesses agree that the man flashed a pistol from behind the hat, shoved it against Long's body and fired. Not, however, before one of the Long party swiped at the gun hand and diverted the gun from Long's heart to his right abdomen.

What happened then is impossible to recreate. Guns roared. Some say that Long escaped the scene before the fusillade began. The evidence suggests otherwise. It was impossible to say for sure, with the entire area obscured by an acrid, stinging blue haze generated by the gunshots.

When it was over, Long had fled the scene down the west staircase and was on his way to a nearby hospital. The thin man in the white suit—physician Carl Austin Weiss—lay lifeless on the floor, blood oozing from his body. As word spread throughout the building that the Kingfish had been shot, bodyguards left their posts to go to the scene of the shooting, emptying their magazines into the still-warm corpse of the man identified as the assassin.[7] The deceased was identified by the coroner. This was done perhaps half an hour after the shooting. Identification was made more difficult because bullets had shredded the physician's prescription pad and other identifying papers.

Meanwhile, at the hospital, Long awaited the arrival of surgeons summoned to perform the necessary operation. But a roadside mishap delayed the physicians en route from New Orleans and the decision was made to proceed with the surgery without them. Chosen by fate to perform the operation was Arthur Vidrine, southwest Louisiana surgeon who had been appointed by Long to head the newly created LSU Medical School and the New Orleans Charity Hospital.

Surgery was performed under the most bizarre of circumstances. The Kingfish's henchmen had been drawn to the operating room like filings to a magnet and they swarmed throughout the hospital.

They lined the walls of the operating room and called out questions to the operating surgeons. Assisting Vidrine were perhaps half a dozen other physicians. As will be discussed later, there is some question as to who actually was in charge of the surgery.

Long's blood pressure had been dropping dramatically and his pulse had been increasing—classic indications that there was internal bleeding. The path of the bullet, diagnosed as having entered the abdomen and having exited through the back to the right of the spine, obviously penetrated the transverse colon, which crosses the abdomen just below the ribs. This raised the specter of peritonitis because of infection by the spillage of fecal matter.

Vidrine and his associates repaired the damage to the transverse colon, cleaned up the spillage in the abdominal cavity and sutured the incision. Spokesmen for the Kingfish were optimistic.

But tragedy waited in the wings.

Those who were present at the operation that Sunday night have drawn a veil of secrecy around the proceedings. What actually happened has never been told in its entirety.

This is unfortunate, because if we are to review what the record shows of the treatment that was provided Huey Long we must conclude that the collection of prominent physicians calling the shots that night displayed an appalling ignorance or disregard of basic medical procedure. Wittingly or not, they insured by their actions in the hospital room that Sunday night that Huey Long would never leave the hospital alive.

For the second time that night, the unthinkable had happened!

First, the flying wedge of skullcrushers sworn to protect Long had allowed a 129-pound stripling to penetrate their security. And now, the combined talents of dozens of physicians who had been summoned from all parts of Louisiana were powerless to save the life of the most important man in the state.

Portions of the record force us to conclude that Long's kidney had been injured, causing an internal hemorrhage. However, no records indicate that this wound was ever addressed. Some have charged that it was overlooked completely. Transfusions given to him later prolonged his life for some 28 hours beyond the operation, but it seems that no one really expected him to recover when it was realized that the blood being given him never found its way into the circulatory system, instead spilling into body spaces where it could do no good.

The hospital records—what is left of them—would seem to indicate that this loss of blood was the cause of Long's death. But because they are incomplete, we cannot rule out the possibility that Long died of other causes. In fact, one physician ruled out an internal hemorrhage and, instead, maintained that peritonitis was the cause of death.

Most physicians disagree with the peritonitis diagnosis because of the relative speed with which Long died. He lived less than 30 hours after the shooting and it is generally believed that it would have taken days, not hours, for peritonitis to run its fatal course.

But no one really knows.

Because the hospital records were stripped of important information and because participating physicians maintained a stony silence in response to inquiries, there can be no definitive conclusion.

When Long finally gave up the ghost, some of the attending physicians pressed for an autopsy but this was blocked, giving additional reason to question the conduct of those in charge of Long's medical treatment.

The morning following the shooting, the coroner of East Baton Rouge Parish convened an inquest to determine the cause of death of Carl Weiss. (Remember that Long was still alive at the time.) No witnesses to the shooting appeared. Two persons who were in the vicinity of the shooting, but did not actually see the event, testified. However, bodyguards and others who were known to have witnessed the affair did not respond immediately to the invitation to testify. As noted earlier, it would be eight days following the shooting before eyewitnesses would finally speak up.

In the meantime, rumors began to surface. Long was shot twice, it was said, and not once, as the physicians maintained. Long's revelations to the U.S. Senate a month earlier that he would be murdered by Roosevelt henchmen were remembered and there was speculation that Washington had a hand in the shooting. Others whispered that it was the bodyguards and not the young physician who did the Kingfish in. Some even hinted that those closest to Long had good reason to will his death. The underworld, it was whispered, was involved.

But still, the survivors of the Long machine maintained then, as they do now, that it was "one man, one gun, one bullet." In the same breath they insist that the alleged assassin, Dr. Weiss, was part of a conspiracy, ignoring the obvious inconsistency of their reasoning. One man and one bullet constitute a unique personal relationship between assassin and target and not a conspiracy.

But such is the nature of political mysteries. The inquest was closed. The case was sealed.

Time has not satisfied the doubts that have arisen. And, in truth, there seems to be abundant evidence that Long was shot not once, but twice. Chief among those who believe this is the Federal Bureau of Investigation, whose Special Agent in Charge of the New Orleans office at the time of the shooting had wired FBI head J. Edgar Hoover one hour after the shooting:

> SENIOR US SENATOR HUEY P. LONG SHOT AT BATON ROUGE LA. TONIGHT WHILE WALKING IN STATE CAPITOL BLDG BETWEEN LEGISLATIVE CHAMBER AND GOVERNORS OFFICE NOW IN LADY OF LAKE HOSPITAL BATON ROUGE LA. IN GRAVE CONDITION UNDERGOING OPERATION. SHOT IN ABDOMEN **TWICE** BODY GUARDS KILLED ASSASSIN REPORTED TO BE DOCTOR CARL WEISS. NO INVESTIGATION BY THIS OFFICE UNLESS ADVISED.[8]

Evidence has been uncovered since the shooting to suggest that Long could have been killed under several sets of circumstances.

But there is one way that he could not have been killed.

And that is the way the "official" investigation would have us believe it happened.

CHAPTER THREE

The Inquest
As Whitewash

East Baton Rouge Parish Coroner Thomas B. Bird moved swiftly to establish the cause of death of Carl Weiss. He convened a coroner's jury Monday morning at the mortuary where Weiss' body lay. The same funeral parlor would receive Long's remains the following day.

Bird expected to hear testimony from at least some of the 11 witnesses who observed the complete sequence of events involving the shooting of Long and the killing of Weiss. In addition to these eyewitnesses, another ten persons were close enough to have heard the shots clearly or to have witnessed part of the action.

The corridor outside the governor's office had been a cramped and crowded place that Sunday night. The corridor measures 11 feet wide throughout most of its 150-foot length, except outside the chief executive's office, where it widens to form a 13-foot bay. The bay is framed by four Travertine marble pillars and it was next to one of these that Weiss stood before the shooting took place.

The area involved in the shooting is about 20 feet long. In this 260-square foot area (20'x13', equivalent to a fair-sized bedroom) some 25 persons were jammed. In addition, some of the available space was taken up by the four marble pillars, with diameters of about 18 inches. Against the wall was an over-sized bust of LaSalle mounted on a pedestal.

It is important to keep this teeming tableau in mind when evaluating the testimony of witnesses. It is doubtful that there is anyone who could have possibly had an unrestricted view and a clear picture of the overall scene. All witnesses are positive in their testimony but it is highly questionable that any of those testifying could have seen all the action they tried to describe.

Eyewitnesses included eight of Long's bodyguards: Joe Vitrano,

George McQuiston, Joe Messina, Paul Voitier, Murphy Roden, Elliott Coleman, Joe Bates and Louis Heard. There were two pro-Long legislators, Representatives C.A. Riddle of Avoyelles Parish and Lorris Wimberly of Bienville Parish. Rounding out the eyewitnesses was Long's hand-picked Supreme Court Justice John Fournet. Fournet was accompanied by his father who was being introduced to Long when the fireworks started, but the elder Fournet did not appear at the inquest and there is no mention of his presence in any news reports.

There were undoubtedly other witnesses. Several men were observed standing close to Carl Weiss. Some have speculated that they accompanied Weiss but there is no mention of their names anywhere and they apparently disappeared during or following the shooting.

When the appointed time for the inquest, 10:00 a.m. Monday, arrived, no eyewitnesses appeared. There is no clear reason why they did not show, although the state's press speculated that Long's followers were abiding by his command issued the night before that no one was to do any talking or give any statements. This would be done by Long when he recovered.

Instead, two of Long's followers who did not actually see the shooting appeared for the inquest. Each had some knowledge of the details, however.

One witness was John DeArmond, one of the Kingfish's protectors who was, strictly speaking, not a bodyguard. He was a supporter and sometime companion of the Kingfish who was carried on the "de-duct" payroll, a fund made up of money taken from the checks of state employees to fund the Long machine.

The second was Charles "Chick" Frampton, favored reporter for the New Orleans *Item*. Frampton collected a second check from the state attorney general's office and was considered to be Long's unofficial press secretary.

The testimony of both witnesses was hardly conclusive, since neither of them had seen the actual shooting.

Frampton testified that he was about to open the doors leading from the governor's office to the corridor when he heard a shot in the corridor. Opening the door, he saw Long holding his side and walking down the corridor, away from the crowd of men milling outside the governor's office. In the corridor, Frampton saw bodyguard Roden and Carl Weiss struggling and then, "half a dozen men began firing at Dr. Weiss."

Although the forum was a coroner's jury to determine the cause of Weiss' death, it was the district attorney, J. (John) Fred Odom who did all the questioning.

He seemed to be particularly concerned with the spacing of shots, whether there were lapses between shots or whether they followed in rapid sequence, without interruption. Frampton estimated that "three or four seconds" had elapsed between the first shot he heard from behind the doors of the governor's office and the others that followed.

When the question was rephrased and asked again later in the testimony, Frampton replied, "It was practically a continuous action."

Clearly, Odom was establishing the possibility that Long could have been shot by an errant bullet fired by one of his bodyguards. From Frampton's testimony, this seemed possible—even likely. He described a scene in which bullets flew wildly from the bodyguards' guns, endangering anyone near. Roden and Weiss grappled in the corridor, both fighting for possession of Weiss' gun. Roden fired several shots at Weiss and these were followed by volleys from other bodyguards.

In the wild crossfire that ensued, Frampton said, "It is a miracle to me that Roden wasn't shot by his own men."

Odom asked Frampton if Weiss was on the floor when the bodyguards began shooting. Frampton replied, "Yes. He slumped down with the gun in his hand."

During the inquest, Coroner Bird read a statement revealing that Weiss' body had 61 bullet holes in it, 30 in the front, 29 in the back and two in the head. A bullet had penetrated his left eye and another had sheared off a piece of his nose.

Merle Welsh, who prepared the Weiss remains for burial, helped Dr. Bird count the bullet holes. Welsh figures that there were more than 61. "When I reached 61," the undertaker remembers, "Dr. Bird sighed and said, 'You can stop counting.'"[1]

I interviewed John DeArmond, who was given a machine gun and told to guard the lifeless body of Weiss. He commented sadly, "The poor man's back looked like a checkerboard," a reference to the pattern of blood splotches against the background of Weiss' white linen suit.

There was friction, suspicion and distrust about the inquest from the start, much of it fueled by Odom's role as questioner. It was a matter of fact that the district attorney had attended a meeting a month before at the DeSoto Hotel in New Orleans which was labeled by Long supporters an "assassination" meeting at which Long's death was plotted. It was a partial transcript of this meeting which Long read to the U.S. Senate. Long claimed that Roosevelt was behind the plot.

After the two witnesses had been questioned and Coroner Bird had recessed the hearing until 4:00 p.m. in hopes the bodyguards would appear, Baton Rouge police chief and Long supporter King Strenzke demanded of Bird, "What is Odom trying to do? Trying to get some publicity for himself?"[2]

Monday afternoon the bodyguards failed once again to appear. Sheriff Robert Pettit, whose office had been taken over by the National Guard when martial law was declared earlier that year, reminded Strenzke that the chief had promised to have the witnesses at the inquest. Strenzke snapped, "The coroner will have to get them himself if he wants them."

Local authorities, charged by law with investigating the homicide of Weiss (and later Long), were up a blind alley. Pettit said he would appeal to the superintendent of the Criminal Bureau of Investigation and ask that the bodyguards be ordered to appear. However, if that official refused to act, Pettit and the rest of the local government were powerless. Long's legislature had stripped the sheriff of virtually all his duties.

Coroner Bird conceded that nothing could be done if the Long forces refused to allow the bodyguards to cooperate. In this event, Bird said, he would have to conclude the investigation and assign the cause of Weiss' death himself.

It was announced that the inquest would reconvene at 2:00 p.m. on Tuesday. The time came and went with no bodyguards appearing. The inquiry was postponed for the third time, to resume on Thursday.

The *Times-Picayune* reported in its Tuesday morning edition:

"Shortly before the hour fixed for resumption of the inquest this afternoon (Monday), several score of state policemen who have been on guard duty at the capitol since the Legislature convened Sunday night were called into a conference at the state house. The subject of the meeting was not disclosed.

"It is reported, however, that strict orders have been issued to bodyguards who participated in the shooting of Dr. Weiss to refrain from discussion of the matter."

On Thursday, Huey Long was being buried and bodyguards were needed at the funeral. None showed up for the inquest. The hearing was postponed a fourth time and rescheduled for 10:00 a.m. Monday, September 16.

Eight days after the shooting the inquest was finally held.

On that Monday morning the courtroom of East Baton Rouge Parish was jammed with spectators. The atmosphere was electric, crackling with tension. Friends and opponents of the late Kingfish rubbed elbows. Both sides were armed and there was little effort to conceal the armament. A member of the deceased physician's family said, "It was man for man and almost gun for gun."[3]

The state's attorney general, Gaston Porterie, arrived a few minutes before the inquest opened. There had been a rumor that he would supersede the parish district attorney in the investigation, but when questioned as to his role in the proceedings, he answered simply, "I am merely here as a looker-on."

Long-sponsored changes in the law had reduced the district attorneys of the state to little more than extensions of the attorney general and, if Porterie chose to inject himself into the proceedings, he could do so. And he would.

By the time of the inquest, many stories had surfaced in Baton Rouge challenging the "official" version of what had happened in the state capitol that

Sunday night. An official statement issued at the hospital reported that the cause of Long's death was a gunshot wound from a single bullet that had entered his abdomen and exited from a point to the right of the spine. The bullet was not recovered, according to hospital spokesmen. Long had died from internal damage inflicted by the projectile.

But this explanation did not satisfy many.

Word had been passed that a bullet had been recovered from Long's body at the hospital. If this were the case, there would have had to be a second bullet inside the body, because of the two penetrations—on the front and on the back—in Long's body. If so, this would have meant that the wounds diagnosed as wounds of entry and exit, respectively, would have been, instead, both wounds of entry. Both bullets would have remained in the body.

A rumor was spreading that Weiss was not the killer. This version had it that Weiss had gone to the state capitol to talk to the Kingfish. Long insulted him. Weiss reacted angrily, striking Long, whereupon the bodyguards cut him down. In the process, deliberately or accidentally, they shot Long.

This interpretation of the events of Sunday night, September 8, spread swiftly. The following Sunday, Walter Winchell reported the story on his weekly radio broadcast. The gun reported to have been fired by Weiss, the broadcaster said, was actually taken from Weiss' automobile and planted at the scene. It was a throw-down gun.

The whole thing was a set-up.

In this climate of hostility and distrust the inquest began to probe the causes of the deaths of Long and Weiss.

Judge Fournet was the first witness. There had been talk that he would be allowed to give his testimony in private, in deference to his position as justice of the supreme court. Instead, he led the parade of 21 witnesses in proceedings that lasted two hours and 30 minutes. The hearing began at 10:10 a.m.

Fournet's testimony was uncomplicated. He had walked towards the governor's office to find Huey and had arrived just as the Kingfish had emerged from the office.

"At that time," Fournet said, "a small man in a white, or almost white, suit, flashed among us and flashed a gun and shot almost immediately."

Fournet put his hand on Weiss' arm to deflect the bullet. Bodyguard Roden grabbed Weiss and both slipped. Weiss and Roden wrestled for possession of the gun. Weiss was attempting to fire again. Shots rang out. Weiss fell to the floor.

DA Odom asked, "Who fired the first shot after Senator Long was shot?"

Fournet replied, "I cannot say who fired the first shot after Dr. Weiss shot Senator Long. The shooting came from in back of me." (Weiss, according to Fournet, was standing in front of him.)

Moments later he offered the possibility that perhaps Weiss had fired another shot. "The first two shots were so close together I thought the doctor fired both shots. Senator Long was of the same opinion. Senator Long told me I kept the doctor from hitting him with the second shot."

It is unfortunate that the conduct of the inquest was so haphazard that the testimony of Fournet was not better established. Had Weiss fired once or twice? Had the second shot come from behind Fournet? Fournet's testimony contradicts itself. The question of whether Weiss fired once or twice is crucial to a resolution of the entire Huey Long shooting.

Fournet's testimony also gave a chilling account of the intensity of the bodyguards' fury:

"I was a machine gunner during the war and machine guns shoot about 600 shots a minute. The shooting sounded as fast as a machine gun. There were two, three or four men shooting at the same time. It sounded like the guns were all automatic pistols.

"...Dr. Weiss went down very slowly. When the first bullet struck him, he quivered and then shots poured in from both sides.

"After the second shot there was no cessation in the shooting—it was one continuous movement. If Dr. Weiss was shot 40 to 50 times he was shot as fast as they could shoot with three or four automatic pistols."

Odom asked, "Was Dr. Weiss shot after he was on the floor?"

Fournet responded, "The shooting was continuous—some may have hit him after he was on the floor."

After Odom concluded his questioning, Attorney General Porterie asked Fournet if there was any conversation between Weiss and Long. Fournet replied that there was none. (So much for the Winchell poppycock about Long insulting Weiss and a responding blow being struck by the doctor.)

In contrast to Fournet's restrained testimony, the appearance of the next witness was so extravagantly dramatic that it galvanized the assemblage, polarizing feelings of the two political factions even beyond the division that already existed.

That witness was the Reverend Gerald L.K. Smith, national organizer and spiritual advisor of Long's Share Our Wealth movement. Smith had been pastor of a Shreveport church, leaving to join Long. He had been chosen to deliver the graveside eulogy for Long and, since the senator's death, had been attempting to establish proprietary ownership of the Share Our Wealth effort in a series of meetings throughout the state. Smith claimed to have witnessed the shooting but his presence at the scene is not confirmed. He also claimed to have been present when Long uttered his final words before expiring but this, too, is doubtful.

Without waiting to be sworn in, the revivalist approached the rostrum and launched into a denunciation of Odom, whom he called "one of the co-plotters" of Long's assassination. He refused to testify. He would do so only when, he said, "a man asks the questions who has not shared in the conspiracies."

A newspaper reported dramatically, "With his eyes blazing and his arms flailing the air, the Rev. Mr. Smith walked down from the rostrum and passed within a foot of District Attorney Odom, who glowered at him."

Long supporters erupted! Some rose to slap Smith on the back as he returned to his seat. Some bodyguards rose, prompting agents of the district attorney to rise also. It looked as if there might be trouble.

Odom was not the only person Smith accused of conspiring to have Huey killed. During the period immediately following Long's death, he nagged at Roosevelt to authorize an investigation, alarming some of Long's associates who were anxious to mend fences with the Washington administration.

Smith also charged that the United States senator from Mississippi, Theodore Bilbo, had carried money to New Orleans shortly before Long's shooting. He hinted that Bilbo was part of a plot. Bilbo replied with an outburst that revealed much of the Mississippian's contempt of Smith and also Long's Share Our Wealth scheme. When informed of Smith's statement, he exploded:

> "When Smith intimates, insinuates or charges that I went to New Orleans with $25,000 in my pocket...he is a contemptible, dirty, vicious, pusillanimous, with malice aforethought, damnable, self-made liar...by trying to fool the Negroes and ignorant white people with fantastic ideas of share our wealth societies...he becomes a public menace and ought to be squelched."[4]

Odom himself rose, bristling with anger. He denied any part in Long's assassination, labeling anyone who said otherwise a "willful, malicious and vicious liar." This caused a rattle of applause from the anti-Long contingent that matched the earlier demonstration from their opposite number.

Odom laughed casually and called the next witness. The tension was broken.

The first of three persons who were not even remotely involved in the shooting was called and the direction of Odom's questioning began to take shape. Dr. William Cook was a Baton Rouge physician who had been summoned to assist in Long's surgery. Cook testified that Long had an abrasion of his lip that bled when the anesthesiologist pressed it with antiseptic.

The scenario implied by Odom's strategy was unmistakable: Weiss and

Long had words; Long insulted Weiss; Weiss struck Long, causing the lip wound. Point for Odom.

But Porterie, the "looker-on," asked Dr. Cook if perhaps Long could not have inflicted the wound upon himself by falling against "an angle of marble or iron?" Cook replied, "Any contusion or trauma could have caused it." Counterpoint.

Following the inquest, the Weiss family would maintain stoutly that the wound on Long's lip was caused by Weiss' fist. Long supporters would just as stoutly maintain that it was a fever blister that was scraped during Long's journey down the bronze and marble staircase following the shooting.

(I interviewed the scrub nurse at Long's operation and she told me that, when asked by the anesthesiologist, "What happened to your lip?" Long replied, "That's where he hit me." I asked her who Long was referring to. She replied, "Dr. Weiss.")[5]

The next witness called by Odom was even farther removed from the subject matter of the inquest than Dr. Cook. Although Cook had not witnessed the shooting, he had at least been at the hospital and had participated in the operation on Long. Odom called Dr. J. Webb McGehee, a local anesthesiologist whose name had not yet been mentioned in any connection with the case.

Porterie "looked on" again by inquiring of Odom, "Speaking in an advisory capacity, do you think this testimony by a physician who was not in attendance is relevant?"

Odom answered that he would demonstrate "something else."

The "something else" that Odom demonstrated was that McGehee had arranged to administer an anesthetic for an operation by Weiss scheduled for the previous Monday morning, the day following Weiss' death. McGehee and Weiss had talked twice about the operation. On Friday, McGehee and Weiss had met in person, probably in the Reymond Building in downtown Baton Rouge, where both had offices. The second time they conversed, according to McGehee, was by telephone at 8:15 p.m. Sunday, about an hour before Weiss was killed.

(There is an inconsistency between what Dr. McGehee told the inquest and what he told the Baton Rouge *State-Times* a few days earlier. To the newspaper, on September 13, he reported that it was his wife, and not he, to whom Weiss talked on the fatal Sunday night and that Weiss asked Mrs. McGehee to relay the message. Whether there is any significance to this inconsistency will probably never be known.)

Although McGehee shed precious little light upon the shooting, his description of Weiss as a physician concerned with the professional aspects of an operation Monday morning obviously argued against the prospects of his harboring plans for assassinating Long that evening. Another score for Odom.

There were a number of witnesses summoned by Odom who really did not see much of the shooting. But their testimony is valuable because they help establish the sequence of shots. Invariably they all pointed to a single shot, a short lapse and then a fusillade. Frampton had estimated "three or four seconds" between the first and second shots when he testified the week before. Louis Le-Sage, Standard Oil lobbyist who saw little of the activity but heard the shots, placed the interval at "not over two seconds." All agreed that very little time elapsed between the first shot and the ones that followed it.

This time lapse is an important element of the shooting. Those who maintain that Long was shot only once—and by Dr. Weiss—maintain that Huey had left the arena before other guns began firing. If this is true, then Long could have been hit only once. If he lingered—ever so briefly—then a second gunshot wound is plausible.

One of Long's bodyguards, Joe Messina, was questioned and gave way to his emotions to such a degree that it was impossible, at times, to understand what he said. Messina was a simple, introverted man who had a religious attachment to Long. His physical appearance was far from appealing. He was short, heavyset and menacing. He was uncommunicative, even to his family.

He is one of the more interesting members of Long's bodyguards. Because of his physical appearance and limited intelligence, many attached evil and devious motives to him. Anti-Long candidates for state office in 1936 accused Messina of killing Long and charged that he had been committed to a mental institution where he spent his time weeping and moaning that he had killed his best friend.

But Messina had no deviousness about him. His wife was Modest (in the French style: "mo-DEST") Marchand, a maid of French extraction who braved family censure to marry an Italian 17 years older than herself. Modest described Messina as a man who never gossiped. She remembers, "I never heard Joe say a bad word about anybody. Nobody. I don't care how bad it was, how good it was, he never said a word. He was a man of few words."

But Joe was, in Modest's eyes, a good man. She was widowed with two children when she and Messina married and she was forever grateful for his generosity in supporting the boys who were not his natural sons. She remembered:

> "Joe was a good provider. He was very
> good to my children, which weren't his, you know.
> When he made money, he didn't forget me and my
> children. He helped me raise them. He was good
> to my boys. When we needed the money he took
> care of us. I always think of the good things."[6]

When he appeared at the inquest, Messina prefaced his testimony with a poignant outpouring of the intensity of his feelings for Long. He told of a plot confessed to by a double agent and informer named Sidney Songy. The plot called for Long to be assassinated on a stretch of highway outside of Baton

Rouge called "Dead Man's Curve" because of the difficulties encountered in negotiating the road at high speed. This plot had been uncovered earlier in 1935 and Long had a hearing convened in the capitol to use as a forum, accusing his enemies of plotting to kill him.

The news accounts of Messina's testimony differ somewhat from each other but all are in agreement that he was emotional, baring his feelings to sob, "in a cowardly way, Senator Long was shot."

District Attorney Odom was tender in his handling of the obviously distraught and discomposed bodyguard. He softly encouraged Messina to continue.

Messina said he saw Carl Weiss shoot Long and "I knew he had been killed. I ran up, pulled my gun and emptied it at the man who shot Senator Long."

Messina had no capacity for the intricacies of elapsed time between gunshots. He knew what he knew and that's all that he knew. Odom asked him, "Roden testified that several shots were fired before he broke loose from Dr. Weiss. Did you fire before he broke loose?"

Messina repeated, "I ran up, recognized Roden and began firing on Weiss."

Odom tried again, "Was Dr. Weiss being held by Roden?"

Messina responded dully, "I ran up and shot the man who had shot Senator Long."

There was a parade of witnesses who offered incidental information about the shooting. Then Odom called Dr. Carl Adam Weiss, father of the alleged assassin. He would be the third witness called by Odom whose testimony was entirely irrelevant to a panel attempting to fix the cause of death of Weiss and Senator Long. But by this time it was obvious that the inquest was a jousting match between pro- and anti-Long forces to prove Weiss was the assassin or muddy the waters sufficiently to cast doubt upon his guilt.

There was no objection to the elder Dr. Weiss testifying.

He took the coroner's jury through the pleasantries and simplicities of a dreamy and simple Sunday that included morning Mass, noontime dinner at the family home, an afternoon at the family camp on a nearby stream and a finale that saw the alleged assassin bathing his three-month-old son and feeding the family dog.

Would such a man, devoted to a homespun, shirtsleeve lifestyle, show up armed in the state capitol? Why, District Attorney Odom wanted to know, did Carl Weiss pack a gun?

The father of the dead man explained it was for self protection. "...Recently there were intruders in our garage."

Odom asked the physician about his son's physical characteristics. He was 29 years old, weighing about 132 pounds and "slight in stature."

Once again Odom was making a case for Carl Weiss, the David against the Goliaths. It took 61 bullet holes to subdue a skinny physician by strong men who could easily have broken him in two.

When Murphy Roden, bodyguard who, along with Carl Weiss, was a central figure in the confrontation outside the governor's office, was questioned, Odom asked for the same information about physical characteristics.

"How old are you?" "Thirty."

"What do you weigh?" "About 150 pounds."

"What is your height?" "Five feet, seven and one-half inches." (Carl Weiss was 5'9". Weiss was lighter, but he obviously had the reach on Roden.)

Murphy Roden was an impressive witness. In talking to both supporters and detractors of Huey Long, no one has ever suggested to me that Roden did anything else but protect Long to the best of his ability. His testimony is considered by most to be accurate and believable.

But there are inconsistencies in what Roden said in 1935 and what he said years later in several interviews granted by him. The same is true of John Fournet. If we analyze these inconsistencies we sense that there could have been an entirely different scenario than what has been passed along to us as the "official" version.

Roden's testimony was brief:

> "Somebody brushed by me, pulled a
> gun, thrust it at the senator's stomach and fired. I
> grabbed him (Dr. Weiss) and we fell to the floor. I
> jerked loose, got up, pulled my gun and began
> firing."

There were no words exchanged between Long and Weiss, according to Roden. Roden fired ten times from his .38 Colt automatic. When asked if others had fired after he had stopped, Roden was noncommittal. "I couldn't say. It was all over in a second. The others were behind me."

How many shots did Dr. Weiss fire? "I am of the opinion that only one shot was fired."

Years later, Roden's testimony would change.

In 1935, he said the gun was pointed "at the senator's stomach" and the assassin fired. In 1963, he remembered that the gun was held "chest high and at arm's length." It was his intervention in knocking down the assassin's arm, according to Roden, that had saved Long from a shot in the heart. (John Fournet had claimed this in 1935.)

In 1963 Roden remembered that Weiss fired a second shot, although he had testified in 1935 that there was only one shot fired by the physician. This second shot, according to Roden, sheared the watch from his wrist.

Roden's recollections about the scene were much more vivid in 1963 than in 1935. At the inquest, he couldn't say whether shots were fired by others after he, himself, had emptied his magazine into the body of Weiss. But his interview with journalist Hermann Deutsch in 1963 provides us a vivid description of whining bullets and whizzing shrapnel in the gunsmoke-shrouded corridor after he had fired all the bullets in his pistol:

> "All hell broke loose...I was being deafened and my eyes were burning with particles of powder from those shots...I could not see any more because of the muzzle blasts from other guns. While I did not learn this until later, shots had passed so close to me that the powder burns penetrated my coat, shirt and undershirt and burned my skin beneath, all along my back..."[7]

To Dave Zinman, another author who wrote about the shooting in 1963, Roden confided, "I got shrapnel in my back from the ricocheting marble chips. They dug it out of my back for six months afterwards." Bodyguard Messina was also peppered with shrapnel.[8]

Why did Roden decide that Weiss had fired twice, not once, as he had said in 1935, when the shooting was fresh in his mind?

It seems that his revised conclusion was prompted by two altogether disassociated and possibly irrelevant facts. According to Roden, the firearm carried by Weiss normally holds seven cartridges. However, when examined after the shooting, the weapon had only five cartridges in the magazine. A shell was caught in the ejecting mechanism.

It was a deductive mathematical conclusion: the capacity of the gun was seven; there were five bullets remaining; 7-5=2, the number of shots Weiss was able to fire.

No one has seen fit to ask Roden why he assumed the gun was fully loaded with the maximum seven cartridges at the time of the shooting. No one has ever asked him if it was not possible that one of the bullets was removed from the magazine of the pistol for testing. A newspaper story acknowledged that investigators were checking to determine if the bullet that was fired into Long's body was poisoned to increase its lethalness.

The second quivery premise for Roden's conclusion that Weiss fired twice is based on the path of the errant bullet that knocked his watch from his wrist. He concluded that it was Weiss' bullet which scarred his wrist and wrenched the watch loose: "The dent on my watch, which was later recovered and which I still have, was made by a small caliber bullet."

Incredible!

A larger caliber bullet, striking his wrist watch at an angle, could easily have made a similar small indentation such as is visible on the watch, now in the possession of LSU.

But upon this flimsy collection of evidence—a seven cartridge capacity magazine from which two cartridges were missing and a dent in a wristwatch—

rests the conclusion that Weiss fired two bullets and not one.

Can we not ask if the shell that jammed in the ejecting mechanism was only the first shot fired by Weiss and not the second? This is not only possible, but highly probable, if we take another, closer look at some of the testimony of Judge Fournet. He told Hermann Deutsch:

> "...At the same instant the shot was fired
> (by Weiss), for Murphy's hand kept the shell of the
> little automatic from ejecting, which is why the
> man whose body was later identified as that of Dr.
> Weiss could not fire another shot."[9]

Well! If the second shot, which tore the watch from Roden's wrist, was not fired by Weiss, then who in the world fired it? Roden and Fournet both agreed that the bodyguards were in the rear of the group of which they were a part. If the bullet came from in front of Roden and Fournet, it could have come from Weiss; if it came from the rear then it could not have been fired by Weiss. It is just that simple.

But if Weiss did not fire that shot, who did, in fact, fire it?

Judge Fournet gives us the answer, again in his interview with Deutsch:

> "...Elliott Coleman from quite a ways
> down the hall fired the second shot I heard that
> night as well as two others...one of Elliott
> Coleman's bullets had shot away Murphy Roden's
> wrist watch, but the next two hit Weiss."[10]

So! Weiss shot once, Elliott Coleman fired the second shot, which knocked the watch from Roden's wrist and presumably ricocheted down the hallway. Coleman was east of Weiss and it is probably safe to say that the bullet ricocheted toward the west. Let us remember that Long was fleeing the scene by attempting to reach the staircase to the west of the melee.

When he testified, Elliott Coleman's description paralleled Fournet's, with one remarkable difference. He described a physical altercation wherein he punched Weiss and perhaps another person.

Coleman told the coroner's jury in 1935 that he fired two shots at Weiss. But, like Fournet and Roden, he would change his mind later. He told Hermann Deutsch in 1963 that he fired only one shot. (Fournet remembered that Coleman fired three shots. One time, three times, what's the difference? No big deal.) But this happened, he maintained, after swinging a punch or two at Weiss. No other witness thus far had mentioned fisticuffs. Did such a conspicuous and seeable action escape the notice of Fournet and Roden, who delivered such clear and positive testimony of the activity?

In 1935, Coleman testified:

> "I struck at the man who shot Senator
> Long but missed him and hit someone else. Roden

grabbed him and they fell against a marble
column. I struck Weiss again as they fell. I then
fired two shots."

But in 1963 the story would change:

"...I reached the young man about the
same time Roden did and hit him with my fist
knocking him down...I fired one shot."

In a letter to author Zinman on June 29, 1961, Coleman wrote:

"I struck Weiss in the jaw, not in the face
and he staggered back against the marble
column...There was one shot fired and Weiss
dropped to the floor."[11]

As if this is not enough confusion, another bodyguard, Paul Voitier,
managed to muddle things a little more. According to Voitier, Coleman did indeed strike Dr. Weiss, but then he threw another punch and "he struck at Weiss
again and missed him and I think he struck Senator Long where the senator's lip
was later found bleeding." (Recall Long's remark to the anesthesiologist when
asked about his bleeding lip: "That's where he hit me.")

What is going on here? Can anyone conclude from the testimony at the
coroner's inquest and from later interviews of witnesses exactly what happened
on Sunday, September 8, 1935? At this point, all witnesses should have been
recalled and re-examined to square these inconsistencies.

Since this was not done, let us conduct our own inquiry and ask a
single question to find the answers we will receive.

Q. HOW MANY SHOTS WERE
FIRED BY DOCTOR WEISS?

RODEN (1935): "I am of the opinion
that only one shot was fired."

RODEN (1963): "It has always been my
belief that it was Dr. Weiss who fired the second
shot."

COLEMAN (1935): "I thought it was
his (Dr. Weiss') gun which fired the second shot."

FOURNET (1963): "Murphy's hand
kept the shell of the little automatic from ejecting,
which is why the man whose body was later identified as that of Dr. Weiss could not fire another
shot."

FOURNET (1935): "I cannot say who
fired the first shot after Dr. Weiss shot Senator
Long. The shooting came from in back of me."

FOURNET (1935): "The first two shots

were so close together I thought the doctor fired
both shots."

Did Weiss fire once or did he fire twice? You pay your money and you
take your choice.

In 1963, Justice Fournet was positive that it was Coleman who fired the
second shot, although in 1935 he had testified first that Weiss had fired the shot
and then later Coleman. Further, he believed, in 1963, that the second shot was
fired while Huey was still on the scene, trying wildly to escape. Reading the
words of that interview in 1963, we see that perhaps this shot found its way into
Long's body.

Listen to Judge Fournet's words:

"Weiss had both hands around his gun,
trying to fire again and this time at Roden; and
Roden, while holding his desperate clutch about
the gun which was waving wildly this way and
that, was trying to get his own gun from his
shoulder holster, and I was still standing there with
my hands outstretched from pushing them, when
Elliott Coleman from quite a ways down the hall
fired the second shot that I heard that night, as
well as two others."[12]

Here is the sequence of events as related at the inquest:

Weiss approaches Long, points his pistol toward Long's heart. Either
Fournet or Roden knocks Weiss' arm aside, so that the bullet Weiss fires
penetrates not the heart but the right abdomen of Long. Long turns, wounded, to
escape from the violence. In so doing, he turns his back to the commotion.

He is fleeing toward the west stairway between the first floor and the
basement. A bodyguard, probably Elliott Coleman, fires at Weiss, oblivious to
the danger he is creating for his brother officer, Roden, who is struggling with
Weiss on the floor. He is oblivious also to the presence of Long, who is in his
line of fire should the bullet miss Weiss and continue on its westward journey.

The bullet missed Weiss and, fortunately, missed Roden too. However,
it strikes Roden's wrist watch, ripping it from his arm.

The bullet has ricocheted. Fournet tells us where the shot landed:

"In that same instant of general confusion that boiled up I heard Huey give just one
shout, a sort of hoot, then he ran like a wild deer. I
bent over to help disarm Weiss and twisted a
muscle in my back so that for a moment I could
not move in any direction. It was then I saw that
one of Elliott Coleman's bullets had shot away
Murphy Roden's wrist watch, but the next two hit

Weiss."[13]

Had the second shot entered Long's back inches to the right, left, lower or upper part of the point where it actually did penetrate, the diagnosis of the physicians would have been simple. It would have been clear that the Kingfish had been shot twice. But the position of the wounds was such that it seemed to indicate that a single projectile entered and exited Long's body.

And the pressure was on to diagnose that it was a single assassin who had done the deed with a single bullet. The location of the wounds seemed to bear this out.

However, had anyone with any knowledge of gunshot wounds examined Long, the theory would have been discarded summarily. Both wounds were small punctures. Neither approximated the ragged, gaping slit that always characterizes the exit wound of a bullet after it has been flattened on the path through tissue, organ or bone.

But no one was of a mind to go beyond the "one man, one gun, one bullet" hypothesis that had been established at the "assassination" conference a month before.

This would be established as the "official" version and would be etched in stone. But Long had been wounded twice, not once. Furthermore, both bullets were inside Long as he fled to the hospital. What would the physicians do when they opened the abdomen of the Kingfish to repair the damage to his battered body?

Would they discover the bullets? Is it at all possible that they could fail to see them? Would they change the diagnosis of "one man, one gun, one bullet?"

CHAPTER FOUR

Rise Of The Kingfish

At the age of 39, Huey Long wrote his autobiography.

His opening words cited the view of Benvenuto Cellini, Renaissance author and artist, that those who have achieved the extraordinary should write their autobiography only after they have reached the age of 60. However, Long offered the justification that his life had been lived at such an accelerated pace that he was much older than his chronological age would indicate and hence was entitled to prepare the story of his life for posterity.[1]

It is fortunate that he reached this conclusion. If he had heeded Cellini's advice and waited, we would have been deprived of his colorful perspective of himself, for he never succeeded in reaching the age of 60. He died less than three years after his work was published.

Long was born August 30, 1893 in northeastern Louisiana in the town of Winnfield, parish seat of Winn. (In Louisiana, political subdivisions known as "counties" in the other states are called "parishes.") Both parish and city were named after Walter O. Winn, prominent lawyer in nearby Alexandria. The area was thinly populated until about 1840 when preferred land along Louisiana's rivers became scarce and settlers had to content themselves with less desirable acreage. The parish was created in 1852. The city was incorporated three years later.

The area was, and still is, an important lumbering center. About 92 percent of the parish acreage is blanketed with longleaf pine. This crop forms the base for sawmills and plants that manufacture plywood, veneers, glue, creosote products and railroad ties. Winn Parish also produces livestock, cotton, salt and some oil and gas.

It also produces—according to a state guide originally published during the WPA years—lawyers. The guide tells us:

"After the parish records were destroyed in a series of courthouse fires, Winnfield became a hotbed of lawsuits and a mecca for lawyers. Many of the state's most prominent attorneys have been products of Winnfield. The best known of these was Huey P. Long. As the late Senator Long's birthplace, Winnfield is today a shrine for many thousands of his former followers."[2]

Without doubt his birthplace had a profound influence on his later actions. It is possible that, had Long been born in another section of Louisiana, say New Orleans, without the Populist heritage of Winn Parish, his career would have been channeled in an altogether different direction. When Winnfield was incorporated its population was almost 7,000. There were few Negroes and the land was worked mostly by tenant farmers.

Winn Parish had a reputation of independence (some called it "contrariness"). In 1861, Louisiana held a convention to consider its role in the Civil War, which had just begun. Winn's delegate was instructed to oppose secession and, for years after, the parish was referred to as "The Free State of Winn."[3]

It was one of the strongest Populist parishes in the state. In 1912, it gave more than 36 percent of its vote to Socialist presidential candidate Eugene V. Debs. By contrast, the parish of East Baton Rouge, seat of state government, cast less than 5% of its vote for the Socialist and the New Orleans area less than 2%.

In the same election Winn Parish voters elected two Socialist parish officials and in Winnfield the Socialists were elected to fill all of the municipal offices.

Long candidly confesses that he was born into a "comfortable, well built, four-room house" which was exchanged for an even better home a year later. The family owned a 320-acre tract of land, of which a small part was under cultivation.[4]

Huey was one of nine surviving children born to Caledonia and the senior Huey P. Long. His mother was regarded in the hill parish stronghold as a radical among radicals. His father was rooted in the belief that the common man was the 20th century counterpart of Negro slaves held in bondage before the Civil War.

The elder Long was apparently one of the Socialist faithful, reading the radical Socialist weekly *Appeal to Reason* and the monthly *National Rip-Saw,* whose publisher remarked about the journal that he had decided to "run up the red flag of the working class and nail it to the mast."[5]

In 1935, an interviewer found Huey P. Long, Senior "smoldering with the resentments that survived, unquenched, from Secession days." He saw the patriarch as "a simple, violent person, still violent at 83." The elder Long told him:

> "Didn't Abraham Lincoln free the nig-
> gers and not give the planters a dime? Why
> shouldn't Huey take the money away from the rich
> and still leave 'em plenty? Abe Lincoln freed the
> niggers without price. Why shouldn't the white
> slaves be freed and their masters left all they can
> use?
>
> "Maybe you're surprised to hear talk
> like that. Well, it was just such talk that my boy
> was raised under and that I was raised under. My
> father and my mother favored the Union. Why
> not? They didn't have slaves. They didn't even
> have decent land. The rich folks had all the good
> land and all the slaves—why, their women didn't
> even comb their own hair. They'd sooner speak to
> a nigger than a poor white. They tried to pass a
> law saying that only them as owned land could
> vote. And, when the war come, the man that
> owned ten slaves didn't have to fight.
>
> "There wants to be a revolution, I tell
> you. I seen this domination of capital, seen it for
> seventy years. What do these rich folks care for
> the poor man? They care nothing—not for his
> pain, his sickness nor his death. And now they're
> talking again about keeping the poor folks from
> voting—that same talk. I say there wants to be a
> revolution."[6]

It was in this atmosphere of bitterness, rebellion and dissent that Huey Long was reared. This willingness to challenge authority, along with a genuine concern for the downtrodden and a desire for the limelight, were to be part of Long's makeup all his life.

Long spent many of his teen years as a traveling salesman. When he decided to become a lawyer is not too clear, but it is obvious that his older brother, Julius, a successful practicing attorney, had much to do with his decision. According to one biographer, Huey's wife was also involved in the decision. He writes:

> "...Julius...had, seven years earlier, com-
> pleted a three-year course in one year at Tulane.
> What one brother had done, Mrs. Long felt,
> another could accomplish. She persuaded Huey to

> quit the road and study law. Julius financed his
> studies and planned his special course of instruc-
> tion."[7]

Julius loaned Huey $400 and, in October, 1914, at the age of 21, he entered Tulane University to study in a three-year law course. Oblivious to the talent that had been thrust into their midst, Tulane registrars got Huey's name wrong and he was enrolled as "Hugh" Pierce Long.[8]

Huey had read law extensively prior to his enrollment in Tulane. He also had been tutored by Julius. He took fewer than one-third the courses offered for a degree and then persuaded the state supreme court to allow him to take a special examination. They agreed and on May 15, 1915, at the age of 21, he became an attorney-at-law, having mastered the three-year course in eight months.[9]

In later years, Long would miss the lack of a college degree and would shop around to obtain an honorary one. He first appealed to his alma mater, Tulane, but was turned down. He persuaded a Jesuit institution in New Orleans, Loyola University of the South, to grant him an honorary Doctor of Laws. Subsequently, he wore cap and gown at LSU on formal occasions when he appeared on the platform with "the other exponents of learning."[10]

For its insensitivity in refusing to grant Long his degree, Tulane would have a steadily worsening relationship with the Kingfish. Some later blamed this slight for the fact that Long established a competing medical school at LSU. As for Loyola, it would suffer at his hands when he would create a dental school at the state university in competition with Loyola's. Some charged that Long established the dental school in reprisal for the university not making enough free time available to him through its clear channel radio station.

A year later Long would use his legal knowledge when he viewed the Louisiana legislature for the first time. The experience would change his life.

He accompanied a friend, State Senator S.J. Harper, to a meeting of the Senate Committee on Capital and Labor, which was considering a bill to restrict the right of recovery for injuries and deaths of workers on the job.

Harper and Long were cut from the same cloth. Harper, an anti-war advocate, charged that World War I was being conducted for the benefit of the vested interests and he suggested that it be financed by conscripting war profits. He was indicted by a federal grand jury and was successfully defended by Huey.

At the legislative hearing, Long had prepared amendments for Harper and sought unsuccessfully to have them adopted. He was rebuffed, ignored and humiliated. Unfamiliar with the legislative procedure, which generally restricts participation to legislators except for those laymen who are recognized, Long was continually told to sit down.

His first brush with the legislative process was an unproductive one. It left him with bitter memories, as his autobiography recalls:

> "It was my first time to have seen a

legislature in session. The formalities, man-
nerisms, kow-towing and easily discernible insin-
cerities surrounding all of the affairs of the session
were, to my mind (untrained to such a scene), disgusting."

A casual conversation with a fellow traveler in a restaurant during his visit with the legislature focused Long's attention (presumably for the first time) on his soon-to-be archenemy Standard Oil. After warning Long that his efforts to fight for the working man at the committee meeting would spoil his career as a lawyer, his companion, a "Mr. Faust," charged that Louisiana "is the worst yet" for industrial oppression. He asked Long, "Why do you think Standard Oil located here?"

When the Senate committee reconvened, Long attempted to be heard to respond to derogatory statements made about him by committee members. Blocked by rulings from the chair, he nevertheless gained the floor and launched into a tirade against the legislature which had, he alleged, for 20 years been dominated by "the henchmen and attorneys of the interests."[11]

This was the quintessential Huey Long: approach the system; by force of logic attempt to win others over to your point; failing that, attack! Attack, vilify and smear your opponents. A more prudent man would probably have retreated or compromised his position but these two courses of action were no part of his makeup.

Long would carry with him a contempt for the legislature for the rest of his life. Shortly after he was elected governor in 1928, he said in a speech reported by the New Orleans *Times-Picayune,* "A deck has 52 cards. I hold the deck and I will deal it myself. In the legislature, I can have bills passed or kill them."[12]

And, of course, Long's aggressive tactics would generate opposition and lengthen the list of his enemies. He tried, after the legislative appearance, to obtain an appointment as assistant United States attorney in Shreveport. The appointment would serve as an opportunity to leave Winnfield and travel to the more fertile legal climate of Shreveport. However, the corporate interests he had attacked now opposed him and, despite earlier assurances that he would be nominated for the attorneyship, he was refused the appointment.

Rather than mend his ways and attempt to soften his opposition, Long brooded, waiting for his chance to retaliate. His autobiography reads:

"Probably that was my evil day. Once
disappointed over a political undertaking, I could
never cast it from my mind. I awaited the opportunity of a political contest."[13]

If Long had not decided long before to enter politics, the legislative committee meeting and his subsequent elimination as a candidate for the federal post probably made up his mind for him. He would run for public office!

However, certain obstacles presented themselves to the young attorney. All statewide offices, where the action was, had minimum age requirements. But one district office, that of Railroad Commissioner, which regulated railroads, truck lines and power companies, had no such restrictions. There really was no decision to be made. Railroad Commissioner was the only major office for which Long was legally qualified and Railroad Commissioner it would be. In March, 1918 he circulated a letter to the editors of newspapers in Louisiana.

He set forth his feelings in the mass media about inequities existing in the distribution of the nation's wealth for the first time, although no doubt he had entertained such ideas long before. His basic premise, that 65-70 percent of the wealth of America was owned by two percent of the people, would stay with him for the rest of his life and he would use this as the rationale for his proposals to redistribute wealth. They would be incorporated into his later "Share Our Wealth" program, which advocated stringent restrictions on the accumulation of wealth and confiscation of fortunes for redistribution to all.[14]

Later that summer he qualified as a candidate for the Railroad Commission against four other opponents.

He won and, from that time forward, politicians would have to reckon with the brash, red-haired lawyer from the hill country of Winn Parish. Huey Long was 24 years old.

The Public Service Commission (the renamed Railroad Commission) would prove to be an excellent platform from which Long would be elected governor. It also provided him a launching pad for his continuing onslaughts against Standard Oil.

If Long's original opposition to the oil giant was philosophical, he soon had occasion to make it a personal battle.

Some of his legal work was done for friends who were involved in oil production by independents in fields located in the Shreveport area. Long took his fee in stock. The oil was purchased and transported to markets by pipelines owned by Standard Oil. The petroleum was purchased principally by the federal government which, after Armistice in 1918, ceased its purchases. Standard Oil reduced its purchases from the independents and, in view of the reduced demand for the product, cut prices.

Huey interpreted this as an attempt by Standard to freeze out small companies and independent operators. It also meant the end of dreams of wealth harbored by him.

He complained:

> "...I had gone to sleep one night with
> transactions all ready to be closed for options and
> equities I had acquired which meant I might some
> day be mentioned among the millionaires, to

awake in the morning to read that nothing I had
was of any value because the pipeline companies
said so."[15]

Campaigning for the governorship in 1923, he candidly confessed to
the Baton Rouge *State-Times:*

"The Standard Oil Company has cost me
a lot of money and a lot of time. As a country yap,
I put $1,050 in oil stock. The company made a
strike and I was advised to hold on.

"...The big oil companies, led by the
Standard Oil, issued notices that they would take
no more oil from independent producers and my
oil stock wasn't worth 40 cents, while oil went to
waste. Do you think I can forget that? Do you
blame me for fighting the Standard Oil?"[16]

Some have contended that Standard Oil had no choice but to cease
buying from independents because the government suspended its own purchases
from Standard after the Armistice in 1918. However, others disagree and
generally side with Huey. Long biographer Carleton Beals remarked that "Standard offered Mexican oil at New Orleans for 50 cents—less than transportation
charges—but when it gained control, boosted the price to $3.25."[17]

It should be remembered that the nation, at the time, was emerging
from a period termed by Henry Adams as "the final surrender of the country to
capitalism," when corporate giants behaved with little or no restrictions from the
governmental establishment.[18]

Long turned upon Standard Oil with unbridled fury. He caused the
Public Service Commission to rule that pipelines in Louisiana were common
carriers and, as such, had to grant access to all producers of oil. He called upon
the outgoing governor, Ruffin G. Pleasant, to convene a special legislative session to give the Commission's regulatory action the authority of law. The governor refused, prompting Huey to attack him forthwith. He cast his lot with John
M. Parker, candidate in the governor's election to be held that fall, because he
felt that Parker would support a pipeline bill.

Because of Long's support, Parker was able to carry the parishes of
north Louisiana by a razor-thin majority against his second primary Democratic
opponent. Later, Long would maintain that Parker had sold out to elements of
Standard Oil and had passed an ineffective pipeline bill. The two politicians
would maintain a bitter rivalry and harbor a mutual hatred during the rest of
their lives. There would be no reconciling the two. Perhaps as objectionable to
Long as Parker's reneging on their supposed agreement was the fact that Parker
did not consider Long's support to be critical to his election. Parker seemed to
have no need of Long's counsel in order to govern Louisiana. Long's autobiog-

raphy tells us:

> "Governor Parker immediately addres-
> sed me a few letters, taking occasion to thank me
> for the support which I had given to his candidacy.
>
> "Before his inauguration, however, I
> was shelved.
>
> "It was here I saw occur a phenomenon
> that has frequently presented itself in the after
> years. Those of us, zealous for reform and who
> had exhausted ourselves in the election, hied back
> to our work to give attention to our several neglec-
> ted affairs. The crowd of wiseacres, skilled at
> flattery and repartee, surrounded our newly elected
> governor. Soon he was convinced that his insur-
> mountable virtue alone had wrought the victory;
> before long he was made to see how much bigger
> his majority might have been but for the 'hin-
> drance' of such 'objectionables' as myself."

Long apparently felt he had destroyed Parker in the fight over the pipeline legislation. Long boasted that, since their altercation, "he (Parker) has never dared to offer himself for an office in Louisiana..."[19]

For his part, Parker later sued Long and collected a token judgement. He later was instrumental in having the Internal Revenue Service revive charges against Long which harassed the Kingfish until his death. Parker, along with other political notables, stood in the rain to attend the funeral of Long's alleged assassin, Carl Weiss. So deep was the rancor between the pair that it hardly paused at the grave.

Long, having now observed firsthand a governor of Louisiana, con-cluded he was worthy of the office and ran for it in the election of 1924. He was defeated but he made a creditable showing, finishing less than 10,000 votes be-hind the first place candidate out of almost 240,000 votes cast statewide. What is most remarkable about the race is that the majority of Long's vote was built up in 21 rural parishes with low populations while he finished poorly in the state's major metropolitan areas.

Long claims that his defeat in that 1924 race was a result of rains that hit the state the previous night. The first precinct reported to Long when the bal-lots had been tabulated was a rural box for the community of Clay. Long received 60 of 61 votes cast. He commented:

> "I'm beat...There should have been 100
> for me and one against me. Forty percent of my
> country vote is lost in that box. It will be that great
> in the others."[20]

Long ran again in four years and this time he would not be denied. He received 126,842 votes, leading the opposing candidates but lacking a majority of the votes cast. Under Louisiana law, a runoff was required if no candidate received more than 50 percent of the vote. However, the handwriting was on the wall and the second place candidate withdrew, making Long governor.

By the time Long had achieved the governorship, he had helped elect other candidates to other offices, providing them with his shirttails to ride on in areas where he was strong. Eventually he would help elect two United States senators, a lieutenant governor, a governor and other assorted candidates.

Long is reputed to have told his bride-to-be, Rose McConnell, that he had his career in politics all planned. He would first be a secondary state official, then governor, then senator and eventually he would be president of the United States. He had chosen the presidency as his eventual goal. He had deductively determined the steps necessary to reach that goal, just as a tourist might decide to drive to New York and then determine what stops along the way would be required to reach that city.

Once elected governor, Huey wasted no time in demonstrating that he would govern the state in his own fashion.

At first, he was not taken seriously. One reason was his youth. He was 35, a stripling politician. A second reason was the slim following he had in the legislature. Of a total of 100 members of the House of Representatives, 23 were elected on Long's ticket; the remainder had campaigned on the tickets of his opponents. Nine senators out of a total of 39 supported him.

However, he managed to get the support of legislators elected on the ticket of one of his opponents and was able to organize the legislature, appointing his friends to committees and electing supporters to leadership positions. He passed legislation that would allow him later to embark upon a highway construction program and to provide free textbooks to school children.

Legislation intended to give him control over Charity Hospital in New Orleans and to appoint additional judges to courts of appeal failed. He had not reached the point where he could pass legislation at whim.

On the Charity Hospital question, Long had promised non-involvement with the institution during his 1924 campaign for governor. A statement issued by his campaign manager promised:

> "Huey P. Long...keenly appreciates the necessity of keeping the throttling hand of petty politics off the neck of this wonderful refuge of the sick...and he will not permit the efficient management of this hospital to be subordinated to the ugly exigencies of partisan politics."

Even some of his closest legislative supporters refused to support Long "in an effort that may plunge the Charity Hospital in New Orleans into politics."

The measure failed narrowly, the first administration-sponsored one to do so.[21]

But Long was nothing if he was not resourceful. On the Charity Hospital measure, he found that he could accomplish what he wanted without legislative action.

Of the eight appointed members on the board administering the hospital, there were two whose terms had expired in 1927. The incumbent governor, O.H. Simpson, had failed to reappoint them or to name successors. Huey immediately replaced them.

There were two members whose terms were to expire in March 1929, eight months hence. Huey asked for their resignations and the pair complied. This gave Long four of the eight votes and, since the governor served on the board as an ex-officio voting member, he now had a 5-4 majority on the board.

He replaced the superintendent with his personal choice, Dr. Arthur Vidrine, whom he also appointed as hospital surgeon. A desire for revenge against two favorite enemies, Standard Oil and the City of New Orleans, prompted his action. He explained the move this way:

> "I'm tired of taking off my hat when I go to New Orleans. They said I couldn't remove Dr. Leake, whose pappy is the Standard Oil's lawyer, from the superintendent's berth at Charity Hospital down there. Well, I put him out, and I came here and I got Dr. Vidrine of Ville Platte to take it. The country people can hold the big jobs just like the city men."[22]

Long could not yet block legislation that was unsatisfactory to him. But he could veto it, and veto he did.

After the legislative business had been disposed of, he cleaned house in virtually every state agency. Many state employees were dismissed. Some were rehired; others were replaced by Long supporters.

When 1928 came to a close, Huey had won every major battle he had undertaken. He had taken over much of the available patronage in the state. State employment, for the most part, constituted a political machine for Long's purposes. He had passed constitutional amendments for road construction over the frenzied opposition of the New Orleans Ring. According to one newsman, "There was no one left to fight."[23]

But Long's inability to get along with his associates for any length of time began to show. He fell out with his lieutenant governor and he broke with a newspaper publisher who had assisted him in his campaign for governor. The publisher blasted the new governor as "the prince of liars."

Long was beginning to tread on thin ice. He enjoyed a majority in the legislature that was made up principally of legislators who supported other candidates in the governor's election. In turning friends into enemies, he was risking the erosion of what was at best a shaky political base.

In March, Huey called a special session and did another foolhardy thing. He proposed a tax of five cents per barrel on the refining of oil, promptly stirring up profound opposition statewide. In Baton Rouge, a community numbering 30,000 at the time—of which an estimated 25,000 were dependent on the payrolls of Esso Standard Oil—there was pandemonium.

When the session convened, a legislature that had cooperated with Long suddenly showed its ugly side. Long had no longer command of a majority. The majority was now against him—and it was hostile.

Long's impetuousness would soon convert that hostility into near-rage.

The Baton Rouge newspapers, neutral until this time, editorialized against Long's proposed tax plan. In retaliation, Long spotted a reporter for the newspapers in the capitol and shouted, "Say, Liter, tell Manship (the publisher of the two Baton Rouge dailies) that if he doesn't lay off me, I might have to publish a list of all the people who are fighting me who have relatives in the insane asylums."[24]

The publisher had a brother in a mental institution.

Long's bodyguard, "Battling" Bozeman, turned on Long and signed a salty and colorful affidavit that Long had attempted to bribe him to murder a representative who was opposing him. According to Bozeman's affidavit, Long told him:

> "'Battling Bozeman, I am the kaiser of this state. When I crack my whip, whosoever dares to disobey my orders, regardless of what they may be, I'll fire 'em.
>
> "'...Battling Bozeman, I am going to call an extra session of the legislature,' and he says, 'This son-of a bitch J.Y. Sanders, Jr. is going to disapprove all of my measures and I want to get him out of the way. I have chosen you to do away with this bastard.'
>
> "I says, 'Governor, what do you mean?' He says, 'I mean for you to kill the son-of-a-bitch, leave him in the ditch where nobody will know how or when he got there.
>
> "'I'm the governor of this state and if you were to be found out I would give you a full pardon and many gold dollars.'"

Bozeman said he refused Long's offer because "I'm not that kind of a man." He concluded his affidavit by saying, "I warn my friends in advance if anything happens to me that nobody can be blamed but Huey P. Long or some of his henchmen."

When questioned by a committee on the occasion, Bozeman threw in for good measure an incident when Long took him into his hotel room and asked him to fetch cigars. When Bozeman returned, he met Long in the hallway outside the room wearing "one shoe and his hat on his head and his B.V.D.'s undershirt."[25]

The fat was in the fire. First the manufacturing tax, now these mad actions. Legislators began to desert him. The Long leadership tried to adjourn the session, realizing there was no chance of enacting the manufacturing tax and hoping to disband before the emotions of the legislature, now decidedly anti-Long, were directed against the governor.

Too late. In a session that was more like a battle royal, the House refused to adjourn. A slow-functioning voting machine was interpreted by anti-Long members as an attempt to tamper with the vote to adjourn. Fists flew. Legislators wrestled with each other. One was struck with a pair of brass knuckles and blood spewed from his forehead.

Panicked, Huey told intimates that he was considering resignation:

"If I stay in office they'll impeach me
and that'll bar me from ever holding office. This
way I'll resign, then I'll run for the Senate next
year and I'll be elected. The people are still with
Huey Long."[26]

The following day the House voted 55-38 to investigate 19 counts in an impeachment resolution. A friend found Huey weeping, face downward, in the Heidelberg Hotel.[27]

However, Long saved himself by his discovery of the key to political survival, used by every governor since, to maintain his hold on government. The key was the Louisiana State Senate. All of Huey's successors have recognized the importance of that body and have relied upon it.

During Long's day, there were 39 senators and 100 House members, roughly 40-60 in proportion. Today there are still 39 senators and 105 House members, 37-63 split. Then, a single Senate vote was worth 2-½ House votes. Today it is worth even more. Simply by reason of numbers, it is easier to lobby the Senate than the House and a bill defeated in the Senate is as dead as one defeated in the House.

Additionally, senators represent more constituents than House members and there is a remoteness from the voters that is not shared by the House members. This remoteness gives a senator a little more leeway in voting his own convictions rather than strictly echoing the view of his constituents.

It would take a ⅔ majority—26 members—of the Louisiana Senate to convict Huey Long. The other side of the coin was that if 14 senators voted "nay" there would be no impeachment. Long was able to gather 15 senators on his side, one more than he absolutely needed. Rather than wait until the Senate heard the charges and have his supporters carry the vote, he had the 15 members sign an affidavit, a "Round Robin," that the impeachment proceedings were illegal and that under no circumstances would they vote to convict.

With that, the impeachment collapsed and Huey got on with the government of the state. A year later, weary of political oppositionists and anxious to resume his timetable of ascendancy to the presidency, he announced to the public that he would run for the U.S. Senate. On the same ballot would be a road building program that he had been denied by the legislature. If—he promised—the people denied him the road program and the Senate seat, he would resign.

They did not deny him and for another five years he continued to run the state, from his Washington-Baton Rouge axis.

During the seven years that Huey P. Long controlled the lives and the fortunes of the citizens of Louisiana, the Pelican State witnessed more progress than it had ever seen before or has seen since. Louisiana was dragged by him headlong into the 20th century despite the outraged cries of the collective power structures of the state. Today, in the 1980s, friend and foe alike will concede that the foundation of the New Louisiana dates back to him.

He did on the local scene what Franklin Roosevelt did nationally. He established social programs that remained the blueprint for human services through succeeding administrations—liberal or conservative, Long or anti-Long. Some would expand, some would shrink, but all governors would maintain the basic fabric of the political structure that Huey built, much as those presidents who succeeded FDR simply modified or swelled programs started by him.

Thousands of miles of roads were paved. Additional thousands of miles of dirt roads were covered with gravel. The three bridges existing statewide in 1928 multiplied to 44 (all toll free) by 1935, the year Long died. During that seven year period, $133 million was spent to lift the citizens of the state from the mud and the dust.

And the capital improvements went beyond roads. There were fish hatcheries, schools, hospitals, institutions and public buildings—first class, well designed and well engineered marvels that survive and function to this day.

Annoyed by detractors who criticized "Longism," Huey suggested in 1932 in a Baton Rouge speech how they could wipe out Longism in Louisiana:

> "...go get you a bomb or some dynamite and blow up that building yonder. Go out and tear up the concrete roads...Tear down the buildings I've built at the University. Take the money away from the school boards that I've given them to run your schools. And when your child starts out to school tomorrow morning, snatch the free schoolbooks out of his hand that Huey Long gave

him.

"Then you'll be rid of Longism in this state and not till then."[28]

There was a price tag, of course. Between 1924 and 1936 the average yearly administrative budget tripled, rising from $22.9 million to $72.5 million. To fuel this increase, taxes were raised dramatically. In 1927, the year before Long became governor, there were 17 kinds of taxes levied in Louisiana. In 1935, there were 45. However, even his bitterest critics noted that the increased tax load fell primarily on the well-to-do of the state.

In addition to the increased cost, there was the deprivation of individual liberties. The *New York Times* observed acidly:

"In reality, Sen. Long set up a fascist government in Louisiana. It was disguised, but only thinly. There was no outward appearance of a revolution but the effectual result was to lodge all the power of the state in the hands of one man.

"If fascism ever comes to the U.S. it will come in something like that way. No one will set himself up as an avowed dictator, but if he can succeed in dictating everything, the name does not matter."[29]

Along with the progress, the state experienced corruption of unspeakable intensity. Like the progress, it was never experienced before and, while others in the state have approached this level since, it has never been matched.

This is no mean accomplishment in a state that is traditionally noted for its free-wheeling approach to political morality.

Road contractors were shaken down for contributions. Oil companies anted up. Even state employees paid portions of their salaries to finance the Long steamroller. Huey's older brother Julius complained bitterly, "It was kick in or get kicked out."[30]

FBI files reveal that all employees during Long's terms as governor and senator were required to contribute 5% of their monthly paychecks to the Long machine. Others maintain that there was a sliding scale that depended upon income. Those earning less than $150 monthly paid 5% of their earnings; those earning more paid 10%.

In addition, state employees were required to buy subscriptions to the *Progress,* Long's house organ and mouthpiece. Long established the publication to counteract the propaganda of the "lying newspapers" who upset him by their continued insistence on publishing news critical of him and his organization.

The proceeds from this extortionate system—a type of United Givers in a political dimension—were generally referred to as "de-ducts," since much of the money consisted of forced deductions from the salaries of state workers.

During Long's lifetime it was understood that the extractive procedure involving state employees took place only preceding and following elections, being undertaken principally to finance political campaigns. However, those businessmen or professionals doing business with the state were bled regularly and entrepreneurs considered the practice a part of the cost of doing business in Louisiana.

The repository (or repositories) of the funds generated was referred to as the "de-ducts box." The custodian of this booty was Seymour Weiss, one of the closest of Long's advisors and confidants, about whom more will be heard later.

It was a measure of the amorality and arrogance of the political power structure of the time that none of the Long leaders, including Long himself, denied that these extortionate practices existed. No one saw anything wrong with it. A former state employee, who was himself assessed by the Long forces, innocently explained to me that the system could be compared to the payment of union dues.

Huey Long defended the system on the floor of the United States Senate, explaining that the de-ducts were entirely voluntary and that workers were not forced to contribute.

The standard of political morality was so low and the collectors so jaded that their justifications for the practice contained a maddening Alice in Wonderlandish tinge of what is best described as a kind of criminal feigned naivete.

In a way, they believed, it was a privilege to be allowed to contribute.

Long leaders felt there were ethical considerations that mitigated the seaminess involved. Huey piously maintained that no "corporate" money reached the kickback coffers, as though shaking down individuals only was a healthy and normal exercise in finance.

Seymour Weiss recoiled in horror and rejected out of hand any thought of lowering the rather high standards that contributors to the de-duct box were required to meet. To biographer Forrest Davis he extolled the moral goodness of the system by stressing that gamblers and prostitutes were not permitted to contribute. "I have refused $10,000 at a time from gamblers," Weiss sermonized.[31]

Huey's younger brother Earl made some estimates of the amount of graft involved in only one phase of state business, highway construction. He charged that there was an assessment against road contractors, "a graft or a dragdown of from four to ten thousand dollars a mile." On a bridge costing between $13-$14 million, Earl estimated there would be a million dollar slush fund.[32]

Brother Julius told all in a two-part series in a 1935 national publication. To Huey's rationalizations that previous custodians of the state fisc had stolen from the till also, Julius compared the corruption that had gone before as "a mouse to an elephant."

He charged:

> "...the funds and property of the state of Louisiana, as well as the services of its thousands of public employees, were used to promote the political position and help the political campaigns of Huey Long."

Huey had the state expend money for exorbitant legal fees, commissions and limousines for his henchmen, described by Julius as "the boneheads" around Huey.[33]

There were few areas that the shakedown machinery failed to penetrate.

Even the press was involved. Those who cooperated with the Kingfish got their share of the boodle. The New Orleans *Item,* an afternoon daily which saw the wisdom of editorially supporting Long and his programs (and even provided a special reporter of Long's choosing to cover his activities), was allowed to belly up and make its own place at the trough.

A Senate investigating committee exposed an arrangement whereby state employees were forced to subscribe to the newspaper, conveniently having the subscription price deducted from their pay. According to committee counsel General S.T. Ansell, about $2,000 was collected from one state department alone for the New Orleans daily. Long, sitting in on the hearing, clarified, "We help those who are with us."[34]

It should be pointed out that the *Item's* arrangement with Long was not unprecedented. Years before, its afternoon opposition, the New Orleans *States,* benefitted from the same arrangement until the publisher got crossed with Huey and the perks were withdrawn. The only newspaper in New Orleans not to be seduced was the *Times-Picayune,* which steadfastly refused to tread the primrose path.

(There seems to be a lesson here, perhaps that morality promotes endurance. Today the *Times-Picayune* still publishes, having cannibalized the afternoon competition in several well-spaced gulps. The other journals have been relegated to an afterthought on the bloated masthead of *The Times-Picayune/The States-Item.*)

No publication ever had a more dedicated and convincing sales force than the one provided the *Item* by the state of Louisiana. According to journalist John Wilds, policemen and firemen solicited subscriptions. Motorists reported being stopped by uniformed motorcycle police and asked to subscribe. The superintendent of Charity Hospital in New Orleans, Dr. Arthur Vidrine, who would operate on a wounded Kingfish four years later, wrote a letter to be used by salesmen in squeezing advertising out of prospective clients.[35]

When a Baton Rouge newspaper criticized the State Highway Commission for right of way payments, the Commission yanked official advertising and placed it in the *Item*, announcing that "news items" about Commission activities would be denied the Baton Rouge competition and placed solely in the *Item*. It was all in the family.[36]

There are differences of opinion about whether any of the plunder wrested from state employees and suppliers stayed with Huey Long personally.

That the Long organization had many costs is a matter of record, such as the role of the group in underwriting costs to help elect Franklin Roosevelt to the presidency illustrates. There were also expenses in feeding the machine. Long supported other candidates and this cost money.

It was expensive to maintain power.

In February, 1934, Long formed his Share Our Wealth organization which would attract membership in the millions, perhaps as many as 7,000,000. It would take considerable funds to maintain this movement. The money would have to come from Long, as it is doubtful that any effort to collectivize the muscle of the have-nots and dispossessed would be in any way self-sustaining.

But regardless of whether or not Long benefitted from the ransom wrung from those who depended on the state for livelihood or profits, there were other lucrative sources of funds for him. These are part of the public record.

Long was legal counsel for the state's Public Service Commission, on which he once served and which he used as a springboard to the governorship. Long biographer Carlcton Beals estimates that Long realized some $75,000 from this account. Perhaps some would question the ethics of a United States senator being retained by a public body regulating commerce in a state that he represented and even controlled, but in Huey Long's Louisiana there seemed to be nothing improper in the arrangement.

He had an arrangement with the State Tax Commission to collect "back taxes." In partnership with an Opelousas attorney, Peyton R. Sandoz, the pair was to receive one-third of all back state taxes collected as a result of their efforts. Long biographer T. O. Harris says that, as of September 4, 1935, a few days before Long was shot, Sandoz reported the firm had earned a quarter of a million dollars with one-half of that amount, $125,000, going to Long.[37]

Long had other retainers from his private law practice, estimated by some observers at $100,000 yearly. Beals speculated that he received fees as legal advisor to a number of large corporations for, according to Beals, "protective insurance," although he provides no documentation for this.[38]

Pressed by colleagues on the Senate floor to reveal his income for 1935 and to disclose what the money was used for, Long hesitated briefly and then replied, "I made about $25,000," and spent it all on "brass bands, football and drinks for my friends."

Long was nettled when, during the exchange, newly elected Senator Alben Barkley prodded, "Did the Senator deduct the funds spent for liquor as a loss?" Long, sensitive to criticism of his drinking habits, snapped, "That's a personal question."[39]

There was much money to be made by the Long organization by profit from insider deals, many involving oil and gas leases. The traffic in "hot oil"—that oil produced beyond state and federal allowables—would eventually lead to the indictment of Long's cronies and, some say, could have revealed the culpability of the Kingfish himself. So profitable were oil and gas transactions from some leases that money would continue to accrue to survivors for two generations without abatement.

The most celebrated case of this sort of deal was the Win or Lose Corporation.

Win or Lose never lost. Although Long's name did not appear on documents, it was hard to believe he was not involved in its formation because of the stripe of the incorporators of the firm. James A. Noe, Senate floor leader, was president; the ubiquitous Seymour Weiss was vice president; secretary-treasurer was Long's secretary, Earle Christenberry. Weiss and Christenberry put up the only cash in the transaction, the sum of $200. For this they received one share of stock apiece, out of a total capital of 100 shares. The balance went to Noe, who transferred to Win or Lose his interests in leases on state-owned land which he had negotiated a month before. Shortly thereafter, Noe transferred 31 shares to Long in a secret transaction.

In August of 1935, less than a year since the formation of Win or Lose and a few weeks before Long's death, the corporation declared a dividend of $2,000 a share, a total of $200,000 in dividends. Huey's share was $62,000, paid in the form of a check made out simply to "cash."[40]

For almost 50 years the leases have continued to produce. They are some of the richest in Louisiana, a state virtually floating on oil.

In 1940, a federal grand jury indicted Noe and Weiss on four counts of income tax evasion in connection with their dealings with Win or Lose. Noe was acquitted; Weiss was convicted and served time.

In July of 1971, a New Orleans oilman filed suit in state district court charging that the incorporators of Win or Lose, along with Long's erstwhile state auditor, Alice Lee Grosjean, conspired to cheat the State of Louisiana out of about $250 million in royalties due from the land.[41]

Ten years later, Texaco would figure in a suit by the State Mineral Board involving the leases. The suit was compromised and netted Louisiana an immediate $18.8 million and a new, more profitable formula for determining the value of the gas marketed by the company. The arrangement was expected to generate an additional $90 million for the state in the ensuing five years. There would be another $80 million in the five years following that. The ten-year total, almost $200 million, was in addition to a $7 million payment to heirs of the original owners, also included in the settlement.[42]

An appreciation of the richness of the Texaco leases and other mineral lands in Louisiana was offered by the *Wall Street Journal*:

> "Huey Long built his populist career battling the oil barons, but in 1934 he secretly threw in his lot with them.
>
> "...the biggest block ended up in the hands of the fledgling Texas Co., which sent its dredges and drilling rigs into a million acres of coastal swamps. Mr. Long's heirs began reaping millions in royalties, which are still rolling in. The driller would grow into a giant called Texaco.
>
> "...For over 50 years, Louisiana has been one of the oil and gas industry's happiest hunting grounds. Producers have sucked out of its marshes and uplands more than 12 billion barrels of oil and 113 trillion cubic feet of natural gas—enough to keep New York City in electricity for five centuries."[43]

The official succession of Long's estate gave his wealth at $100,000. Listed against this amount was $27,000 in debts, the major portion being a mortgage against his home. The $62,000 dividend from Win or Lose in August was never shown and it never was found.

Many believed that Long was well-heeled when death overtook him. A week before his death, he said in a radio speech that he was "lousy with money." Supreme Court Justice John Fournet said Huey had told him that he had $4 million in hand for his presidential election, contributions from both Republicans and Democrats.

The Baton Rouge *State-Times* speculated after his death that Long's net worth might have been $5 million, although "the more conservative would go no higher than $2,250,000."[44]

It is doubtful if there will ever be any agreement about the amount of money Huey Long was really worth. Most of his supporters and many of his admirers will readily concede that a lot of money found its way into the coffers of the Long machine. However, there is a difference of opinion whether Long benefitted personally from this flow of wealth.

Elmer Irey, treasury agent who headed the section charged with gathering information on Long's finances, believed strongly that Long was indictable on charges of income tax evasion and that only the grim reaper saved the Kingfish from a conviction and a jail term.

What happened to the vast sum of money collected for the Long machine remains a mystery. He dealt in cash as a rule. Rare was the occasion when a check was written that could be traced to him. Much, if not all, of the cash was kept in the de-duct box, ostensibly under the watchful eye of the chancellor of the ex-chequer, Seymour Weiss, in the Roosevelt Hotel in New Orleans.

When Long moved to Washington he was supposed to have taken the box with him, placing it in a safe at the Mayflower Hotel. Later he moved it to the vault at the Riggs National Bank.

According to Weiss, Long advised him the day before he was shot that he had moved the box to a new location, which Long did not confide to him. While Long lay dying, Weiss several times urged him to reveal the whereabouts of the box. To Weiss' persistent queries, Long would only reply, "Later, Seymour, later."[45]

But there was no later. He died, apparently without revealing the new location.

There are many who said the money never left the Roosevelt Hotel. One of these was Harvey Fields, onetime law partner of Huey and successor to him on the Public Service Commission. Fields paints a picture of Weiss, as Long lay dying:

> "...besieging and begging Long, as he
> lay on his back, floating between two worlds, to
> give him the keys to the lock box, urging that there
> were papers he desired to secure, intimating to the
> senator that life and spirit were about to leave his
> body, that death was near."[46]

Long's widow was also of the opinion that the de-ducts box was safe with Weiss and, following the death of her husband, went to the hotel to have the safe opened. She expected to find the Win or Lose dividend and perhaps other valuables.

There was nothing. The cupboard was bare. The mystery of what happened to Long's wealth, like the mystery of his death, would never be solved.

CHAPTER FIVE

The Paranoids Are Out To Get Me

Times-Picayune capitol correspondent George Vandevoort spent as much time reporting on and observing Huey Long as any newsman. He was on hand the night that Long was shot in the state capitol and confided to a colleague this scenario of a portion of the happenings that night:

> At the capitol, Huey left a meeting with some of his supporters. As he walked down the marble corridors of the building, he boasted to those accompanying him, "I've fixed that nigger son-of-a-bitch." An eavesdropping bystander who had been observing Long went to a telephone and called the home of Carl Weiss. The doctor listened intently and then hung up. He went to the dresser, took a gun from a drawer and put it in his coat pocket. He then went into the nursery, kissed the feet of his sleeping child and left the house.[1]

The reference to fixing "that nigger son-of-a-bitch" stems from one of the motives attributed to Weiss in supposedly attempting to take Long's life. The story was that Long was preparing to accuse Weiss' father-in-law, Judge Henry Pavy, of having "a little too much coffee in his milk," a euphemistic Louisiana expression used to describe people who had traces of Negro blood.

The reporter Vandevoort is no longer living. The reporter to whom he confided this information and who passed it along to me knows no more about the story than what he related to me and I have written here.

Any attempts to speculate about the source of the tale or to obtain additional information are pointless. How could Vandevoort have known this information? Did it come from Weiss himself, perhaps passed along to Dr. J. Webb

63

McGehee, or from one of the other persons to whom Weiss talked that night? Did Carl talk to his wife, Yvonne, and did she perhaps communicate the story?

I don't know. No one will ever know.

I have passed it along because it provides answers, of a sort, to some of the questions that have been asked about that night. Why would Weiss want to kill Long anyway? Why did he choose that night? Did he act alone? Were others involved?

Vandevoort's information answers these questions.

Q. Why did Weiss want to kill Long?

A. Because Long was preparing to use the racial slur against Judge Pavy, a slur that would extend to Weiss' wife, Yvonne, and their child.

Q. Why did he choose that particular night?

A. Because, having learned that Sunday morning that Long was preparing to gerrymander his father-in-law out of a judgeship, he had brooded all day. When he received the telephone call, he was thrown into a rage, losing control and setting out to destroy Long.

Q. Did he act alone?

A. No. He was part of a cabal and one of the group was staked out at the capitol. This was the person who called Weiss.

Vandevoort's report provides a case for Weiss as the assassin. Elements of his story are advanced by many, including the Long hierarchy of the period, who believed that Long was murdered by Weiss in collusion with others.

This conspiracy aspect was used to good advantage by Long's political heirs, who promptly dubbed their opponents for statewide office in the January primary election "the assassination ticket."

Fifty years later the possible existence of a conspiracy was given a kind of belated credibility and dignity when Huey Long's oldest son, Russell, a United States senator at the time, speaking at ceremonies commemorating the death of his father, observed, "I don't believe it was the act of a single individual. In my judgment, there might have been other people involved in one respect or another."

He speculated, for the first time, that the reason for the killing of his father was the repeal of the poll tax when Huey was governor, which was interpreted by some as a concession to Negroes, bringing down upon Long the wrath of right-wing segregationist elements in Louisiana.

Russell promised to reveal more about the plot at an appearance at the New Orleans Press Club the following day but his appearance added no new information. Despite the source, it is hard to take this explanation seriously. In the first place, Long had convinced the white voters of the state that there were other devices for disenfranchising Negroes and the principal value of the poll tax repeal lay in the enfranchisement of thousands of poor whites who could not afford to pay the $1 assessment.[2]

The utility of the Vandevoort scenario is that it provides a reason why a man who behaved rationally and normally all day—nay, all week, all his life—doing nothing to lead anyone to believe he was planning, or even capable of committing, such a crime, would suddenly discard the veneer of sanity and become a killer.

If something happened to create a mental imbalance—something that would cause Weiss to become temporarily insane, inflamed with anger and altogether out of patience with Long—then we have an acceptable explanation of Weiss' behavior. And certainly the telephone call described by Vandevoort gives us this catalyst.

The story also supports a theory held by many that Long was killed as a result of a conspiracy and that Weiss was an agent of the plotters.

Judge Fournet spotted two persons standing alongside Weiss before he accosted Long. A Baton Rouge dentist who claimed to have knowledge of a group plotting Long's death told me that he believed Weiss was part of a network and that the group had monitors at the capitol that night to see that he did what he was chosen to do.[3]

Dr. Tom Weiss, brother of Carl, told me, in answer to my question as to why his brother would even show up in the capitol that night, "I don't know. Maybe somebody got into the car with him, put a gun to his ribs and said, 'Okay, let's go do it!'"

The conspiracy hypothesis places the Long assassination in the company of other celebrated killings such as those of Abraham Lincoln and John F. Kennedy.

Long was a man hated by many. It is not hard to consider seriously that his death was the result of a conspiracy. Quite the contrary. If there was the slimmest shred of evidence, the barest indication, that Carl Weiss could possibly have joined with others to do away with Long, it would be altogether believable—not only believable, but the logical and natural culmination of Long's lifetime of violent confrontations, premonitions, fistfights and forebodings of impending disaster.

In April, 1935, less than six months before Long's death, a hulking anti-Long state representative took the floor of the House on a point of personal privilege. He expressed a concern that was growing more and more prevalent among the citizens of the state. As he spoke, the legislature was in session during the second of four special sessions that would be held in 1935. Legislation had been proposed that would place the entire election machinery of Louisiana under the control of Huey Long.

The legislation shocked even the most hardened capitol observers. The speaker, Mason Spencer, predicted to his colleagues:

"I am not gifted with second sight, nor
did I see a spot of blood on the moon last night,

but I can see blood on the polished marble of this
capitol, for if you ride this thing through, you will
travel with the white horse of death."[4]

Huey Long was haunted by fears of death from the time he was elected
governor in 1928 and perhaps before. Eventually this paranoia would reach
manic proportions. He was rarely without bodyguards. One carried a Thompson
submachine gun in a paper sack. Huey himself carried a gun, sometimes two,
which he had laced into waistcoat pockets. He referred to the weapons as
"sandwiches."[5]

He was the first governor in the history of the state to hire bodyguards.
He was ridiculed for it constantly. His enemies taunted him about his excessive
concern for his own safety.

In 1928, as the newly inaugurated governor, he telephoned the mayor
of Baton Rouge to report a strange character who continued to ride around and
around the governor's mansion. The report was checked out. It was an ordinary
motorist running up the mileage of his new automobile. At the time, it was
necessary to break in new automobiles by driving at reduced speeds for a
specified period.[6]

Much of Long's fear was generated as a result of his own actions. He
created enemies the way most men collect acquaintances. For the most part, he
divided those with whom he came into contact into two classes: those he could
subdue and those he would destroy. Few were allowed to co-exist.

He became resentful of opponents. The resentment bubbled into hatred.
His hatred, fueled by fears of possible retaliation, forced him to attack, oftentimes when the victim was of little or no consequence or already neutralized. In
his attacks, he employed the most ruthless and brutal means he could devise.
Victims would retaliate and Long would meet reaction with reprisal. This resulted in a series of vendettas that left a trail of embittered victims whose hatred for
Long knew no bounds.

His vindictiveness fed on itself.

Rebellion against his Draconian measures infuriated Long, causing him
to devise even more paralyzing strategies which were met, in turn, with increased resistance. On and on, ad infinitum, or—more accurately—ad September 8, 1935.

Long's earliest concerns for his safety were groundless and they even
contained an element of humor. There was no substantial organized opposition
to him when he first assumed the governorship. Many considered him to be a
flash in the pan, a momentary phenomenon with little staying power.

He was able to elect his speaker of the House and Senate president pro
tem, key legislative posts, with little problem, once he had forged a coalition of
defeated candidates for governor. At the outset, whatever opposition there was to
Long was not so deep as to consider doing him bodily harm.

This changed a year after his election. In his autobiography, Long claims that he made peace offers to his political opposition shortly after his election, to insure that the legislative session would be "one of harmony, good will and progress for the state."

According to him, his terms were unacceptable to his opponents. They warned him that they would let him run the state for about a year. After that, they would consider impeachment.[7]

Whether that conversation ever happened, Long was in fact impeached a year later and he did a great deal to help bring it about. His animosity toward Standard Oil had surfaced before the close of his first year in office, when he attempted to slap a refining tax on the oil giant. He borrowed more misery than he bargained for and impeachment charges were filed. He was saved by the Senate's "Round Robin."

Long would never forget the impeachment and he would never let up the fight against those who had hounded him. Perhaps other men, less gifted and less determined, would have reassessed the actions that precipitated impeachment and attempted to win over, or at least neutralize, the opposition. No way! Huey had attempted that course a year before and was not about to make the same mistake.

No, sir! No more Mister Nice Guy! The gloves were off.

It was not an olive branch he extended to his foes. It was the back of his hand.

Wary of the time when his opponents would mobilize for another impeachment, he announced, "I'll just have to grow me a new crop of legislators," whereupon he began recall efforts against some of the impeachers. At the same time, he bestowed political plums upon those who had buttressed him in his hour of need.

Most of all, he did not forget Standard Oil. He would nurse his hatred of the corporation, allowing it to fester and ferment until, years later, he would revive the tax that had caused his impeachment in 1929.

After he survived the impeachment, Long conducted a campaign to achieve a kind of political hegemony that would eventually extend his power and influence into every area of Louisiana life touched by the body politic.

He would be ruthless in his campaign, granting no quarter to opponents. Each foray would result in a new batch of foes and more bruised feelings. By 1935, he had uncounted enemies, many of whom made no secret of their desire to rid the state of him, by fair means or foul.

They were a diverse group, having little in common except status as targets or victims of the Kingfish.

School teachers who had lost their jobs because of their politics; property owners whose assessments had been raised arbitrarily or for spite, revenge, or personal gain of the lackeys of the Kingfish; elected officials who allowed their authority to be eroded because of fear of his wrath; legislators who endured personal insult and humiliation because they were impotent and power-less, unable to survive if the Kingfish offered opposition to them; members of the Long machine who fawned and toadied, facing continuing shame and abasement to Long's demands—these were the enemy.

To these must be added those who expediently allied themselves with Long and found that they were dancing with a bear. It would have been suicidal to execute any unplanned move that did not have the bear's concurrence. Long's public career was riddled by feuds with former friends and associates. Invariably they escalated into vendettas.

Huey played no favorites and made no exceptions. No one escaped his wrath. Not even his immediate family and close friends were immune from his retribution.

Befriended by his oldest brother, Julius, who paid for his college educa-tion, Huey rewarded him by considering running against him for district attorney of Winn Parish.

His rupture with brother Earl, who fought Huey's fights in childhood, was healed only at Huey's bedside as he lay dying.

Julius struck back by a vicious and devastating series of articles in a na-tional publication in which he hit at Huey's morality. Both Julius and Earl gave damaging testimony about Huey to a Senatorial investigating committee inquir-ing into Huey's affairs.

Long even fell out with an entire legislature—that of the State of Texas.

In 1931, he launched a plan to solve a knotty problem facing cotton farmers in Louisiana. Following the crash of 1929, cotton prices plummeted. Political and economic leaders devised schemes to deal with the problem, which was essentially one of overproduction.

Characteristically, Long's solution was bold and direct. Others danced around the problem, suggesting reductions, controls and other mild approaches. Huey's solution: cut production entirely!

Rather than mess around with artificial shortages, Long proposed to create a genuine shortage. If no production of cotton happened for an entire year, then surpluses would be used up and the demand for cotton would rise. Along with this would be a natural rise in prices. Cotton farmers would watch the good times roll.

There were certain problems connected with this approach, to be sure. Chief among them was the question of how farmers would subsist for an entire year with no income. There was also a difference of opinion whether the glut of cotton could be wiped out by the withholding of a single year's cotton produc-tion. Synthetic fibers such as rayon were being developed, so there was some anxiety about whether keeping cotton off the market would not create a demand for these items, further aggravating the problem.

But Long's idea had sufficient merit to attract a lot of support in cotton growing states. Obviously, it would not work unless all of the states involved would cease production simultaneously. Everything hinged around Texas, which contributed one bale of cotton out of every four that found its way to market.

The Texas legislature was intrigued by the plan and invited Long to Austin to address them. If the Kingfish would have shown up in person, there is no question that he would have sold the plan, so great were his personal powers of persuasion. But he was foiled by one of the enemies he created, Lieutenant Governor Paul Cyr.

Long could not leave the state in Cyr's hands unless the lieutenant governor was willing to promise not to throw his weight around as acting governor in Long's absence. Cyr was unwilling to give this assurance and Long had to content himself by using radio to address the Texans.

When the legislature and Governor Ross Sterling of Texas did not act immediately on Long's plan, he began to lose patience. He charged that Sterling was a pawn of the rich. One Texas legislator told Long to mind his own business and "run Louisiana if your people have no more sense than to permit you." Long charged that Sterling had "money up to your eyes and every luxury" and that the governor was "deaf to the cries of the children of destitute farmers."

The argument really got hot.

Later he charged that the Texas legislature had been "bought like a sack of corn" to vote against the cotton plan. The Texas Senate passed a resolution branding Long "a consummate liar." Texas eventually passed a crop reduction plan, but it was far from being the bold plan advanced by Long.[8]

One of Long's most intense feuds was with Governor John M. Parker, whom Long had supported for the governorship in 1920.

Parker had the last laugh. In the summer of 1933 he was granted an interview with Franklin Roosevelt to discuss the "alleged graft rings" in Louisiana. It was following this visit that the President ordered a resumption of the federal inquiry into Long's income tax matters.[9]

Long managed to hold onto control of Louisiana following his impeachment and he maintained his hold until his death. His fortunes, however, waxed and waned. The degree of his control varied.

For several years following his escape from conviction, he held the line against his enemies but, in the fall of 1933 and winter of 1933-34, the anti-Long sentiment in the state reached fever pitch. Violence was everywhere. If there had been a single individual with assassination tendencies at any one of a dozen confrontations, Long's demise would have been an accomplished fact.

In Minden, armed citizens and Long bodyguards narrowly avoided a shootout. At Donaldsonville, he was booed. At Alexandria, he was egged. Throughout southeast Louisiana, signs on bridges bearing the names of Long and his successor to the governorship, O.K. Allen, were torn down and the pair hanged in effigy. In East Feliciana Parish, north of Baton Rouge, $10,000 was offered to anyone having the courage to bring Long across the parish line.

At Monroe, unsupportive citizens were beaten at a Long-sponsored rally. One eyewitness recalls:

> "Some little bald-headed fellow—must have been in his forties—raised his arm and stood up. Huey said to sit down. He answered, 'No, I won't sit down,' and Huey said, 'Escort that man out of here!' And four or five or six great big burly men, bodyguards, they all jumped on this poor little man and beat him with their fists. And I stood right there looking at it. I was horrified that such action could occur. But it did happen. They literally threw him out bodily, returned to the stage and Huey continued his harangue.
>
> "There were about six men jumped on this one fellow, beat the bejesus out of him with their fists. One man in particular—just beating on his old bald head."[10]

Huey's bodyguards were quick to resort to violence and it extended not only to enemies but newsmen and innocent bystanders as well.

A newsman who waited patiently in the lobby of the Roosevelt Hotel in New Orleans to interview Long was halted by one of the senator's bodyguards, who explained pointedly, "The senator doesn't like to be around reporters." The reporter replied that his city editor had asked him to solicit a comment from Long on a matter currently in the news but before he could give his explanation, he was lifted bodily from behind and pushed through the revolving door at the hotel exit.[11]

An Associated Press photographer took a picture of Long and was promptly struck by a bodyguard. His camera fell to the pavement. The photographer stopped to pick it up and Huey commanded, "Let him have it!" The bodyguard hit the photographer again while other protectors smashed the camera to bits. The photographer, severely injured, was taken to the hospital where a physician said that the blow, had it landed a little lower, could have killed him.[12]

In the spring of 1934, Huey's enemies believed that the end of the dictatorship was near. They decided to press their luck. Still willing to work within the system, still believing that the dictatorship was assailable, they laid plans to wrest from Long's control the legislature in Baton Rouge.

Well in advance of the session that was scheduled to convene in May, opponents began lining up the necessary votes to unseat the Long-supported speaker of the House, Allan Ellender. Of the 51 votes needed, Long's enemies had 48 signed pledges. They believed the remainder would jump aboard the bandwagon when their strength became apparent.

After the speaker had been replaced, they believed the groundswell that would develop because of this show of power would result in the Long-backed lieutenant governor, John Fournet, being addressed out of office, giving control of both houses to anti-Long legislators. "Addressing" a public official out of office was a Louisiana device that provided for removal of statewide officials below the rank of governor by legislative action. No reason or cause was necessary.

All of this legislative maneuvering was simply prologue to the main event, the unfinished business of 1929, impeachment and conviction of the chief executive. In 1929 it was Long. In 1934 it was O.K. Allen. He would be impeached by the House and the impeachment would be upheld by the Senate. There would be no round robineers this time.

The plan was foolproof. There were chants of "It won't be Long now!"

But the plan was never carried out. Try as oppositionists would, they could never get the additional three votes to put the movement over the top. Long's opposition had much idealism, or, more correctly, naivete, in its ranks. The opponents never quite grasped the realities of practical politics. Every time they managed to get a new recruit, they lost one of their committed votes.

The movement collapsed.

The anti-Long faction saw its dreams of a legislative coup vanishing in the face of Long's political maneuvering and it infuriated them. The mood turned bitter. The peaceful opposition threatened to explode into violence when it became apparent that they had been outfoxed once again by the Kingfish. Any attempt to seize control of Louisiana politics by legal means was doomed to failure.

On the day before the legislature was to convene, the antis convened their own session in a downtown office building in Baton Rouge. It was the same building in which Carl Weiss' office was located. It housed some business and professional people who supported Huey Long but, for the most part, it was a hotbed of his enemies.

On that Sunday, May 13, 1934, Long had no friends in attendance at the meeting.

Those who showed up shared a single goal: rid the state of Huey Long! They were armed, most of them. They had come to Baton Rouge for action and not talk. They would settle for legislative action, but if they were denied the prospect of getting what they wanted by parliamentary and legal devices, they were willing to entertain other, stronger, extra-legal remedies.

They were prepared to storm the Kingfish in his aerie in the nearby Heidelberg Hotel, braving the machine gun nests that were reported to surround Long in his quarters.

Cooler heads prevailed. When the hopelessness of their situation became clear, the plotters left, mumbling and cursing the aborted coup. Long was spared—for the time being.[13]

But the violent brew that was being concocted in Louisiana continued to steep. Long did nothing to temper it. Instead he aggravated the situation. He did nothing to defuse the ticking infernal machine that by now was beginning to make itself heard. He taunted his opposition. He flaunted his power, delighting in provoking his enemies to the breaking point.

And some were beginning to break. Following that legislative session, five rifle shots were fired into the front of Long's New Orleans home by men who sped away before they could be identified.

In retrospect, it seems a wonderment that Long lived through the fall of 1934. But the most spectacular happenings were yet to come. If the citizenry had not been goaded sufficiently by outrages of the Kingfish up to now, he would give them even greater opportunity to show their hatred.

A little more than a year before his death, Long embarked upon a series of adventures that held within them such ready prospects for violence that there could be only one result: insurrection. The legislator who delivered the "blood on the capitol floor" speech in April had also observed, in the same outburst, "White men have ever made poor slaves."

In predictable fashion, Long took no notice of the simmering rebellion except to tighten the screws on his enemies, notably the city of New Orleans.

At the legislative session in May, 1934, when the coup fizzled, he stripped New Orleans of control of its own police force, placing it in the hands of a state-appointed "non-political" board. The state highway department withdrew funds earmarked for highway construction in the municipality. The city was deprived of any power to assess its own property.

The bankruptcy of New Orleans had begun. But even stronger measures were in the offing.

On September 11, 1934, an important election was scheduled to be held in New Orleans. Two congressmen would be elected; a seat on the all-important supreme court was up for grabs; one of Long's bitterest enemies (once a strong ally) on the Public Service Commission was running for re-election.

Earlier in 1934, Long was rebuffed by the electorate of New Orleans when he sponsored a candidate for mayor. Still smarting from the January defeat, he set into motion plans to insure that he would not be bested a second time in a single year.

This time Long would go beyond legislative action. He would use military force.

Many felt that Long had everything he needed already, since he controlled the state and the city of New Orleans as well. He could do anything he wanted. According to one biographer:

"...Huey Pierce Long became owner of

Louisiana in fee simple, with all reversionary
rights and hereditaments, in full trust and benefit,
to have and to hold, in paramount estate and
freehold, for the balance of his days."[14]

On July 30, two weeks after the legislature adjourned, Governor Allen issued a proclamation declaring "partial" martial law in New Orleans. He seized the voter registration office, stationing national guardsmen with mounted machine guns in the windows and on the counters of the office.

The city of New Orleans reacted. At first, its resistance was directed along legal lines. City fathers obtained an order restraining the governor or adjutant general from taking over the registration office, a meaningless gesture, since this was already a *fait accompli*. However, process servers were turned away when they attempted to serve the order on the adjutant general at the national guard military barracks.

Failing in their legal maneuvers, New Orleans officials themselves turned to force. To the already existing 900-man police force were added 400 special deputies. The force was equipped with machine guns, tear gas and arsenic bombs.

Facing them, entrenched in the voter registration office and armed with cannons, trench mortars, gas grenades and other implements of war, was the National Guard. Like comic opera armies facing off on the borders of neighboring banana republics, the two military gangs confronted each other.

The spectacle attracted the attention of the national press.

It also attracted the undivided attention of the White House.

When the confrontation started, the Special Agent in Charge (SAC) of the New Orleans office of the FBI routinely wired Washington each evening, giving a detailed summary of the particulars of the confrontation that day. FBI files reveal that the U.S. Attorney General's office became interested and asked to be added to the mailing list of the daily communiques.

Eventually the White House was brought into the network and details about the daily activities of the two armies were sent to Marvin McIntyre, appointment secretary to Roosevelt.

Throughout Long's lifetime, the Federal Bureau of Investigation normally had little interest in him. The bureau kept a file on his activities but there were few entries in it. While the Internal Revenue Service charged after Long with great zeal almost from the moment he was elected to the governorship, FBI files do not reflect any abiding interest in his monkeyshines.

To the contrary, FBI Director J. Edgar Hoover kept himself detached from Louisiana—at least officially, and responded in curt, stereotyped language to pleas from city officials that the bureau unleash its resources to curb Long. Invariably, Hoover answered any such requests with the chilly reply, "No investigation warranted because no federal law violated."

But it seemed, during those days in the summer of 1934, that the White House was fishing around to see if it couldn't find some kind of federal law that the Kingfish was violating so that it could move against him. The interest of the FBI in the situation involving the voter registrar's office, as reflected by the number of reports compiled by the FBI and furnished the White House, had become more intense.

Documents in the FBI file obtained under the provisions of the Freedom of Information Act confirm the FBI's concerns (probably the White House's concerns) that the confrontation between New Orleans and the State of Louisiana would spill over and damage federal property, notably the U.S. Post Office, which was in close proximity to the voter registrar's office.

Roosevelt seemed ready to move against Long if he could manufacture a plausible and defensible reason. His advisor, Raymond Moley, recalls that the President toyed with the idea of federal intervention into Louisiana affairs. His justification would be that the Constitution guarantees all citizens a republican form of government and that such freedom was long gone from Louisiana, a casualty of the oppression of Long and his cohorts.[15]

For a time it seemed the feds might intervene between state and local authorities and make the confrontation a three-cornered affair.

While the White House watched and waited for its opportunity, the military situation developed into a standoff. The occupation forces of Generalissimo Long did not budge from their captured territory in the voter registration office. The forces of the city of New Orleans were not inclined to mount an offensive to recapture the office. The two sides glared and glowered at each other like actors in a Gilbert and Sullivan opera bouffe.

To rekindle the fire and allow the pot to boil again, Field Marshall Long decided it was time to open a second front.

He had Governor Allen call the legislature into special session. It was the worst session of all those called during the Long years. The docket represented the most repressive measures ever introduced in the legislature.

All of the 27 pieces of legislation introduced at the session were referred to a single committee. Testimony was given by a single witness, the Kingfish. In little more than an hour the committee passed the bill.

Long's testimony was effective, but hardly enlightening: "Now, this is a bill to purify the ballot and do away with the dummy candidate business. It's a good measure and ought to pass." Upon a cue by Long, an administration supporter would move passage and pass they did, with one "nay" vote by a lone anti-Long committee member.

When the bills reached the House floor, Long was on hand, dashing about from desk to desk like a sheep dog herding his charges, nipping, barking and growling. At first, the acquiescent herd of Long lackeys went along quietly. But so flagrant did his disregard of legislative decorum become that the normally compliant and submissive representatives rebelled. They invoked Rule 10, which prohibits all but members from entering the floor when the House is in session. Normally the rule was not followed and reporters, supporters and even lobbyists were allowed to circulate freely among the assembled lawmakers.

The pro-Long speaker pointed out that invoking the regulation would mean the expulsion of the newspaper reporters also. No matter, the House, with new-found courage, replied. Throw them all out! Violence erupted. Long threatened a mutinous representative to bring him back in line. The representative threatened to slap Long's face. A photographer attempting to record the exchange was coldcocked and floored by two of the dozen bodyguards protecting Long. A fight broke out on the floor between several legislators.[16]

But the ruckus was little more than an interlude, a sideshow to the main drama. It neither delayed nor stopped the Long steamroller. All the bills were passed out of the House and, later, the Senate. The whole proceeding had taken 77 hours and when the lawmakers departed, the grip of Huey Long around the state—and particularly the city of New Orleans—had been tightened even more.

Long had been granted increased power over elections; he had been authorized to use the state militia for any purpose that suited his fancy; he had been presented with a state constabulary; his Attorney General was given broader powers over local district attorneys.

As the *piece de resistance,* Long had ramrodded through the legislature a resolution to investigate vice conditions in New Orleans. It was so juicy an assignment, this opportunity to confront vice in the wicked city of New Orleans (and in an official capacity, yet), that Long was forced to flee the state capitol and hide out in a fishing camp to escape the hordes of legislators clamoring for appointments to the Sin City Investigating Committee.

The investigation was clearly aimed at helping the Long candidates in the September 11 election.

On August 31, Long rode into New Orleans to begin the investigation. He entered as Caesar might have returned to Rome, preceded and followed by truckloads of armed national guardsmen. The guardsmen escorted him to his home and formed a corridor through which Long marched. A photographer attempting to record the scene was roughed up.

The hearings began in a climate of intimidation that was both tragic and comic. The committee's first move was to hire Long as its legal counsel. The next was to arrange for a radio station to broadcast the proceedings. (First things first.) The hearings were conducted in a high rise office building in quarters rented by a state agency. Newsmen and spectators were barred from the proceedings by some 50 national guardsmen.

Witnesses were hauled before the tribunal by the showboating Huey. The proceedings were broadcast to a bored and disinterested citizenry who were hardly shocked when it was established that there were whorehouses operating in the city and that gambling and police payoffs were actually going on! One reporter commented that it was "old stuff" and that any citizen of New Orleans could have told the committee the same thing.

When it was deemed that the committee had smeared the city administration sufficiently, the group left. Almost concurrently with the committee's adjournment, Long escalated the military situation. He had Governor Allen sign a mobilization order moving 2,000 national guardsmen into New Orleans, virtually the entire membership of the militia. Facing this military machine was the hastily assembled Army of the City of New Orleans.

The situation was loaded with tension. What would happen if an incident occurred that would start the sides to fighting? Certainly Long's troops, in a pitched battle, could be expected to carry the day. They outnumbered the defenders. They were trained and organized. They had the weight, the authority and the resources of state government on their side.

But there were other factors that had to be considered and these might have placed the outcome in doubt.

Could the national guardsmen be counted on to fire upon the citizens? This was no crack militia, spoiling for action to break the back of insurrection in some strange and alien environment. Instead, they were simply the reserves, the home guard, many of them probably neighbors of those they would be called upon to attack and subdue.

And how would the rank-and-file citizens of New Orleans react to an outbreak of hostilities? Would they, as the good citizens of Baton Rouge would do four months hence, arm themselves and occupy public property on their own initiative?

And what of the federal government? Would President Roosevelt seize the opportunity to break the back of the Long machine by using military force? A generation later President Eisenhower would foil Arkansas Governor Orval Faubus by nationalizing the militia that Faubus had mobilized, thereby forcing them to switch their allegiance from the state to the central government. Certainly Roosevelt must have understood that this was one of his options.

It was a heady and electrifying moment and certainly the peril of the situation was not lost on Long. He had pushed the city of New Orleans to the brink of armed conflict. Legislative humiliation and punishment were one thing. Armed warfare, with the imminent prospect of bloodshed and loss of life, was quite another.

Long had sown the wind and the dragon's teeth. He would reap the whirlwind and suffer the armed men.

Long's behavior was that of a deranged and unbalanced man. His constant goading and agitation of the city of New Orleans seemed designed to force the community into some precipitous action from which there could be no turning back. If he persisted in his actions and carried them any farther, the blood would surely flow.

How far would he go?

As it turned out, there were limits beyond which even Huey Long would not go and one of these was the conscious, final provocation of armed conflict among fellow citizens. Even a hardened enemy such as Franklin Roosevelt conceded this restraint to Long when he told Joseph P. Kennedy (father of a President and two U.S. senators), "If there was a demagogue around here of the type of Huey Long to take up anti-Semitism, there would be more blood running in the streets of New York than in Berlin." The reference was to Hitler's anti-Jewish actions on his ascent to power in Germany in the 1930s.[17]

Civic leaders and business interests intervened. Alarmed at the potential damage to the image of New Orleans and its effect upon those with dollars to invest in the city's future, the marketplace prevailed upon both sides to sheath swords and declare an armistice.

A collision was avoided. The election went off without further incident.

Incredibly, the election returns reflected no resentment on the part of New Orleanians for the rude intrusion by Long into the affairs of their city. They booted his enemy, Francis Williams, off the Public Service Commission; they re-elected two Long congressmen and they elevated his lieutenant governor, John Fournet, to the supreme court.

Reports of Huey's demise had been greatly exaggerated. He was alive and well, more powerful than ever. It was time for him to relax, to consolidate his gains. Defeated in January by the city of New Orleans in his efforts to elect a mayor, he swept the city cleanly in September. A prudent man would have eased his grip on the state. He would have readjusted the reins.

But Huey Long was not a prudent man.

As long as New Orleans was managed by his enemies, he would not relax his campaign to destroy the city. As long as a single enemy existed in the state, he would not rest. As long as Standard Oil continued to operate beyond his control, he could not sit still. Consumed by bitterness, motivated by revenge, he summoned the legislature into special session two more times during the balance of the year.

In November, he called his second special session of the year and it followed a pattern that seemed to have been established. More and more, special sessions had taken on the flavor of instruments of reprisal. The pattern would continue during 1935, escalating until his death.

The November session saw 44 bills passed in exactly the same manner as in the August session. All bills were referred to a single committee, argued by Long alone and passed at breakneck speed. The House committee reported all the bills favorably in one hour and 42 minutes. The Senate Finance Committee bettered this performance, passing the package in one hour and 21 minutes, less than two minutes per law. The procedure was described by one reporter as setting an "all-time, all-American record."[18]

The bills—like earlier bills—were an outpouring of the Long thirst for power and his desire for petty personal retribution against political enemies. One bill provided for a "civil service commission" which was given unlimited power over municipal police and firemen. The newly created body could fire and hire non-elected officials. Several months later the commission fired the police chief of Alexandria, the city where Huey had been pelted with eggs in 1933.

His attorney general had been disbarred by the state bar association. Huey had a rival bar association established.

One bill took authority for regulating utilities away from municipalities and vested it in the Public Service Commission. The commission promptly hired Long as special legal counsel.

The salary of the anti-Long district attorney of East Baton Rouge Parish was limited by statute to $4,000 yearly.

The governor was given the power to fill all vacancies in all elective offices.

Long had extended the power of the state (and, hence, his own power) to police and fire chiefs in Louisiana; to the payroll of the New Orleans Sewerage and Water Board; to the bar association; to debtors of all kinds; to utilities and to homestead associations.

He also advanced the date of his approaching senatorial re-election from November, 1935 to January, 1935. Once re-elected, he could concentrate on his campaign for the presidency in the fall of 1935 without jeopardizing his seat in the Senate.

Long rested on his oars for a month. He had New Orleans crippled. City fathers were dazed, impotent and barely hanging on to the ropes. But he suddenly remembered some unfinished business in Baton Rouge: Standard Oil and the irksome East Baton Rouge Parish government. He dealt with these troublesome problems in the same way he had come to deal with most problems. He had a special session convened.

In December, Long had Governor Allen summon legislators to another extraordinary session to deal with his enemies.

During the session, legislation was passed to stack the governing body of Baton Rouge with a pro-Long majority; to require that the appointment of all deputy sheriffs beyond the number of five be approved by the Criminal Bureau of Investigation, Huey's recently created police force; to bring all of the 15,000 school teachers in the state's public school system under the spell of a "budget committee" which would approve all educators or they would not be eligible for employment. This extended to all teachers, those yet to be hired and those already employed.

But the most remarkable action taken by the December legislature was directed at Standard Oil. It was effected by a maneuver so slick that the corporation was not even aware it was being shafted until the bill was passed.

An innocent-appearing bill was introduced which provided for the codification of existing licensing laws. Half a dozen statutes were combined into one law. There were no new provisions. It was simply a consolidation.

The bill passed the House committee, the House floor, the Senate committee and was up for final passage on the Senate floor. Before the question was called, however, an administration floor leader offered an amendment to the innocuous law. It was 100 pages of single spaced typing that re-enacted the manufacturer's license tax that had resulted in Huey's impeachment in 1929.

The secretary of the Senate mumbled a few incomprehensible words to comply with the constitutional provision that all legislation be "read." Cries of "question" were heard immediately, a vote was taken and the bill passed handily. When it returned to the House it was railroaded in similar fashion.

The chief lobbyist for Standard Oil was not in the Senate when the bill was passed. He had left the chamber to telephone his superiors that the session was grinding to a close and there had been no anti-Standard Oil legislation passed. The oil company fired him shortly thereafter and some years later it was revealed that he and Long's principal bagman, Seymour Weiss, were boyhood friends and close business associates. When Long made peace with Standard Oil a month or so later, he forced the company to rehire the lobbyist.

Long had finally brought Standard Oil to its knees. The tax for which he was impeached in 1929 breezed through in 1935, although it would eventually spawn even more dreadful consequences than in the earlier year. Passage of the legislation would be the final straw on the overburdened back of Baton Rouge. Its enactment unleashed the pent-up hostilities of the community, pushing it to the brink of revolution, infinitely farther than Long's shenanigans pushed the city of New Orleans.

Men would take up arms. They would drill and maneuver in paramilitary formation. They would plot and scheme to rid the state of Long.

When Long moved to tax "the Standard," as the company was referred to, he hit the nerve center of Baton Rouge. In that community of 30,000 people, Standard Oil was the principal employer. Several thousand Baton Rougeans worked at the refinery.

But its importance to the city went far beyond this.

There were few in Baton Rouge who were not touched in some way by the presence and the operations of the plant. Everyone depended, to some degree, upon Esso Standard Oil paychecks. The hours of banks and merchants were regulated by the plant's paydays—they stayed open later on paydays to cash checks and to sell to the newly-paid employees. Even lawyers and other professionals who had no direct dealings with Standard Oil prospered from their location in an affluent community made so by the Standard.

Baton Rouge was a company town. In attacking Standard Oil, Long had violated the soul of the community. He had finally committed the one act the people would not abide. He would pay dearly.

Perhaps when Long first assumed the governor's office, fears for his personal safety were groundless and probably prompted by paranoia rather than fact. But, as the expression goes, "Just because you're paranoid, it doesn't mean that nobody is out to get you." When the year 1935 came rolling in, his concerns were well founded. He was a prime target for assassination. Plots were being hatched throughout the state. They were especially rife in Baton Rouge.

That there would be attempts upon his life was a foregone conclusion. Even Long himself was aware of that. He told a Senate colleague, "If there were just a few people plotting it, I think I might live through it. But these people are determined to kill me and I'm not going to live through it."[19]

The only questions remaining to be answered were where, when and by whom the deed would be done.

CHAPTER SIX

Public Enemy
Number One

FBI Agent A.C. Hayden, in a memo to his superiors in Washington dated March 7, 1940, reported that Mr. Don C. Miller of East Kalispell, Montana, had visited Baton Rouge and had stopped at the grave of Huey Long. According to Agent Hayden:

> "The guide, in pointing out spots of interest about the capitol, described the death of Long, according to Mr. Miller, and advised that 14 people were connected with the plot to kill Long. He related that the conspirators had been led by President Roosevelt and advised that Roosevelt was in Baton Rouge at the time of the death of Long."[1]

If this is surprising to readers, it will be even more surprising, if not downright shocking, to learn that there were—and still are—many in Louisiana who believed that the President engineered the death of Huey Long.

In the late '40s, after I had returned to civilian life from the Pacific and the U.S. Marine Corps, I attended a seance with a professor from Tulane University in New Orleans. We had engaged in a classroom discussion that touched on spiritism, the belief that dead persons can communicate with the living. The teacher asked if I could locate a seance. This I did and one Friday night we attended—he, his wife, my fiancee and members of my family.

There were a number of standard seance personalities there: an Indian, several historical personalities, one of the Doctors Mayo—and Huey Long. The ghost of Long took the occasion to explain the circumstances of his death. He stated unequivocally that the orders for his death came from Washington. The allegation didn't cause a ripple among seance-goers. The news was hardly of blockbuster proportions, since virtually everyone in the audience had been exposed to the story and many believed it. It was not news.

Huey Long himself was convinced that Franklin Roosevelt was encouraging plans to assassinate him. He read a transcript to the Senate on August 5, a little more than a month before he was killed, of a meeting in New Orleans of his opposition. He tied the entire assemblage to the President, whom he scornfully referred to as "Franklin Delano Roosevelt, the first, the last and the littlest." Long quoted one of the conferees as saying, "I would draw in a lottery to go out and kill Long. It would take one man, one gun and one bullet."

Long ended his speech by pledging, "Louisiana will not have a government imposed upon it that represents murder, blackmail, oppression or destitution."[2]

Journalist and author of the 1930s and beyond, Adela Rogers St. Johns, writing in her autobiographical *The Honeycomb,* claims that Long told her in the summer of 1935 that in 1936 he would be President or he would be dead.

"Unless he has me shot first, I will be President," he told the reporter. Mrs. St. Johns relates that Long confided the possibility—really, the certainty—of his assassination during dinner in a Washington restaurant less than a month before he died. The "he" referred to by Long was Franklin Roosevelt.

She recalls another occasion where she listened on a telephone extension to a conversation between Long and Roosevelt. Long's safe had been rifled and an important letter had been stolen. According to Mrs. St. Johns, Long told Roosevelt:

> "Send me back that letter. You're not going to let me live until the election anyhow, so what'd you want with it?...I know you for a treacherous and deceitful man...God damn you for a treacherous and deceitful man."[3]

Some believe that the hands-off posture adopted by the Federal Bureau of Investigation reflects Roosevelt's desire that no investigation be made into Long's shooting and death. Surely, if Roosevelt had passed the word that the Bureau should look into the shooting, the agency would have abandoned its "see no evil, hear no evil, speak no evil" policy inherent in the stock FBI turndown to demands that it investigate the matter.

The Bureau was deluged with correspondence from all over the nation urging that it take a look at the shooting. Many of the letters blamed Roosevelt and Postmaster General James Farley for Long's death. A memo to J. Edgar Hoover dated 12:20 p.m. September 13, from one of his chiefs, refers to a conversation with the Special Agent in Charge (SAC) of the New Orleans office. The New Orleans SAC referred to newspaper articles "to the effect that numerous telegrams are being sent to the President of the United States demanding that the Department of Justice institute an immediate investigation relative to the assassination of Senator Huey Long."

One anonymous letter to the FBI four years later stated, "If Huey Long had of (sic) lived Roosevelt would not be serving his 2 (second) term."

To all requests that it participate in an investigation, the FBI stoically responded that the Bureau had no jurisdiction, since there was no violation of federal law. It designed a mimeographed form letter to respond to such inquiries. The format allowed space for the name of the respondent and salutation and was personalized to the extent that it referred to "your letter dated————." From that point forward, all inquiries received the same answer.

A threat to kidnap the infant son of the slain Carl Weiss was mailed to Weiss' widow and was turned over by the family to the Post Office Department. This department gave it to the U.S. Attorney's office in New Orleans, which then referred it to the FBI. The badly-written letter warned Mrs. Weiss:

> "You had better keep close watch on that
> merders (murderer's) boy for he may come up a
> missing wich (which) would service (serve) all of
> you just what you deserve."

The "Lindbergh Law" had been passed in 1932 following the kidnapping and death of Charles Lindbergh's infant son. This made kidnapping the jurisdiction of the federal government when the victim was taken across state lines, which could or could not have been a possibility if the Weiss child had been abducted.

However, the FBI was of no mind to get involved under any circumstances.

SAC Magee wrote the Director about the Baby Weiss kidnap threat:

> "While the import of the anonymous
> communication might be construed as a threat to
> kidnap, there appears (sic) to be no facts which
> would warrant investigative jurisdiction by this
> office and I so informed Assistant United States
> Attorney Warren O. Coleman. He stated that he
> will retain the anonymous communication in the
> files of the United States Attorney for any purpose
> it may serve in the event that the son of Carl Weiss
> or any of the immediate Weiss family were subse-
> quently kidnapped."

The Post Office originally made the hair-raising suggestion that the Weiss family report the threat to the state court. With a pro-Long attorney general, a pro-Long supreme court and with district attorney's and sheriff's operations tightly supervised by the state administration, one can imagine the risk of placing the potentially explosive assignment in the hands of a state court, even considering that Long had never quite managed to subdue all of the judiciary in Baton Rouge, the domicile of the Weiss family.[4]

The tragedy of the handling of this matter is that the FBI was prepared to sit on its hands and allow a child to be kidnapped, rather than risk participation in any kind of investigation bearing on Long's death. (Anything beats getting involved!)

Many believe there is a great deal of reason to support a theory that those surrounding Franklin Roosevelt had Long killed. When Mrs. St. Johns was skeptical that Roosevelt would actually have ordered Long's killings, Long told her there were many around the President who would gladly have arranged the job if they felt their boss was interested in having it done. In the Watergate matter, years later, one eager Nixon henchman was prepared to do away with a presidential enemy when he construed a vague, offhand statement as meaning that the President wanted him out of the way.

The prospect of Long possibly succeeding in his quest for the presidency in 1936 concerned Roosevelt's camp to the point of panic. One writer observed:

> "It was a terrifying idea (that Long held the balance of power in the 1936 election), and dreadful fantasies seized the minds of all the national committeemen: The Kingfish riding high, General Jim (Farley) in prison on trumped-up charges, the nation careening to revolution because of New Deal policies carried beyond control.
>
> "It is interesting to speculate on what might have happened but for the Roosevelt Luck.
>
> "With the White House as a stronghold, Huey might well have eliminated some of his enemies by the gun and it is certain that he would have jailed some Washington figures and driven others out of the country..."[5]

Such was the terror inspired in his enemies by the redoubtable senior senator from Louisiana.

A violent climax to the relationship between Long and Roosevelt would have been predictable and it is doubtful that it would have surprised too many people. Had a person had a sophisticated enough computer and had he been in possession of sufficient data concerning the personalities and backgrounds of both Roosevelt and Long, the inevitability of a collision between the two would have been apparent. Just as a physicist or astronomer, armed with facts about two moving celestial bodies, could accurately forecast that they would both seek to occupy the same space at a given time, it was certain that the two personalities would collide.

Roosevelt and Long were both political animals, sharing somewhat similar political backgrounds. Both were elected to public office at relatively early ages. Roosevelt won election to the New York Senate at 29 and Long was elected to the Louisiana Railroad Commission at 25.

In 1928, both were elected governors of their respective states.

Both were Democrats, although it is possible that both were willing to desert their party and start a new one if they were unsuccessful in achieving desired ends through the original party.[6]

Long had no doubt that he would be elected President. Recall that he told his bride-to-be, Rose McConnell, that he would first win office as a secondary state official, then governor and eventually he would be President of the United States.

From his earliest days in Louisiana, reporters felt he had "a presidential complex." When campaigning for the Senate in 1930, he said he was "headed for the White House."

In February, 1930, when ex-President Calvin Coolidge and Mrs. Coolidge visited Baton Rouge, Long questioned him concerning the quality of the Hoovers' housekeeping. He was concerned that they might have neglected the White House. He said, possibly with tongue in cheek:

"When I was elected, I found the governor's mansion in such rotten shape, I had to tear it down and rebuild. I don't want to rebuild the White House."[7]

Roosevelt obviously had similar goals. Elected to the state Senate of New York in 1910, he ran unsuccessfully for the vice-presidency with Ohio Governor James M. Cox in 1920. In 1924, he seconded Al Smith's unsuccessful bid for the presidential nomination and supported Smith again in 1928 when Smith actually did receive the nomination. Roosevelt became governor of New York, succeeding Smith, in 1928.

Long and Roosevelt were alike in only a few ways, one being a common desire to serve in the nation's highest office.

They were complete opposites in many other ways. Journalists wrote colorful copy constrasting the style of Roosevelt, the Squire of Hyde Park, and Long, the Redneck of the Bayous. But the contrasts were largely superficial and unimportant. Underneath, they shared a lust for power which forced them into a contest for the nation's highest office, the presidency.

It was a competition from which there could emerge only one winner.

Roosevelt was an aristocrat, a patrician to the manner born. Long was vintage redneck, boisterous and outrageous, possessed of great wit and homespun charm that could be turned off and on at will. He had little patience for manners and the polite demands of society.

But if Roosevelt held the edge in breeding, those who were able to observe both held that it was the Kingfish who possessed the superior mentality.

Professor Raymond Moley, member of Roosevelt's own "brains trust," who knew both men, wrote admiringly of Long, "I have never known a mind that moved with more clarity, decisiveness and force."[8]

No less a person than H.G. Wells, mindful of the social graces and bearing of the time, pronounced that Long was a "Winston Churchill who has never been to Harrow."[9]

Another political and social commentator and philosopher, Raymond Gram Swing, said just about the same thing. Swing was no friend of Long's. He considered the Kingfish one of the harbingers of fascism in the U.S. Nevertheless, he warned, "he is uneducated and devoid of culture today, but let there be no mistake, he is an almost neurotically intelligent man." He reminded that Long had been praised by Chief Justice Taft and Justice Brandeis of the Supreme Court. America might have more polished lawyers, Swing concluded, but few with greater talent.[10]

Long and Roosevelt shared a commitment to redistribute the wealth. Long's commitment was one of great longevity, reaching back into his formative years. Roosevelt's did not square with his background, prompting a certain suspicion by some that it represented no true, ingrained conviction, but was instead born of political expediency.

They differed on a timetable for redistribution of wealth. Left to Long, fortunes would be nationalized and redistributed right now or, as a compromise, overnight. Roosevelt proposed a milder, more polite, more gradual, less disruptive approach.

But these were essentially differences of strategy and timing. Both were committed to the basic principle of taking from the rich and giving to the poor. If Roosevelt was capable of packaging his program in trappings that would not alarm the Establishment and, on the other hand, Long could not resist the temptation to shock and even terrify authority, are these not simply differences in technique and not in kind?

They were surface distinctions.

At the bottom, deep inside their psyches, both men were capable of strong feelings that would give rise to strong actions. Long's vengeance and talent for retribution were overt, open and visible for all to see. There would be no misplacing the credit (or blame) for his actions. The victim was sure to know who brought about his misfortune. Long displayed his anger with vigor and with relish.

Roosevelt was reserved. He sought no credit for having done a distasteful deed, for having torpedoed an enemy. He was circumspect. But the anger and the capacity for reprisal were there, nonetheless.

As Long had confessed in his memoirs, once disappointed over a political undertaking, he could never cast it from his mind. So had Roosevelt made a similar candid admission. He wrote a Cabinet member, "I have an unfortunately long memory and I am not forgetting either our enemies or our objectives."[11]

James Farley, legendary Democratic party strategist (who guided the Roosevelt political fortunes to two terms as President and eventually broke with him), considered Roosevelt "sometimes a spoiled boy...(with a) few petty attributes which were continually getting him into trouble."[12] Roosevelt was capable of a less spectacular, but perhaps a more frightening, quality: a steely-cold silent anger that he could mask when necessary, publicly observing the social amenities but inwardly plotting retribution even as he guffawed and patronized his intended prey.

Long was a special enemy to Roosevelt, a kind of *bete noir*. He hated Long with a passion reserved only for the Kingfish. Elliott Roosevelt related his father's feelings after a meeting with Long:

> "'That,' Father said to me afterward, 'is a man totally without principle.' Ickes went further. 'Long,' he snapped, suffered from 'halitosis of the intellect.'
>
> "The Kingfish was no joke to my parent. To his keen eyes, Huey Long had much in common with Mussolini who, by promising the impossible, had made no scruples about the route he would choose to get there. Not long after their encounter, Father began to look for means of unhorsing Long and his cronies, who ran Louisiana."[13]

Roosevelt tolerated many enemies, General Douglas MacArthur and "The Radio Priest," Father Charles Coughlin, being notable examples. But he had little patience for Long. He moved to smash the senator from Louisiana. The word was passed to deny federal patronage to Long and his machine in the state. "Give it to Long's enemies!" FDR ordered.

Later he would unleash the power of the United States government, including the reluctant FBI and the eager IRS, to bring Long to heel. When Roosevelt could no longer manage Long politically, he ordered that federal investigators be sent to Louisiana "to prove the financial shenanigans of Huey Long and company." Son Elliott speculates that his father "may have been the originator of the concept of employing the IRS as a weapon of political retribution."[14]

Roosevelt, crippled by polio, could offer no physical threat to Long. Nevertheless, he cherished a fond wish to clout the Kingfish with a couple of well placed haymakers.

The President told Joseph Kennedy:

> "If I could, the way I'd handle Huey

Long would be physically. He's a physical coward. I've told my fellows up there that the way to deal with him is to frighten him. But they're more afraid of him than he is of them."[15]

Long was equally bellicose. He bragged:

"I can take him. He's a phony...he's scared of me. I can out promise him and he knows it. People will believe me and they won't believe him. His mother's watching him and she won't let him go too far...He's living on inherited income."[16]

(Long's reference to FDR's mother probably stemmed from his one and only visit to Hyde Park, the Roosevelt family's palatial estate. He was invited by Roosevelt as a political gesture. Present was Sara Roosevelt, domineering and outspoken matriarch of the family, who was repelled by Long as a stereotype of a low class politician. She asked, in a voice loud enough to be overheard, "Who is that dreadful person sitting next to my son?" Grandson Elliott, the family historian, adds, "taking care not to lower her resonant voice, she exclaimed, 'Why, they look like a lot of gangsters!'")[17]

Long and Roosevelt had differences stemming from their first joint venture, which involved Roosevelt's nomination and subsequent election to the presidency.

Long felt he was responsible in no small measure for these two landmark events in Roosevelt's life. While the President and his advisors could hardly argue with the fact that Long's help was beneficial, they were reluctant to give him the entire credit for the election and were understandably loath to turn the presidency over to him. The senator and the President parried several times, Long trying to win Roosevelt over and Roosevelt trying to charm and pacify the Louisiana senator, with neither quite succeeding.

When this dialogue failed, the gloves were taken off. It became a fight to the death, no quarter asked and none given. It could only end with the capitulation or elimination of one of them.

Although Roosevelt and Long served as chief executives of their respective states at the same period, there was little contact between them as governors.

Long invited Roosevelt to the New Orleans meeting of the National Governors Conference in 1928, an invitation Roosevelt declined because he was being treated at the time for polio at Warm Springs, Georgia. Furthermore, Roosevelt's opponent for the governorship had not yet conceded the election and FDR felt it might appear presumptuous for him to accept the invitation.

There was also a fatuous exchange of views between Roosevelt and Long in 1931 over the proper way to prepare and consume potlikker, the juice that remains in a pot after greens and other vegetables are boiled. The dish is a hearty and nourishing favorite of the rural South.

Long provided comic relief for newspapers throughout the nation by extolling the virtues of the concoction, even offering advice about the best way to prepare it. He dictated the etiquette for eating potlikker in combination with cornpone, a Southern cornbread made without milk or eggs. Cornpone, the Amy Vanderbilt of the Rednecks declared, should be dunked and absolutely not crumbled.

It being the silly season, the editor of the Atlanta *Constitution* offered an opposing view, stating authoritatively that cornpone should be crumbled and not dunked. The newsman went so far as to suggest that Long himself, in private, was a closet crumbler.

Into this inane debate dashed Franklin Roosevelt. Aware of the great power Long held in Louisiana and the Kingfish's growing attraction throughout the South, and hungry for any kind of publicity that might help him capture the Democratic nomination for president, Roosevelt worked out a comic compromise between the Louisiana governor and the Georgia editor: refer the matter to the platform committee of the next Democratic National Convention.

Roosevelt's patronizing of Long during the potlikker exchange was part of a strong effort to enlist the support of the Kingfish to help him win the Democratic nomination for the presidency. Both Roosevelt and his campaign manager, James Farley, paid particular attention to Long. Although Long had not formed his Share Our Wealth Society yet and lacked national recognition, he had a strong following in Louisiana and throughout the South. He would be valuable as a friend and formidable as an enemy.

But Long was far from sympathetic to Roosevelt when he arrived in the Senate in 1932. Upon taking his seat in that body, he told reporters that, as far as Louisiana was concerned, Roosevelt "would have no chance with us." But Huey's opposition to the New York governor was softened through the influence of other Progressives in the Senate, Democrat and Republican alike, who were attracted to the Roosevelt candidacy.[18]

Roosevelt buttered up to Long.

In Atlanta, he even sounded Hueyesque when he declared publicly, "The millions who are in want will not stand by silently forever while the things to satisfy their needs are within easy reach." To Huey he wrote, "You and I are alike for the rights in behalf of the common man of this country."[19]

And Huey bit. He was won over. Politics had made another pair of the strangest of bedfellows.

He declared for Roosevelt, promptly receiving a telephone call from Farley asking for the Kingfish's help in lining up delegations. He became Roosevelt's man in the South, immediately working Mississippi, Arkansas, Oklahoma and other Southern states. He became part of the strategy team. Farley asked him to arrive early in Chicago for the convention and to help with the nomination strategy.

Long sincerely believed that he was the key element in Roosevelt's successful bid for the nomination. Roosevelt's failure to recognize his assistance and to reward him adequately for his efforts rankled him until the day he died. During a filibuster in the Senate less than three months before his death, Long charged that Roosevelt would not have been elected had not the Kingfish obtained the nomination for him. Long said:

> "I have yet to hear it denied that Mr. Franklin D. Roosevelt would not have been nominated at the Chicago convention without the help that we were able to give him, which he would not have had if I had not been with him."[20]

Long's claims are not without foundation.

In the spring of 1932, Roosevelt seemed to be far out in the lead for the nomination. A win on the first ballot was possible. But then his hold began to slip. Al Smith defeated him 3-1 in the Massachusetts primary and then showed unexpected strength in Pennsylvania. In California, House Speaker John Nance Garner ran ahead of Roosevelt. Long's announcement in Roosevelt's favor portended solidarity in the South but the campaign was in deep trouble in other areas.

The trouble would continue throughout the Democratic National Convention, which opened in Chicago in June, 1932. More than half the delegates were pledged to the New York governor. However, he needed more, since the rules of the convention required a two-thirds vote to nominate. This Roosevelt did not have. It was possible that Governor Roosevelt and ex-Governor Smith would deadlock, creating a situation ripe for a dark horse who would triumph over both candidates.

Huey's delegation at the convention was challenged by his opponents in Louisiana, who offered an alternate slate of delegates. With help from the Roosevelt delegates and with his own testimony before the Credentials Committee ("Democratic party in Louisiana? I *am* the Democratic party in Louisiana!") his delegation was seated.[21]

Huey offered the Roosevelt forces a solution to the two-thirds hindrance and, if they had stayed with him, it would have meant the end of the problem, although it could have created fresh ones. It was Huey's nature, when an obstacle presented itself, to simply eliminate the obstacle. Don't go around it. Don't try to reshape or refashion it. Eliminate it! And so, he proposed to abolish the two-thirds rule to provide for a simple majority to nominate, which Roosevelt already had.

At a meeting on June 24 with the Democratic leadership, Long delivered a spell-binding presentation that attracted national attention and persuaded the group to sponsor a resolution to repeal the two-thirds rule.

An admiring but horrified Farley commented:

> "He delivered a stem-winding, rousing stump speech that took his listeners by storm. This was perhaps Huey's first entry onto the national scene and he went over with a terrific bang...It was a coat-flying, arms flailing, fire-and-brimstone speech which overwhelmed everyone within earshot. The fat was in the fire and for the time being, at least, Huey was Cock of the Walk."[22]

Roosevelt, at first supportive of Huey's idea to change the rule, sensed that it would have repercussions when it came to the floor. He dropped his support. The decision almost cost him the nomination and once again he needed Huey to rescue him.

(Ironically, in 1935, when Long and Roosevelt were bitter public enemies, the two-thirds rule looked like it might once again threaten Roosevelt. The rule was originally written into convention regulations because the South insisted on it. It would help the region block the nomination of a candidate not to the liking of the conservative South. It was Long's plan to deny Roosevelt the nomination at the 1936 convention by draining enough votes from Southern delegations so that the President would not be able to gain the necessary two-thirds majority. In 1936, at the convention, with Long in the grave, Roosevelt forces abolished the requirements, with the active assistance of Louisiana's delegation.)

When the first ballot was tabulated, Roosevelt was close but he still lacked more than 100 votes to reach the two-thirds majority. The second and third ballots showed little improvement. The chinks and flaws of the Roosevelt movement began to show. It seemed, for a while, that it would collapse entirely.

Huey moved in to shore up Roosevelt's crumbling fortunes. He crashed the Arkansas delegation, threatening Senate leader Joe Robinson and the others if they deserted Roosevelt. The Mississippi delegation was held in check only by his efforts. He warned Mississippi Senator Pat Harrison that he would campaign against him for re-election if Harrison did not hold fast his delegation for Roosevelt. His influence was also felt in other Southern delegations.

The Solid South remained solid.

On the fourth ballot, California switched its support from John Garner to Roosevelt.

It was all over. Roosevelt was nominated.

Credit is properly given to publisher William Randolph Hearst for putting Roosevelt over the top, since he called the shots for the delegation from California. However, had Long not kept the Southern delegates in harness, even the later infusion of California delegates would not have averted a wholesale desertion from Roosevelt. Arkansas, had it not held fast for Roosevelt, voting early in the roll call, would have given an early signal to others that Roosevelt had peaked and was on his way down.

It could have started a rout.

And Roosevelt would soon have the smell of a loser.

When the convention adjourned, the Roosevelt forces would have preferred that Long return to Louisiana, not so much because the state needed any persuading to vote for Roosevelt, but because the Democratic National Committee would have rested easier knowing that Long's energy was contained in Louisiana and would not be unleashed upon the balance of the nation. It could not afford to have a loose cannon such as Long rolling about the decks of the Roosevelt bandwagon as it barnstormed the country.

But Huey could never be excluded from any undertaking in which he chose to be included. This extended to the presidential campaign.

Hardly had the oratory died down when the Kingfish was off and campaigning. Having scrutinized the talents of the national leaders of the party, Long felt that he was as competent and as qualified as any of them. He was prepared to unload on an unsuspecting nation a demonstration of the fine points of political campaigning—Louisiana style.

Farley was cool to Long's involvement in the campaign, believing that the Kingfish was simply planning his own campaign for President and was using the Roosevelt effort for on-the-job training. Long's aspirations to the presidency were common knowledge.

Nevertheless, uninvited, Long arrived in New York accompanied by bodyguards and raring to go. He occupied a series of connecting rooms in the Waldorf-Astoria that accounted for an entire floor. He left the hotel to descend upon Farley's headquarters with his characteristic bombast and showmanship. He unveiled a campaign plan so grandiose that the Democratic pros recoiled in horror.

Essentially, it involved the Democratic National Committee providing Huey with a special train equipped with the loudspeakers he had learned to use so effectively in Louisiana on sound trucks. He would travel the length and breadth of the United States, visiting each state, promising immediate cash payment of the soldiers' World War I bonus if Roosevelt was elected.

That there was no money available for such a scheme did not bother him. That a simple spearcarrier in the ranks of the presidential campaign should not outshine the candidate would never have seemed to him to be an issue. The fact that he had no idea whether Roosevelt favored cash payment of the bonus apparently was a trivial detail which merited no serious consideration.

Farley's advisors blanched when they learned of Huey's plans. However, no one wanted to meet Long head on, dismissing his harebrained scheme out of hand. Instead, the powers at the committee mapped out a modest itinerary for the redneck activist which took him into states believed already lost, or so firmly committed to Roosevelt that Long's mercurial temperament, unpredictable behavior and fiery disposition could do little harm.

It would also keep him away from the critical areas where the campaign would be won or lost.

If the Democrats were surprised at Long's effectiveness at the convention, they were overwhelmed at what he accomplished on the road. The road show was, according to Farley, "a curious hodgepodge of buffoonery and demagogic strutting, cleverly bundled in with a lot of shrewd common sense and an evangelical fervor in discussing the plight of the underprivileged."

When Farley and Roosevelt learned the vote-getting power of the Kingfish, they concluded that the margin of victory would have been far greater had they used Long more sensibly than they did.

Looking back, Farley believed that if the campaign had sent Huey into the thickly populated Pennsylvania mining districts, Roosevelt would have carried the state by a comfortable margin. The Democratic leaders were forced to understand that Long was more than a regional phenomenon and had great appeal to the troubled and downtrodden, wherever they existed—North, East, South and West.

Farley understood and put the knowledge to good use. He said, "We never again underrated him."[23]

Long was an effective campaigner for Roosevelt. He was also cheap. He cost the Democrats nothing. He raised his own campaign funds and even covered expenses for other areas.

He told the Senate on April 15, 1935, that he raised $69,000 from Louisiana sources for the Democratic campaign. He paid his own expenses and even left some money in South Dakota and Kansas for the less-talented Midwesterners who lacked his fund-raising skills. He gave more to a "low-ceiling fellow that wore glasses" in New York. This party emissary promised Long political patronage and even gave the Kingfish a list of jobs he would control.[24]

Long went back to Louisiana and passed the hat, coming up with more money from his friends to help the Roosevelt effort. Later he confessed ruefully that not only did he not get the jobs, but to add insult to disappointment, one of the contributors was indicted by the Feds.

When Roosevelt won the presidency, he won many things: recognition, prestige, many problems and all the pomp, circumstance and trappings that go with the nation's highest office.

He also won Huey Long, who would be "the problem child of the New Deal." There would never be agreement between the two politicians. And soon the disagreements would flare and explode upon the public scene.

Even before Roosevelt was inaugurated, Long served notice on the incoming President from the Senate floor that if he did not carry out the program advocated by the Kingfish, there were those in the Senate who would do it themselves.

He continued to snipe at Roosevelt past inauguration day.

By June of 1933, Roosevelt had had enough. In a celebrated meeting between him and Long, the inevitable break occurred. With Farley and Marvin McIntyre, the President's appointment secretary, looking on, Long stated his position: he wanted patronage; he was to be the chief conduit for all federal patronage into the state of Louisiana and perhaps for other areas as well.

Throughout most of the conversation, Huey wore a bright-banded straw hat, which he removed only to add occasional emphasis to his remarks by irreverently tapping the President's knee. Midway through the meeting he did remove the hat, but only after Farley, Roosevelt and McIntyre had time to absorb the full meaning of the arrogance of Long's gesture.

Farley describes the scene:

> "I saw McIntyre standing there with his
> teeth clenched and I thought for a moment that he
> was going to walk over and pull the hat off Huey's
> head. Later, he told me that was exactly what he
> started to do."

Farley felt that "each of us present knew at the time it would have far-reaching consequences." It was the end of any pretense of compromise or cooperation. The battle was on.[25]

Historians have expressed curiosity as to why Roosevelt decided to come down as hard as he did on Huey Long. He tolerated other bosses and demagogues, such as Frank Hague of New Jersey, patronizing and humoring them. Historian Arthur Schlesinger has concluded that Roosevelt had been "genuinely persuaded that Long was far more dangerous to the country."[26]

When Long left the White House that day in June, he was a marked man. The full power of the presidency would be brought to bear against him. The patronage he demanded would be withheld from him and dispensed through his bitterest enemies. He would also be hounded and harassed when Roosevelt would order the Internal Revenue Service to revive a dormant income tax investigation.

As early as 1930, during the administration of Herbert Hoover, the IRS had been on Long's trail. He had not yet taken the oath of office as senator. The investigation was prompted by a flood of letters to the President and to the IRS from Long's enemies in Louisiana. The letters had a common theme: "Long and his crowd were stealing $100 million and what was the Treasury Department going to do about it?" The flow of letters eventually became a torrent. The letters reached Elmer Irey, Treasury Section Chief.[27]

In the summer of 1932, Irey contacted the agent in charge of the Dallas IRS office, Archie Burford, asking him to investigate Long's dealings. Burford's report was blunt. Long and his people, Burford said, were "stealing everything in the state—and they're not paying."

Irey sent 32 special agents into Louisiana (out of a total of 200 in his unit) and they began gathering evidence. The intensity of the probe was described in January, 1933, by the Memphis *Commercial Appeal* as "bearing many earmarks of political persecution." His bank accounts were studied. He was shadowed. His telephone was tapped.[28]

Hoover's Treasury Secretary, Ogden Mills, ordered the investigation suspended following Roosevelt's election to the presidency, leaving it for the incoming administration, since the Democratic Long was considered to be one of "their babies." A report was typed and the unit awaited further instructions.

Apparently the Democrats were prepared to live and let live, to let sleeping dogs lie. There would be no action against their "baby." The FBI files contain an undated news clipping from the *Chicago Tribune* quoting Farley, in the midst of masterminding the winning of the Democratic nomination, as saying, in effect, "Yes, we know all about Long and the investigations and charges and elections down in Louisiana, but what we are interested in at this time is delegates. He's for Frank Roosevelt."

When the need for delegates had passed and Long had grown from Democratic Baby to New Deal Problem Child, Farley would be of a different mind.

Some of the enemies Huey had made were agitating for action against him by the IRS.

In January, 1933, Huey savaged a banking measure authored by Virginia Democrat Carter Glass in the Senate. Long filibustered against the bill, hurling many personal references about Glass. Following a particularly bitter attack on him, the diminutive and peppery Glass, eyes flashing and face flushed, charged Huey in the Senate, being stopped by Majority Leader Joe Robinson. Glass was deterred, but not before he had cursed Long as a "damned thieving son of a bitch," which Huey, 15 feet away, could not fail to hear.[29]

Seven months later Glass would strike back. In August, 1934, he asked Irey, "Haven't you gotten that son of a bitch from Louisiana yet?" Irey explained that the investigation was on hold and there was nothing he could do without orders. Glass promised that the T-man would receive the authorization. Guy Helvering, IRS Commissioner, called Irey and reported that the Roosevelt White House was inquiring why the investigation of Huey Long was not proceeding.[30]

But still there was no authorization to renew the probe.

Former Louisiana governor and Long enemy John Parker wrote Roosevelt's vice-president, John Nance Garner, on April 12, 1933, vowing support for the New Deal and pleading for a federal investigation of Long and his henchmen. Parker claimed to have evidence that Long was a "dangerous paranoic" and suggested that the Kingfish be permanently incarcerated in the hospital for the criminally insane in Washington. Later that summer, probably about the same time that Roosevelt and Long had their celebrated meeting, Roosevelt met with Parker. After a lengthy recitation of the sins of Long, Parker convinced Roosevelt to resume the income tax investigation.[31]

Parker is also believed to have provided information that resulted in the indictments of key Long aides following the Kingfish's death.

Beginning in the fall of 1933, the hounds of the tax collectors pursued Long unrelentingly, without let-up, without surcease. The unit charged with the responsibility of investigating Long had also investigated Al Capone, underworld boss of Illinois. The news media made much of the coincidence.

But the zeal with which they pursued the gangland figure was mild compared to the Long investigation. Forrest Davis, Long biographer, observed, "The persistence with which they (IRS) had tracked down Al Capone wasn't a patch on the way they dogged Long and his associates."[32]

No one knew this better than Huey. On the floor of the Senate on January 7, 1935, he said, "They (the newspapers) simply said in their headlines that inasmuch as they had put Al Capone behind the bars, now they had time to come and get Huey P. Long."

Huey told his colleagues in the Senate:

"You have seen them send their hordes
of income tax sleuths, investigators and spies by
the hundreds to Louisiana. You have seen them
take them off the Lindbergh case; you have seen
them take them off the oil cases; you have seen the
chase of the hounds..."[33]

The chase continued throughout 1933 and into 1934. According to Irey, almost every contract let in Louisiana under Long's administration as governor and, presumably, that of his successor, Oscar K. Allen, had been tainted by graft. All told, the IRS unit had investigated 232 individuals, 42 partnerships and 122 corporations for a total of 1,007 tax years. Capone's case was not looked into nearly as thoroughly.[34]

Frank Wilson, Treasury man who helped break the case against Capone and who figured in testimony against Bruno Richard Hauptmann, kidnapper of the Lindbergh baby, concluded that there was an ironclad case against Long for some $100,000 of income which had been unreported and hence, on which no taxes had been paid. Martin Sommers, writing for the *Chicago Tribune*, fixed Long's assets at not less than $1 million, accumulated from a $6,000 annual salary as governor and a $10,000 a year salary as U.S. senator.[35]

Insiders in the IRS were confident that they could return an indictment against Long. Many considered a conviction of the Kingfish by a Louisiana jury to have been impossible. But, nevertheless, the IRS had high hopes. They pointed to the indictments against some of Huey's lesser lights and one indict-

ment against one of the greater lights, bagman Seymour Weiss. The only indictments tried before Long's death, that of a state senator and his nephew, a
state representative, resulted in a conviction.

The government was prepared to move.

On September 7, 1935, in a hotel room in Dallas, T-men Burford and
Irey, along with former Texas Governor Dan Moody, met to consider asking for
an indictment against Long. Moody, the personal choice of President Roosevelt
to prosecute Long, told the others he would seek an indictment of the Kingfish
the following month.

But the Kingfish had run out of months. The following day arrived on
schedule, however, and Huey Long was shot. Less than 36 hours later he would
be dead.

The reaction in Washington to his death was not one of sorrow. Elliott
Roosevelt reported, "The President and his Cabinet felt no pity, but a sense of
relief." In an off-the-record interview with journalist Max Lerner, Roosevelt said
simply, "We had the menace of Huey Long and somehow we were rid of him."[36]

Columnists speculated that Long's death was one more example of
"Roosevelt Luck," which seemed, like a lucky charm, to pay off at the oddest
times, delivering the President from adversity. Others felt—and some still feel—
that it was more than luck, that perhaps the President had helped it along.

CHAPTER SEVEN

Sands Point: The Kingfish As Crawfish

Throughout Huey Long's unconventional life there were constantly occuring all sorts of bizarre happenings, many of which were characterized by violence. On those occasions when the Kingfish was protected by bodyguards, he came out on the long end of the incidents. There were other times when he was hard pressed.

Physical courage was never one of his attributes. Growing up, he left his fighting to his younger brother, Earl. On occasion in the Senate, Long would call attention to his lack of fighting ability and he would profess a disdain for violence. Yet both his public and private life were punctuated by one tumultuous incident after another.

When he campaigned for the United States Senate in 1930, he suspected that an uncle and the former husband of his secretary, whose relationship with Long was whispered about, would embarrass him with lurid revelations about his private life. He had them kidnapped and held incommunicado.

He once fought with an elderly former governor, J.Y. Sanders, Sr., in the lobby of the Roosevelt Hotel in New Orleans. Long threw a punch at Sanders while bodyguards immobilized the septuagenarian ex-governor. Sanders broke loose and chased Long through the lobby and the pair disappeared into an elevator. Long later displayed a fragment of Sanders' torn shirt as proof that he had gotten the better of the old man.

Long called a one-legged state representative a "low-lived, white livered scoundrel." He managed to wrest the representative's walking stick from him and exhibited it later as evidence of another victory.

Newsmen and photographers figured in much of the violence around Long, as a rule being on the receiving end. At least one newsman was sent to the hospital after bodyguards, urged on by Long, fractured his jaw. However, on one occasion a newsman himself planted a punch firmly on Long's jaw after Long insulted him.

Many of the violent incidents in which Long was involved were the results of problems with liquor. He told the *New York Times* in February, 1935, that he had stopped drinking. The reason, he said, was because:

> "I used to have a fight and then meet a man and forgive him and get all over it. That was the way it worked at first and that wasn't so bad. But then I began to find that as I got older I couldn't drink without fighting with people."[1]

Years before that he told a friend, "I've been under the influence of liquor more nights of my adult life than I've been sober."[2]

As early as seven years before he assumed the governorship, Long's drinking seemed to be common political gossip. At a special legislative session in September of 1921, the House of Representatives was debating a resolution petitioning Congress to modify the Volstead Act, which prohibited the manufacture and sale of wines, beer and spirits to the general public. The resolution asked Congress to permit the manufacture and sale of low alcoholic content drinks such as wine and beer.

A joker of a legislator from the Fourth Ward of New Orleans, in those days a legend of free-wheeling living, shocked observers when he announced that he was not too sure he would vote for the resolution. His reason involved Huey Long:

> "I don't want to make it any easier for certain people to get liquor. Yesterday I saw this self-anointed holy arch-deacon of politics, Huey Long, who was in Baton Rouge attending the session of the Railroad Commission here, drunk and lit up like a Christmas tree. If we make it any easier for him to get liquor, there will be no more living in this state any more."[3]

The House exploded in laughter.

When he served in the U.S. Senate, his colleagues constantly needled him about his drinking habits. During a prolonged filibuster on June 12, 1935, he interrupted his discourse to comment:

> "Here is a book somebody laid on my desk and wants me to read...If it is good for me it is good for the balance of the people. If it is good for man, it is good for beast. It is entitled, 'The Liquor Problem and its Solution,' but I am not going to read it now because it is not any part of the argument."[4]

As governor, when prohibition was still the law of the land, a bottle of liquor was delivered daily to the governor's mansion from a downtown Baton Rouge pharmacy. In exchange for the liquor, a mansion attendant would give the delivery boy the price of the spirits and a prescription attesting to the fact that the liquor was for "medical purposes."[5]

The most damaging assessment of Huey's drinking has been given by his older brother Julius. Julius charged, "He is never in his real element until he is fully loaded with booze." Julius added that Long moved his wife and three children to Shreveport soon after he became governor and that, when he stayed in the mansion, separated from his wife and children, he had "drunken parties with his puppets."[6]

At one point he seemed to have the habit beaten. Then it returned to grip him again. He told a reporter for the Hearst newspaper syndicate, Adela Rogers St. Johns, "I had to lick my lust for likker and I've done it. But sometimes I think I'm gonna die for it." So saying, he picked up a bottle of gin, crashed it through a window and then, according to the reporter, shook and sobbed in her arms.[7]

Huey stopped drinking in early 1934 and hopped off the water wagon about a year later.

A Washington tax lawyer confessed to a Louisiana cousin that he and Huey drank heavily during the time both had lodgings in the Broadmoor apartments in the nation's capital. The tax lawyer complained that the first time he and Huey uncorked a bottle, "I couldn't stay with him." The second time the pair met, the tax lawyer reported, "I stayed with him until I had to pour him in bed." He then confided what Huey himself had often confessed: "He's not a very good drinker." The drinking bouts took place in June, 1935.[8]

By July, it became obvious to everyone that Huey had resumed drinking.

On July 2, 1935, he narrowly missed being struck on the jaw at the crowded dance terrace of the Shoreham Hotel in Washington. Long claimed his clumsy dancing had caused him to step on the toes of a younger dancing partner. But Tracy Ansell, a young lawyer whose father was a complainant in a half-million dollar libel suit against Long, had another story. Young Ansell said Long approached his table "in a way which caused resentment" and Long's bodyguards held Ansell's arms while Long escaped.[9]

Later in July, Long staged a publicity stunt in the Hotel New Yorker. He imported a bartender from the Roosevelt Hotel in New Orleans, promising to show New Yorkers how to concoct a Ramos Gin Fizz, a uniquely Louisiana drink.

Following the Kingfish's instructions, the bartender blended a drink. It was not right. Fix it again! It took five fizzes and two hours before he was satisfied with the mixologist's product. He held the last gin fizz up, announcing,

"And this, gentlemen, (is) my gift to New York." With this, he downed the cocktail as he had done the previous four, while flashpowder popped and pencils scratched to record his behavior.[10]

The queerest episode of Huey's career happened early one Sunday morning, August 17, 1933. It turned out to be a gaffe of the highest order and fueled the gossip mills of his enemies for months thereafter.

Long had been invited to attend a charity function at the exclusive Sands Point (Long Island) Bath Club by songwriter Gene Buck. Following a session at Buck's home, Huey, along with Buck's other guests, left for the club. Included in the party were Edward P. Mulrooney, one-time New York police commissioner; Jack Curley, boxing promoter and Alford J. Williams, former Navy pilot and Fordham University football player. Except for Long, all were accompanied by their wives.

Some 600 guests attended the charity affair. It was sponsored by the National Charity Amateur Air Pageant, an event that would be held in October.

Sometime around 4:00 a.m., Long visited the restroom of the club and exited shortly thereafter with one hand held to a bleeding cut above his left eye. His original explanation was that he had been "ganged up on." Later, he said he had been set upon by gangsters. Other explanations for the wound would be forthcoming. The Kingfish was placed in a taxicab and returned to the Hotel New Yorker in downtown New York. At the hotel a physician dressed the wound, closing it with two stitches.

The assault on Huey set off waves of laughter and ridicule, most of it generated by the press. One newsman remarked, "The wound was trifling, but no lowgrade injury in recent history save, perhaps, only the pistol shot that Theodore Roosevelt stopped while campaigning in Milwaukee in 1912 so captured public imagination."[11]

At first, Long refused to comment on the incident. He left New York to travel to Milwaukee that same Sunday to attend a convention of the Veterans of Foreign Wars. Asked about his bandaged eye, he snapped, "Nothing happened on Long Island." However, Monday he broke his silence and issued a statement.

The delay in commenting on the affair, Long explained, was occasioned by his efforts to investigate the matter and track down the assailants. He described his encounter in dramatic fashion. It had involved three or four men, at least, one of whom was armed with "a knife or something sharp." Long adroitly ducked just in time to escape the full force of the weapon, which managed to graze his forehead. His exit was initially thwarted by one of the attackers who blocked the door, but Long was able to "wriggle clear" and escape from them.

Dazed, blood streaming down his face from the cut, he staggered from the restroom, mobilized his friends and stormed back to the restroom to confront his attackers, now that the odds were evened. But the assaulters had fled.

The boxing promoter in Long's party, Curley, said that he drove Huey and host Buck back to Buck's home. Curley was fuzzy about the details of the encounter. He told the *New York Times* that he believed Long "was struck in the washroom of the club," but otherwise professed ignorance of the circumstances. Yes, the Kingfish was groggy when he was helped from the restroom. No, he did not believe the senator's claims that he was ganged. Curley said he was of the opinion that only one person followed Long from the restroom.

The president of the club showed proper restraint when he was asked about the scuffle. He recalled seeing the Kingfish at the club with friends and remembered that "an incident had occurred," but he knew no details about it. A day later he was less restrained and amplified on his knowledge about "the rather unfortunate occurrence to Senator Long." In a statement given through tightly clenched teeth, he set the record straight:

> "The facts are these: Senator Long apparently got into an argument in the washroom with a gentleman not a member of the club. The fight that resulted between them and which caused Senator Long's injuries followed this argument.
>
> "Senator Long's statement about being 'ganged' is, of course, not worthy of comment."

A wave of mockery and twitting followed Long throughout his travels. The vision of the feisty Kingfish being pummeled like an ordinary drunk in a restroom was too juicy for the press and his many detractors to let go of.

In Milwaukee he was introduced to 4,000 veterans, delegates to the Veterans of Foreign Wars encampment, as "the friend of all downtrodden." When he rose to speak, he revealed his aggravation with the press. He began, "When I picked up your *Milwaukee News* I knew where all the polecats had gone." Obviously they were all working for the *News* and writing stories about what had happened at Sands Point.

The veterans cheered him and, encouraged, he complained of the presence of photographers at the meeting. They were removed amid "a tangle of tripods and cases." Glaring at newsmen, he charged that anyone foolish enough to believe what was printed in the newspapers "should be bored for the hollow horn." (The "hollow horn" is an imaginary malaise that Louisiana farmers believe affects cattle. When conventional veterinary treatment fails to draw a response from ailing cattle, the horns of the sick beast are drilled to release whatever it is that is causing the ailment.)

Embarrassed VFW leaders issued a statement apologizing and disclaiming responsibility for Long's remarks.

Long left Milwaukee by train for New Orleans, hounded and shadowed by the press at every step of the journey. A reporter who got on the train at Jackson, Mississippi was rebuffed when he asked a question about Sands Point.

Another asked if Long would accept an offer of $1,000 a day to appear in a freak show at Coney Island. He was ignored.

Clearly, Long was rattled.

He brushed by a ticket conductor on the way to the dining car, pushing the conductor into the laps of two nuns whose tickets he was collecting. Asked about the incident, Long denied the charge. From his New Orleans home he pouted, "Just say for me I don't pay attention to such lies and neither does anybody else in Louisiana." The conductor confirmed the whole story for newsmen. The nuns maintained a vow of silence.

And still, the pressure of the press continued. They gleefully kept the matter alive on page one.

When Long arrived in New Orleans on the Wednesday following the Sunday encounter, he had had enough. He was in no mood to bandy words with the press. He arranged to have 10 security guards meet him at a suburban stop prior to arriving in downtown New Orleans. He wanted to avoid the pesky newsmen.

But the press had anticipated his move. He was met at the stop by a delegation of newshawks. Long commanded his guards to attack reporters and photographers: "Hit 'em! Don't let them take my picture!" The guards drove the newsmen back, restraining photographers so that they could not use their cameras. One reporter threw a parting gibe regarding the freak show appearance by the senator: "Are you going to sign the Coney Island contract?" Long glared at the reporter and left.

Huey withdrew, shunning contact with the press while a nation roared. The Sands Point management barred him from the club forever, terming the whole affair "an undignified mess." The *New York Times* questioned Long's claim of having been ganged up on by pointing out that it was an exclusive club and "usually regarded as free of rowdies or others with a propensity to 'gang up' on a national legislator."

Mulrooney, a member of Long's party, said he saw no gangsters or thugs at the club that night. Sands Point Police Chief Steve Weber said that he had "looked the place over pretty thoroughly" and had not seen any rough characters.

Long blamed a banking conglomerate, the House of Morgan, by name, for the assault on him. He was reported to have said, "A member of the House of Morgan sneaked up on me with a blackjack. The doc took two stitches over my left eye."

At the time, Long was having his problems with a now-defunct weekly magazine named *Collier's*. The magazine had consistently reported on Long's activities through its executive editor, Walter Davenport. At first favorable, Long sensed a change in the tenor of the articles when he leveled his criticism at the House of Morgan. After Sands Point, he published a circular in the form of an open letter to Al Capone, bootlegger and racketeer then serving time in a federal prison. Long suggested that Capone could obtain a speedy release from prison by confessing that he was the one who ordered the attack on him at Sands Point.

There were other nominations for the honor of having hung one on the Kingfish.

Al Williams, the former Naval ace who had been part of Long's party, coyly denied that he was the assailant, although he sported a bruised hand, stained with iodine, which he not too convincingly shielded from reporters. Another flier, Clarence Chamberlin, advised that he was in the washroom at "just about" the critical moment, but saw nothing. Chief Weber of the Sands Point police force "smiled genially" while denying that he had struck Long. A Park Avenue lawyer and a prominent architect were named as suspects; both denied the charges but added that they would be happy to take credit for the deed if they had done it.

In Philadelphia Jack O'Brien, a retired boxer, cleared up part of a mystery associated with the incident. Long said he was the victim of a gang; the club maintained that there was a lone attacker involved. O'Brien recalled that he was knocked out in 1902 or 1903 by Joe Walcott, and ringside customers saw only one opponent standing over him. O'Brien saw four or five and sympathized with the Kingfish since no one believed him, either.

New Orleans boxer Tony Canzoneri, in training in New Jersey to regain his lightweight boxing title, offered his services to Long as a trainer to teach him boxing.

As it turned out, Long had been training at the New Orleans Athletic Club, even before Sands Point. One of his trainers was Jimmy Moran (nee Brocato), onetime prize fighter and, at the time, a bodyguard to the Kingfish. The club's magazine *Punch* reported, "The distinguished senator reports every morning to Athletic Director Irwin Poche" and the senator would return to the nation's capital in the fall of 1933 "about 15 pounds less and fit as a fiddle."

Collier's magazine, tiring of being the butt of Long's barbs, struck back. The associate editor of the publication began to lay plans to present a medal to the unknown hero who assaulted Long. Started in fun, the editor was encouraged by a stream of contributions to finance the undertaking. A medal was cast depicting Long sporting a black eye and boxing gloves as he reclined in a washstand. Copies of the medal were made and offered for sale by Louisiana enemies of the Kingfish to help finance their continuing efforts to oust him from the Senate.

In a bit of black humor, one of the medals was sent anonymously to the family of Dr. Carl Weiss following Long's shooting and death.

A year after the assault, the Sands Point Bath Club erected a bronze tablet in its washroom to commemorate the time and place of the assault on Long.

Although the Sands Point incident was one of the most publicized happenings in the Kingfish's political career, it would have little historical significance were it not for the fact that revelations since then indicate that the episode had consequences extending beyond simple crude restroom humor.

There still remained questions to answer. Who attacked Long? Why was he attacked? The "why" has since been well established, although it was, and still is, alluded to in muted tones. Some referred to an insulting remark directed at an occupant of the restroom. Another explanation involved Long's boorish behavior toward the date of one of the male guests of the club, who sought to settle the matter within the confines of the toilet.

But the most likely reason for Long's comeuppance, and the one accepted by most of those who had reason to know Long's ways, involves a particularly disgusting habit he had when he was drunk and his bladder was full to overflowing. William "Fishbait" Miller, longtime Democratic doorkeeper in the House of Representatives, described the habit thus:

> "Huey Long had an unfortunate way of expressing himself when displeased or in his cups—like a dog, he would point and urinate. Once, in the members' men's room, he pretended to miss his mark in the urinal and hit another senator with whom he'd been having words a short time before. The victim tried to slug him, but Huey fended off his blow with one hand and walked out laughing."[12]

Long was unaccompanied by his bodyguards at the Sands Point club, but one of his security contingent confided to Long biographer Dr. T. Harry Williams years later:

> "He was always kind of sloppy and that night he had been drinking. He went to the restroom and to the urinal...He just swung it too far and hit the fellow's shoes and he socked him."[13]

This is the version, whispered and embellished, that is generally believed in Louisiana. Long's accidental or purposeful lack of control when urinating was a matter of record and well known.

This is the "why" of the Sands Point incident. The "who" is equally intriguing and links Long to the underworld. Verified by a number of sources, the explanation as to who was involved in the set-to explains many things that have happened in Louisiana since that occurrence in August, 1933.

Two independent sources maintain that Long was befriended by Frank Costello, rackets kingpin nicknamed "Prime Minister of the Underworld" for his finesse and tact in dealing with sticky situations.

Frank Costello was far and away the class act of the racketeers. "Uncle Frank" to many, he was born Francesco Seriglia in Calabria, Italy in January, 1893, some seven months before Huey Long. At an early age he migrated to New York's lower East Side, where he grew up with other budding racketeers such as Lucky Luciano (nee Salvatore Lucania), Meyer Lansky and Benjamin "Bugsy" Siegal.

In his 20s, he was picked up for carrying a pistol under his coat and was hustled off to jail. From that time on, he disdained the use of guns and learned to rely entirely on personality, charm and wits—all of which he had in abundance. He would spice these endowments generously with payola and the result was a trap that seduced many an ambitious public official.

Costello would become the intimate of politicians of high degree— even a President or two. In later years, his next door neighbor at his Sands Point home would be former President Harry S. Truman. Through his connections with New York's Tammany Hall, Costello was ushered in to meet Franklin Roosevelt at the 1932 Democratic convention in Chicago. Costello was described to Roosevelt as a New York businessman and a substantial campaign contributor.

At the same time, Costello enjoyed an excellent rapport with some of the biggest racketeers of the time: Owney Madden, Vito Genovese, George "Big Frenchy" DeMange, Vannie Higgins, "Big Bill" Dwyer and Waxey Gordon.

The high regard in which he was held by Luciano resulted in his installation, in the late 1940s, as undisputed boss of one of the "families" that operated the rackets. Luciano helped engineer the Judas-like killing of Mafia chieftain Joe "the Boss" Masseria, whose faction he was associated with, in favor of rival Salvatore Maranzano. In time, Luciano had Maranzano wasted by assassins with guns and knives and he had the entire "family" to himself.

On February 10, 1946, Luciano was deported to Italy, the land of his birth, and Costello took over his interests.

It was Costello who predicted that prohibition would end and so he converted to gambling. It was Costello who foresaw the backlash of the public if competing mobs did not cease the bloodletting that characterized the 1920s. The result was the National Crime Syndicate—law and order, gangland style. Costello bribed and elected judges, district attorneys and at least one mayor of New York. But he shied away from dope and refused to become involved in prostitution. While head of the Syndicate, he decreed that those operations were strictly off limits and prohibition became known as "Costello's Law." At first it seemed to work, but eventually, like all reforms, it went by the boards.

In his book *Uncle Frank,* Costello biographer Leonard Katz matter-of-factly tells us that Long, in a men's room in Long Island, found the urinal being used by someone else. "Long took careful aim between the other fellow's legs and let fly. He missed. The man on the receiving end of his stream beat him bloody."

At another point in the biography, Katz quotes a New Orleans link to the mob, Peter Hand, who served in the state legislature during the Huey Long years. Hand says:

> "One time Huey Long went up to New York and poor Huey was a coward and he went into the powder room of one of those clubs. I think it was Long Island somewhere and somebody punched him in the mouth and Costello, that is one of Costello's friends, saved him from getting a beating..."[14]

Prolific crime writer Hank Messick, who has written dozens of books about crime and criminals, tells a similar story, although some of the details vary from Hand's version. In his biography of Meyer Lanksy, Messick reports that Long was drunk and urinated on the trousers of a stranger next to him. This happened in a Manhattan hotel. The stranger was syndicate gangster "Trigger Mike" Coppola, henchman of Vito Genovese who was working his way up in the New York rackets during the 1920s and 1930s.

Coppola was a beast and a sadist who beat his wife. He also impregnated her on occasion and demanded that she have an abortion each time she became pregnant. The operations were performed under the most sordid of circumstances. Mrs. Coppola lay on a kitchen table while Trigger Mike watched the procedure, all the while receiving sexual gratification from the squalid spectacle.

Messick claims that Long was saved from certain death at Coppola's hands in that restroom by the appearance of Frank Costello, who emerged from a nearby stall and convinced Coppola to lay off the Kingfish.

Coached by Costello, Coppola apologized to the Kingfish, "I didn't know who you wuz. As far as I'm concerned, you can piss on Roosevelt if you want to."[15]

I was struck by the similarity of Katz's and Messick's versions—except for the location—so I called Mr. Messick to ask if possibly he may have misplaced the location of the incident from Long Island to Manhattan. I sent him my data for checking. He responded that his information had come from the IRS through a diary provided the government by Coppola's wife, Ann. One of Messick's major works was *Secret File,* detailing the success of the IRS in crimebusting. He was allowed access to the Service's files to prepare his manuscript. The diary was one of the file items.

Ann Coppola was a reluctant witness against Trigger Mike. In reprisal, she was kidnapped, beaten and left to die on a lonely beach. She recovered and continued her testimony. Her diary helped convict her husband. In Rome, she left a suicide note written in lipstick on a mirror saying:

"Mike Coppola, someday, somehow, a
person or God or the law shall catch up with you,
you yellow-bellied bastard. You are the lowest and
biggest coward I have had the misfortune to
meet."

A dozen Nembutal capsules and a few fingers of Scotch later she breathed her last.[16]

There are many versions told of the Sands Point incident and all are true—in part. The stories have been told and retold, magnified and inflated to the proportions of a legend. But, as with most legends, there is the germ of truth in all of them.

I feel that I have reconciled all the elements of the story and have the added advantage of having interviewed a source close to the Costello family who received the story from "Uncle" Frank himself. Here it is. My source has insisted on anonymity.

Sands Point was a desirable homesite for New York racketeers. Costello himself bought a home there in 1944, although he cautiously put the property in the name of his wife, the former Loretta "Bobbie" Geigerman.[17] On the night of August 27, 1933, Costello was at the Sands Point club. He was in the restroom when Long entered and sprayed the occupant of the urinal. The abused man struck Long, opening a gash over his left eye. He was prepared to do even more damage when he was stopped by Frank Costello, who emerged from a nearby stall.

Long's assailant was a pilot, attending the charity function at the club, sponsored by the National Charity Amateur Air Pageant. He was formerly in Costello's employ during prohibition days.

Costello's bootlegging operation was a masterpiece of organization, elevated to the precision of a military action. Legal Scotch whiskey from England was unloaded at the rocky and desolate, fog-bound French islands of St. Pierre and Miquelon, ten miles off the coast of Newfoundland. From this point the liquor was transferred to "rummies," vessels operated by bootleggers which transported the load to "Rum Row," a staging area for bootleg vessels off Long Island beyond the three-mile limit. The liquor was offloaded to speedboats, which then dashed for the coves and inlets of Long Island and other coastal points.

As the Coast Guard increased its surveillance, bootleggers such as Costello had to devise newer and bolder methods to foil the authorities. Costello had a fleet of 160-foot long vessels built with low freeboards to reduce visibility, capable of making up to 17 knots. Clandestine radio stations along the U.S. shoreline guided the movements of the smuggling ships and kept them posted on Coast Guard activity.

An important part of Costello's activity was air cover and this was the responsibility of the pilot who attacked Huey Long. The seaplane would spot

Coast Guard cutters closing in on speedboats and suggest diversionary action. On one occasion, the plane laid down a smokescreen to allow a bootlegging vessel to elude an advancing Navy warship.

Costello's intercession on Long's behalf would benefit the racketeer greatly. In 1933, much of his income was accounted for by slot machines. The end of prohibition had wiped out bootlegging as a source of revenue and the resourceful Costello replaced it with gambling. But this new source of wealth would soon be endangered when, in December, New York would inaugurate a new mayor, Fiorello LaGuardia. An unrelenting war on the slot machines would begin. Within a year, the machines would be off the streets of New York and in warehouses awaiting shipment to other areas inhabited by more understanding public officials.

That area turned out to be none other than the state of Louisiana, the Kingdom of the Kingfish.

In 1940, Costello testified to a New York grand jury that Long invited him to move his slots to New Orleans. He repeated the same information to the Kefauver Committee when it barnstormed throughout the nation in the '50s. He told the committee that Long wanted to raise about $40,000 for the relief of orphans, widows and other disadvantaged people. Costello agreed to pay a licensing fee for the machines.

Sometime in 1935 (the IRS placed it in the month of July), Costello moved his slots into New Orleans and continued to operate them until the middle '40s. He claimed to have only 600 machines in the city at the peak of operations, although the Internal Revenue Service estimated that about 1,000 were imported into the city in 1935 and that, by 1945, the number had grown to 5,000. Along with the slots he sent his four brothers-in-law, the brothers Geigerman, to be supervised by "Dandy" Phil Kastel, right hand and detail man for Costello.[18]

It is difficult to estimate the amount of profit generated by the slot machine operation in New Orleans. In 1944, Costello declared on his income tax that he had earned about $71,000 from that source and in 1945 he earned $62,000. This was at the peak of the slot machine operation. However, in 1939, the government indicted Costello for income tax evasion, charging that from 1935 to 1937 he had made a profit of over $2 million from slot machine operations.

In 1945, the *Times-Picayune* estimated that the machines in operation in New Orleans and adjacent parishes represented an investment of slightly less than one million dollars. In 1944, the newspaper figured, the 6,200 machines in the area had grossed $32,840,000.

Did Long intend to profit personally from Costello's slot machine operation? Many have insinuated that he did, but there is no evidence that this is the case. There is convincing evidence that Long intended the slot machine operation to be a legal one, much as it would be in Las Vegas later. This was brought out during the Kefauver Committee proceedings, when Costello testified that Long had invited him to bring the slots to New Orleans. This testimony provoked the wrath of New Hampshire's Senator Tobey, who charged that Costello and Long had conspired to break the law. Costello disagreed:

> Costello: I think you misrepresent it, sir, with all due respect to you: that you say that a governor of Louisiana tried to violate a commercial purpose—which is not true. He did it, just like you have a race track up in New Hampshire and if you went there and passed legislation, you are doing it practically for the state. You are not doing it for a selfish purpose.

> Tobey: But the law didn't allow the use of slot machines in Louisiana and the law does allow pari-mutuels in New Hampshire.

> Costello: But they had to pass legislation to allow it.

> Tobey: Sure, they did, but they never legalized the slot machines in Louisiana.

> Costello: Well, they probably would, if he lived.

> Tobey: He didn't live; that's another story.

Throughout the Kefauver hearings, Costello demonstrated a fierce loyalty to Long. He defended the Kingfish whenever the deceased senator became the topic of questioning. He objected when Tobey accused Long of breaking the law. Tobey charged, "Well, you put the machines in, didn't you!" Costello fired back, "Then I broke the law! He never broke it."[19]

There is speculation that Long had other brushes with the underworld, although none of them is as well documented as his dealings with Costello.

Long's association with William Hale "Big Bill" Thompson, corrupt mayor of Chicago about the time when Huey served as governor, raised many eyebrows. Thompson was the only guest speaker at Huey's inaugural in 1928. Older brother Julius Long charged that Huey copied much of the methods he used in politics from Thompson. This is hardly a sop to good government, since Thompson was owned, controlled and directed by Al Capone. When Thompson died, his estate was initially estimated at $150,000. Shortly after his death, additional wealth began surfacing. Boxes crammed with currency and securities yielded almost $1.5 million in cash. Bank boxes yielded additional wealth and the authenticated total of his wealth, including real estate holdings, topped $2 million.

Several writers have placed Long in the company of such underworld elite as Meyer Lansky and Lucky Luciano at the Chicago Democratic Convention of 1932. However, there is no mention anywhere of either of these racketeers ever having any association or influence with Long thereafter.

Costello remained the favored racketeer. Far into the 1940s he and his slot machines, along with other coin operated devices, would flourish. He was observed on several occasions in conversation with Huey's younger brother, Earl, who was elected twice to the office of governor. These observations were made in New Orleans' Roosevelt Hotel, which was owned by Huey's aide, Seymour Weiss. "Dandy" Phil Kastel, who oversaw Costello's New Orleans slot machine holdings, was a long-term tenant in the hotel.

Costello would enjoy a virtual monopoly on such activity. His "Chief" slot machines were absolutely off limits to law enforcement authorities. In 1937, an FBI memo reported that the New Orleans Chief of Detectives had said, "I know better than to touch the slot machines." Pinball machines had invaded the New Orleans area in the middle '30s and their novelty threatened to eclipse the one-armed bandits. However, the police would allow no more than one pinball machine in an establishment where Costello's slots were located. A captain of detectives was reported to have clipped the wires of pinball machines in an outlet where more than one machine was operated alongside Costello's machines.[20]

A native New Orleanian, Hamilton Basso, remembered that the one-armed bandits made their appearance in March 1935, three months earlier than the FBI said. Basso reckoned that the take for the six months in 1935 between the installation of the slots and the death of Long netted $2 million in profits. If the gaming devices were as widespread as he reported, this could easily have been so. Basso recalls:

> "There are slot machines wherever you go—in saloons, clubs, drug stores, soft drink establishments, cigar stores, even in the lobbies of some of the buildings. Everybody plays them—school children, housewives, workmen, bankers, lawyers, the whole town."[21]

Costello lived out his years in relative peace, never having been deported and generally enjoying the esteem of law enforcers and breakers of the law alike. He died of natural causes (not necessarily the rule of the Mob) at age 82, in 1973.

A small-bore Brooklyn mobster of the late '40s and early '50s, "Crazy Joe" Gallo, noting the leverage that Frank Costello enjoyed in Louisiana, asked a fellow hood in a telephone conversation taped by authorities, "Who gave Louisiana to Frank Costello?"[22]

To which the proper answer must be: "The Kingfish, Joey. It was the Kingfish!"

CHAPTER EIGHT

The Natives Are Restless

The year 1935 dawned on a Louisiana that was in the firm and apparently unshakable grasp of the Kingfish.

But this was on the surface.

Beneath the veneer of complete control was a fomenting of insurrection that was beginning to show. It had begun to seethe and stew when Long first embarked upon his journey toward absolute domination of the state following his escape from impeachment in 1929. It simmered and bubbled when Long called the special sessions of 1934. Soon it would erupt, a final, desperate reaction to his excesses, particularly his reprisal against Standard Oil.

But 1935 had been, overall, a very good year, despite its inauspicious beginnings, when the Old Regular machine in New Orleans had decisively beaten back a challenge from a Long-sponsored candidate for mayor of that city. In spite of that single setback, when the year had run its allotted course and the complete tally was in, Louisiana was the property of Huey P. Long.

He had extended his power into the conduct of elections, insuring that it would be very hard indeed to elect someone opposed by the Long forces. Not impossible, you understand, but very, very hard. He had taken control of local police and firemen around the state. He had brought the recalcitrant city of New Orleans to its fiscal knees and all that remained was the single, inevitable knockout punch.

But, sweetest of all, he had finally evened the score between himself and his enemy of long standing, the Standard Oil Company.

This was the profit and loss statement: much profit, little loss. But there remained a few entries to be made.

For openers, Standard Oil refused to be tamed. Stung by the action of

112

the legislature in imposing the manufacturing tax, the company announced that it would curtail its operations in the state. It would immediately lay off employees. Part of the plant's equipment would be dismantled and moved to another location where the political climate was benign and where Kingfishes were unheard of. Rumor had it that 1,000 of the 3,300 employees of the plant would be let go.

New Orleans was fighting back, too. It sought relief from some of Long's restraints and that relief soon arrived. Thanks to the actions of a friendly federal court, the city was, for a time, left free to sort out its tangled finances without the hot breath of the Kingfish breathing down its municipal neck.

There was trouble on a third front. The net of the Internal Revenue Service was tightening around Long, obviously orchestrated and encouraged by the White House. In the fall of 1934, federal indictments were handed down against several Long supporters. A state senator and a state representative, uncle and nephew, respectively, were charged with failing to pay taxes; Abe Shushan, collector of kickbacks from contractors and others friendly to the Long administration, was indicted on similar charges.

But the shock waves were reserved for the indictment of Seymour Weiss. Long relied heavily on Weiss, one-time shoe salesman but now without peer in the affections and esteem of the Kingfish. He was treasurer, confidante, apologist and advisor in matters political, social and sartorial to the Kingfish. The same task force that had put Al Capone in prison had been assigned to handle Louisiana and some remembered that the strategy had been to first knock off those around the racketeer before attempting to nail him.

The heavy hand of Washington even extended to the crossroads and boondocks of Louisiana. The Roosevelt administration was systematically denying Long and his allies any kind of federal patronage, funneling it instead through his most dedicated enemies. Moreover, any community in Louisiana interested in resisting Long's domination learned that the federal government had unlimited funds available to sustain and encourage them, just for the asking.

Most disturbing of all was the growing threat of assassination, always a prospect but now becoming more and more a reality. The *New York Times* reported:

> "Long is protected like an Oriental potentate. A day and night guard has been thrown around the state house and the governor's mansion. A half dozen or more sit outside the door to the governor's office—where Long, on occasion, sits in the governor's own chair. The Senator never goes abroad without his personal staff of strong-arm men in attendance. He has increased the strength of his secret state constabulary, and guns

and permits to carry them have been passed out to
many employees in various departments."[1]

The heart of Long's opposition was Baton Rouge but opposition was to
be found in every area of the state in greater or lesser degrees.

The capitol city was panicked by the news that Standard Oil would pull
up stakes and leave. Huey had threatened to nationalize Baton Rouge, to convert
the city to a miniature District of Columbia. He had predicted that grass would
grow on Third Street, the city's main thoroughfare. Now it would come to pass.

Huey was unmoved by Standard's threat to vacate the state. He roared,
"If they got to leave this state...they can go to hell and stay there." However, he
held out the possibility of a compromise if "they want to give Louisiana oil the
proper treatment." Long had not forgotten the company's decision to suspend
purchases from independent oil producers, a move that had dashed his hopes of
being numbered among the millionaires.[2]

A compromise was, in fact, being worked out between Standard Oil
and Long. But this failed to satisfy the people of Baton Rouge, especially the
employees of Standard who, having had their emotions inflamed to fever pitch,
would settle for the unlikely goal of nothing less than complete capitulation by
the Long forces.

A paramilitary organization of "Square Dealers" was formed, composed mainly of Standard Oil employees. It immediately issued a sweeping ul-
timatum to Governor Allen to convene a special legislative session to repeal
"every dictatorial law." They warned the governor, "We are not asking this, we
are demanding it!"

The group paid lip service to non-violence but its leaders talked
bloodshed and death. One leader said, "I know of worse ways to die than fighting Huey Long." Another demanded that every legislator in the state be hanged,
"commencing with our governor" (who was, strictly speaking, not a legislator).
He volunteered the opinion that the state was being "run by a maniac."

In a highly rhetorical but unconvincing repudiation of violence, Square
Dealer President Ernest J. Bourgeois explained, "It is not our purpose to assassinate or murder anyone." However, he qualified, "When the time arrives for action...we will break the tyrannical power of the dictator of this state within the
near future."[3]

The threat of force by the citizens was being met by the threat of more
force by the authorities.

Governor Allen responded by posting additional guards around the
capitol and governor's mansion and on the streets of Baton Rouge. The city
crackled with tension.

Huey, speaking on a broadcast aired by CBS, told the nation that only
by adopting "divine laws" of economic justice for all could America avoid
having him for President. The growing peril around him was on his mind as he

added, "if I live."[4]

Into this bubbling cauldron of hostility and strained emotions Allen tossed an ill-timed catalyst. It would cause the people of Baton Rouge to throw off the last vestiges of restraint and take up arms against their oppressors.

At the last special session, the governor was given the power to appoint 13 additional members to the East Baton Rouge Police Jury, which governed the parish. The existing jury, which numbered 13, was anti-Long by an 11-2 majority. The appointment of 13 new Long supporters by Allen gave the Long forces a 15-11 majority.

The new Police Jury met on Thursday, January 24, minus the 11 anti-Long members, who boycotted the gathering as a protest. It immediately fired all 225 parish employees, replaced the troublesome district attorney as its legal counsel and removed the sheriff as custodian of the courthouse itself.

The following day the city erupted. At about 4:00 p.m., a crowd of some 300 men armed with crowbars, shillelaghs and, according to the *New York Times*, "other more lethal weapons" seized the courthouse and held it for three hours. Women joined in the occupation. Wives and daughters supplied the occupying forces with coffee, sandwiches and ammunition. Some of the females carried weapons. One girl of about 16 was seen carrying a rifle.[5]

The exact reason for the uprising is not entirely clear. It is doubtful that the Police Jury's action, as distasteful as it was, would have provoked hundreds to leave homes and jobs to engage in a paramilitary action. Many believe it was caused by the arrest of a Square Dealer who had been privy to discussions dealing with violence against Long. There was speculation that, under pressure, he might be prevailed upon to tell all he knew, implicating others.

It later developed that the member was actually a double agent and did, in fact, testify about these plans at a Long-inspired inquiry held a short time later. The agent, one Sidney Songy, had a history of living on both sides of the law. According to the FBI, he was a former informant to Prohibition agents and was also investigated for impersonating an FBI agent.

Once the intoxication of storming and occupying the courthouse had worn off, the Square Dealers reflected on what they had done. They were at a dead end. They had no plan to go further. It was a headstrong act, perhaps symbolic, but born of frustration and devoid of any real meaning or purpose. Where could they go from there? They went home.

Reprisals from the Long forces were swift in coming.

Asked how he intended to deal with the uprising, Huey replied, "If they want a fight, they'll get one."[6]

Late that Friday night the dissidents got their fight. Governor Allen declared martial law for the city and called out the state militia. Strict regulations against assembling, carrying firearms and criticizing the government were posted on telephone poles throughout the community. Anyone violating the regulations was dealt with swiftly.

Allen's proclamation left no doubt that the administration held Standard Oil completely responsible for the chaotic state of affairs. The document charged:

> "Whereas the chief leaders and largest numbers of those exercising such violence are officers and agents of the Standard Oil company, whose officials are apprised of such misconduct and who decline to do anything to prevent the same, and
>
> "Whereas employes (sic) of said Standard Oil company are intimidated by superior agents to do acts of violence which the said company, though informed as to same, declines to prevent..."[7]

The FBI Special Agent in Charge reported to J. Edgar Hoover that a man driving a car in which ammunition was found was shot by a militiaman and "as a result the situation is very strained."

National Guardsmen set up machine gun emplacements around the capitol and patrolled the city streets. It was the second time in six months that they were pressed into service to deal with rebellious natives. But the Baton Rouge confrontation had much more serious implications than the one in New Orleans. In New Orleans the issue was basically political, the one-upmanship of rival political machines; in Baton Rouge it was a citizen's revolt.

It was estimated by the *New York Times* that the Square Dealers numbered several thousand men and women, although many of these could not be considered combatants. The *Times* reported the scene in military terms. It estimated the "forces of Senator Long and his ally, Governor Allen" to be more than 2,000. In addition, the pair had access to "a constabulary unlimited under dictatorship statutes."[8]

Saturday morning the fragile calm was broken.

Long ordered a local judge to conduct a hearing on his charges that enemies, including Standard Oil, were conspiring to assassinate him. As co-conspirators, he named a number of city officials, the manager of an anti-Long congressman's office, several sheriffs of adjoining parishes and others. An estimated 128 subpoenas were said to have been issued, of which 108 had been served by the eve of the hearing, scheduled for the following Friday.[9]

That same Saturday, in the afternoon, in defiance of restrictions on assembly and the carrying of firearms, an armed group of citizens from Baton Rouge and the surrounding area assembled at the parish airport. But, their ranks riddled with informers for Long, the Square Dealers had been lured into a trap. They were surrounded by the state militia and were routed. One of the demonstrators was wounded and one state employee considered to be a "Long spy" was severely beaten.[10]

Blood had been shed.

Following the Battle of the Airport, an apprehensive calm descended on Baton Rouge. Then, a week later, Long convened an open hearing on his charges that his enemies were conspiring to murder him.

His star witness was Sidney Songy, the same Sidney Songy who was at the same time a member of the Square Dealers and informant for the Long forces, whose arrest was considered to have set off the coup to occupy the courthouse. He was now unmasked as a Long plant in the ranks of the rebels. Another witness was George "Red" Davis, a former Baton Rouge deputy sheriff.

Songy testified that on Wednesday of the previous week, the night before the Long-stacked Police Jury met, a group of citizens gathered. Murder was on their mind. They considered rushing Long in his suite at the Heidelberg Hotel. The plan was abandoned after a careful consideration of the risks involved. The attackers would first have to make their way past a machine gun trained at the elevator door on the floor where Huey stayed. Once past this obstacle, they would have to overcome a half dozen bodyguards who stood between the hotel corridor and Long's suite, located in a cul de sac at the corner of the hotel.

An alternate plan was devised, Songy testified. It was to ambush Long at a portion of highway called "Dead Man's Curve" south of Baton Rouge, where it was necessary for automobiles to reduce speed to negotiate the stretch of highway.

Davis, the ex-deputy sheriff, testified that he had been offered $10,000 to kill Long. The money was proffered, according to Davis, by a fellow deputy sheriff. Davis was provided with a sheriff department's car and furnished a rifle by relatives of the sheriff who owned a hardware store. He testified that he had tried several times to shoot Huey through windows at the capitol and the mansion, but could not get close enough because of state troopers.

Davis was well known to others involved in similar plots to kill Long. On an earlier occasion, because of his alleged sharpshooting abilities, anti-Long forces had retained him and had staked him out on the Mississippi River levee some distance from Huey's aerie in the Heidelberg. He lost his nerve, unable to pull the trigger when the moment of truth arrived. His co-conspirators spirited him out of town.[11]

Those accused of plotting to kill Long rested on their constitutional rights and said nothing.

Long took full advantage of this opportunity to get in a few licks against Standard Oil and other enemies. "There were four sheriffs and a district attorney mixed up in (the plot)..." he charged.[12]

The hearing was adjourned.

And, incredibly, that was the end of it! There were no criminal charges.

There were no prosecutions. There was no further investigation. Just as the inquiry was begun on the whim of the Kingfish, so was it abandoned.

The reasons for Long's failure to follow up are obscure.

There is no doubt that he believed the plot was genuine. His bodyguards also believed it. Perhaps, as he had done with the vice hearings in New Orleans, he simply used the hearing as a forum for propaganda to torment his enemies. Perhaps he felt that he would eventually be murdered, as he often predicted, and, fatalistically, felt powerless to stop the unfolding of events that would result in his death.

Perhaps.

Long's opponents were generally inclined to downgrade the importance of the hearing. They claimed—and still claim today, most of them—that on any street corner in Baton Rouge, citizens could be heard talking about murdering Huey Long, since that seemed to be the only way possible at the moment to rid the state of him. But this, they insisted, was simply empty talk. The most vocal of his opposition were the pillars of society, the *creme de la creme,* the attorneys, physicians, judges and other professionals. Who among them would harbor such dark intentions? In the light of subsequent events, who, indeed?

Murder and assassination were in the air, a contagion that seemed to turn the most innocent action into a threat and which attached overtones of violence to the most meaningless exchange.

The president of the Square Deal Association wrote J. Edgar Hoover in March of 1935. The reason for the letter was to "provide a lead to any investigations you might care to instigate in the event I am ever murdered." Ernest J. Bourgeois, ex-Standard Oil employee, added, "We are living in a city where the police are under the domination of America's new Public Enemy Number One, Huey P. Long."[13]

But even as oppositionists protested and discounted the existence of plots, the plots themselves continued to mount. They were real. The talk was far from empty.

The *New York Times* speculated that, of the 64 parishes in the state, "more than half a dozen are rumbling with revolt." [14]

Hodding Carter, anti-Long Louisiana newspaper publisher, wrote, "There are many sane, thoughtful citizens who believe that only through a .45 can the state regain its political and economic sanity."[15]

Noting the incendiary character of the Louisiana situation, Will Irwin, writing in *Liberty* magazine, speculated that Louisiana "is at the mercy of an incident." He continued, "We may see Long's half-unwilling militia, backed up by irregulars from his machine, trying to suppress guerilla warfare."[16]

Whether Irwin had inside information or was simply speculating, his observation was accurate. In the summer of 1935, an organization was formed in Central Louisiana to retake the government by force. The group had members in

West Feliciana Parish, northern neighbor to East Baton Rouge, who met regularly to discuss ways of eliminating Huey Long. Armed guards patrolled highways to apprehend Long supporters and state employees entering the parish.[17]

In Baton Rouge, off-duty sheriff's deputies met regularly to discuss killing Long. One citizen, in his teens at the time, cleaned weapons for attending deputies, weapons that consisted of "everything from pistols to double barreled shotguns."[18]

A sniper was staked out in a parking garage cater-corner to the Heidelberg Hotel, patiently waiting for Long to leave the front entrance on a day it was known he would be traveling to New Orleans. The cordon of bodyguards ruled out the prospect of a stranger getting close enough to do Long harm (although this was not the case when Carl Weiss did just that) and it was concluded that the deed would have to be accomplished by a marksman. A getaway boat was stashed by the bank of the nearby Mississippi River.

Long, surrounded by bodyguards, left the hotel just as a cloudburst began. The party went back inside and another plot fizzled.[19]

The most celebrated and best documented plot on the life of the Kingfish involved a two-day meeting of anti-Long businessmen and public officials July 21 and 22, 1935. The meeting was held in the DeSoto Hotel in New Orleans. Its purpose is still being debated.

Attendees included a former governor, the anti-Long members of the congressional delegation, federal appointees of President Roosevelt, prominent businessmen and public officials of a number of Louisiana's parishes.

Most of those who attended the meeting insist that it was a caucus to plan for the upcoming January elections when a new governor would be elected and Huey Long would stand for re-election to the United States Senate. Admittedly, there was talk of killing Long, according to one public official, but it was common to have such discussions on the streets and in any political meeting. The talk was "without serious intent."

Others hold that the conference was an assassination meeting, with the principal business being to reach a decision about the best way to kill Huey Long.

The leading exponent of this version was Huey Long himself.

Early in August, 1935, he took the Senate floor on a point of personal privilege to reveal to his colleagues just how bitter the relationship between him and Roosevelt had become. He read from a document which he claimed was a verbatim transcript of the DeSoto Hotel meeting in July. He laid the blame for an impending assassination attempt at the doorstep of his Public Enemy Number One: Franklin Delano Roosvelt.

There was no bluster accompanying the Huey Long that a shocked Senate heard on August 9, 1935. He was subdued—understandably so, perhaps, when one considers that he was discussing the prospect of his own murder.

He quoted one participant at the meeting as saying, "I am out to murder, kill, bulldoze, steal or anything else to win this election." Another voice: "It would only take one man, one gun and one bullet." And finally, the clincher: "I haven't the slightest doubt that Roosevelt would pardon anyone who killed Long."

It was a bemused and frightened Kingfish who unburdened his fears before his colleagues, probably the first public outpouring of those emotions of his political life. He was scared. "I read that language after midnight when I was alone in my room and got a little bit more shaky, but it is funny in daylight."

He wound up his report by restating his opposition to the Roosevelt administration, which he termed as a government representing "murder, blackmail, oppression and destitution."[20]

Long was certain that the New Orleans conference was called to plot his assassination. Most of his supporters believed likewise. The opposition maintained that the meeting was simply political in nature.

Actually, it seems that both points of view are correct—to a degree.

At any large gathering, be it class reunion, political convention or social function, rarely is the official and stated purpose of the meeting the only agenda. There are sub-groups that have individual meetings and hidden agendas. A political convention will feature meetings-within-a-meeting of those with like, although limited, interests. The delegates from the South will caucus individually; women will discuss women's issues to the exclusion of men. Other groups will gather for their own separate talks.

The DeSoto meeting was like this.

There were some 150 delegates to the meeting, whose purpose was to decide upon a ticket to oppose the Long administration candidates in the January election. And such a ticket was decided upon.

However, within that meeting there was a sub-meeting of some 15 hard-core Long opponents and they discussed, in the most candid of language, ways to rid the state of Huey Long by violent means.

Former Governor John M. Parker, erstwhile and continuing Long enemy appointed by Roosevelt to head a New Deal recovery committee, opened the meeting with this bald statement: "Well, it looks like the only way we can get rid of Huey Long is to assassinate him."

The plans discussed were varied. One involved "a Chicago gangland deal" consisting of driving alongside Huey's car and spraying him with bullets. Another called for an ambush similar to the one planned for Dead Man's Curve earlier in the year. One straightforward but unimaginative scenario involved a delegation of enemies arranging an appointment with Long at his Heidelberg suite and simply pushing him out the window. Strangest of all was a bizarre scenario involving importation of a drug addict from Chicago who would figure out his own way to kill Long.[21]

It is hardly believable, but once again there was no attempt on anyone's part to determine the validity of these appalling disclosures. For the second time that year, Long had revealed the existence of a scheme by political opponents to take his life and had failed to take any action to bring to justice the conspirators. He did nothing to avert what he apparently sincerely believed would be his eventual assassination, except to posture and grandstand at the mock hearing he staged in Baton Rouge in early February and to attack Roosevelt in the Senate.

He knew his opponents were out there.

Perhaps a little effort on his part could isolate and identify them. Perhaps persistent probing would have disclosed the identity of a most unlikely assassin, a gentle, soft spoken, ear, nose and throat specialist who, although native to Baton Rouge, had spent most of his adult life outside the city, studying and practicing in New Orleans, New York, Vienna and Paris.

Even as early as the spring of 1935, Carl Weiss was confiding to some that he believed something was going to have to be done about Huey Long. Some believed that the solution might even involve murder.[22]

CHAPTER NINE

Seymour And
The Princefishes

There were—and still are—many in Louisiana who believe that the assassination of Huey Long was an inside job, engineered by those around him who, for their own reasons, felt they would be better off with the Kingfish dead.

This belief is occasioned by the generally inept and shoddy way everything connected with the assassination was handled. The actions of those who were in positions of authority around Long and who could have reasonably been expected to see that all the facts of his shooting and death were made public did nothing except invite suspicion of themselves, their actions and their motives.

None of his followers seemed inclined to make a clean breast of the matter. The cloak of secrecy and guilt thrown over the whole affair caused many to conclude that, if a complete investigation had been undertaken, it would unquestionably have led to those in the Long hierarchy. The whole thing smacked of a coverup.

The assassination of Long was made a campaign issue in the gubernatorial election in January. Long supporters dubbed the opposition the "Assassination Ticket," because the head of the ticket, Cleveland Dear, had been in attendance at the July meeting in the DeSoto Hotel where Long charged his assassination was being plotted.

Dear, in return, accused Long's own people of murdering him. In a radio address he flatly charged that one of the chief bodyguards entrusted with Long's safety was in an asylum for the insane and constantly cried, "I killed my best friend."[1]

So potentially damaging was the charge that six of Long's bodyguards sponsored a full-page newspaper advertisement to deny the charges.

The nature of the shooting itself, coupled with events following Long's death, provides a very strong foundation for a belief that Long's palace guard was responsible for his death.

The fact that an assassin could get within striking distance of Long is, in itself, cause for amazement. The zeal and the protective nature of his bodyguards when danger threatened was well known. They guarded him as a jealous dog defends its master. It was steadfastly believed in Washington and Baton Rouge that no one could ever get close enough to do harm to the Kingfish.

One of his entourage was known to carry a submachine gun in a brown paper sack to deal with an attack in numbers. At times, his guardians were estimated to number as many as a score. Some were former prize fighters. Most seemed to exhibit a predilection for violent action.

They moved with military precision. International News Service noted the elaborately-orchestrated movements of the bodyguards when Long left his office in the nation's capital one day in August, 1935:

> "Long came out, accompanied by his usual bodyguard, a burly ex-trooper from Louisiana. This bodyguard dropped about 10 feet behind his chief. Three other guards dropped in, about 20 feet behind the little procession.
>
> "'Come on! Step it up here!' snapped the bodyguard in charge as the trio allowed the senator to step into the hall at the head of the little group.
>
> "'Don't let that man go down the hall alone.'
>
> "And this intense order was snapped for a 50-foot trip of the senator between the doors of his office in the Senate office building!
>
> "Prior to this, Long rarely had more than one bodyguard in attendance, never more than two. From then on, he was never without three and most of the time there were four men with him. They were all powerful men, too. Their hips bulged as if with a small package."[2]

The bodyguards accompanied Long everywhere. They sat in when he was interviewed by newsmen and they usually were with him when he went to nightclubs.

When Long died, there was no autopsy which would have established conclusively the cause of death and would also have determined the number of bullets that entered his body. The .32 caliber bullet that Long forces claimed passed through his body was never exhibited, although it must be assumed that it would have been recovered from the scene of the shooting.

If it was not recovered, then it should have been. The bodyguards were shooting with .38 and .45 caliber weapons. Weiss' pistol was a .32. Despite the bits and pieces of spent bullets and casings at the scene, it should have taken no great effort to separate the .32 caliber slug (or slugs) and casings that were supposedly fired from Weiss' gun from the larger bullets.

If the bullet had been recovered, many unanswered questions would be answered. Recovery of the bullet would certainly have reinforced the Longite claim that Weiss fired at Long. Many believe the slug or its jacket were never displayed because they never existed.

And then there was the mess at the hospital. No one seemed to be in charge. Decisions were made by consensus. There was bickering among the doctors. Some have concluded that it was preordained that Long would never leave the hospital alive.

According to one writer, underworld figures Frank Costello and Meyer Lansky met several weeks after Long's death in the Arlington Hotel in Hot Springs, Arkansas to assess the Louisiana situation. Costello remarked to Lansky, "We could have saved him, but I didn't see much use in it. The doctors had their orders to let him die."[3]

A strong accusation, to be sure, and hardly worthy of mention, were it not for the fact that complete medical records that might have proven the charge to be a lie have never been made public and physicians in attendance stubbornly refused to answer questions. When facts are withheld, speculation flourishes and invariably takes on the ugliest of interpretations.

And, finally, there is no denying that some of those around Long benefitted from his death. They were decidedly better off as a result.

When Long died, federal indictments were pending against several of his leaders, notably Seymour Weiss, for income tax evasion. The state was at war with the Roosevelt administration. Public works funds were being withheld by federal authorities. But after Long's death, the feud ended and, miraculously, an era of peace and harmony between state and nation was ushered in.

Before Long's body had been lowered into the grave, members of his organization caucused to confect a deal with the Roosevelt administration. Paul Maloney, United States congressman and Long stalwart, solemnly pronounced, "The battle between Senator Long and President Roosevelt is over." Maloney was to take a peace offer to Washington and lay it on the table before President Roosevelt: the Long organization would support Roosevelt if the feds would drop the income tax fraud investigation, funnel patronage through them once again and also reopen the spigot to provide public works funds.[4]

"Laissez les bon temps rouler!" Let the good times roll! And possibly, along with the good times, Huey would likewise roll over in his grave as his political heirs made their peace with the Kingfish's archenemy, Roosevelt.

Asked to comment on the prospect of such a truce materializing,

Treasury Secretary Henry Morgenthau, Jr. pooh-poohed it. "We don't start any tax cases for political purposes and we don't stop them for the same reason."[5]

But public works officials took a more tolerant view of the matter. They said something could be worked out as far as the money was concerned, if objectionable laws passed under the Long regime were repealed.

And, nine months after Long's death, despite Morgenthau's statement of principles, the United States Attorney asked the United States Court to dismiss most of the indictments against the Long crowd. A howl went up, not only in Louisiana, but throughout the country. The whole unsavory spectacle was promptly labeled "The Second Louisiana Purchase."

In keeping with this newfound peace and harmony, Governor Richard W. Leche, who had been elected against the "Assassination Ticket" in a landslide victory in January, convened the Louisiana legislature in Dallas, where Roosevelt was visiting the Texas Centennial Exposition. The legislators passed a resolution praising divine Providence for providing "a great leader, Franklin D. Roosevelt, who saved the nation from ruin and chaos." They even criticized the Republican candidate for President, Kansas Governor Alfred Landon, for entertaining the idea of running against Roosevelt, proposing that Landon withdraw from the presidential race and make Roosevelt's re-election unanimous. (C'mon, do the decent thing, Alf.)

Adding a bit of nostalgia, the LSU marching band, which made the trip along with the legislature, played Huey's campaign song, "Every Man a King."

To insure that sleeping dogs would continue to snore, Governor Leche, despite a campaign promise to investigate Long's murder, had a bill killed that would have done just that. The measure provided a $100,000 appropriation for an investigation and was introduced on May 31, 1936. A day later, the author of the resolution, Representative Ben R. Simpson, withdrew the measure.

When asked why he had the bill withdrawn, Leche replied that the primary responsibility for investigating the slaying rested with the widow, Mrs. Rose Long, who had been appointed to serve out the remaining days of her husband's Senate term. Leche added that, since both Long and Weiss were dead, he didn't feel that it would help Huey or the state to go into an investigation. Interesting, since Leche headed the Long ticket that charged the opposing "Assassination Ticket" with having conspired to kill Long.

The Kingfish is dead! Long live the Princefishes!

The Princefishes wasted no time in carving up the empire that Long left. There was much to be done and it had to be done fast.

Without doubt, the first order of business was to set into motion the machinery to obtain federal forgiveness for Long's lieutenants for the indiscreet financial transactions that had caused them to be indicted. This was attended to as described previously, the "Second Louisiana Purchase."

Next came the business of preparing for the upcoming statewide elections. There would have to be candidates chosen for governor, lieutenant governor and all the statewide offices. Governor Allen could not succeed himself, so it would have to be a new face. In addition, there would have to be someone to sit in the late Kingfish's Senate seat. His unexpired term would last until January 1, 1937 and a full six-year term would begin at that time.

Huey left no heirs apparent to his throne. He operated with no table of organization. There was no pecking order. Everything radiated from the Kingfish himself, as spokes from the hub of a wheel, as rays of light from the sun. It would be every man for himself in dividing up the spoils and taking command of the machine left by the Kingfish.

The survivors of the organization began to joust and jockey for positions in the organization that would supplant the original Long juggernaut. As could be expected, there was infighting during this episode of the long knives.

State Senator Jimmy Noe, one of Huey's fellow investors in the Win or Lose Corporation, announced that he would seek the governorship. He was joined by the Reverend Gerald L.K. Smith, Long's organizer for the Share Our Wealth movement. The ticket included Wade O. Martin, Sr., whom Long had elected to the Public Service Commission to replace former ally Dudley J. Le-Blanc, as a candidate for Long's full six-year term in the U.S. Senate. Smith would travel to Washington with Martin to become his secretary, carrying on the Share Our Wealth work in the nation's capital.

Supreme Court Justice Fournet endorsed the ticket, as did outgoing Governor O.K. Allen, who would run for Long's unexpired term in the Senate.

But these best laid plans ran into a stone wall made up of the two strongest men in the Long organization, Seymour Weiss and Robert Maestri. Weiss has been mentioned in these pages before and more will be said presently. Maestri was a true-blue supporter from New Orleans about whom a great deal will also be said further along in this work.

No! said the pair. The ticket would be composed of Richard W. Leche, a former secretary of Governor Allen and later elevated to a judgeship on the court of appeal, for governor and Earl K. Long, younger brother of the Kingfish, as lieutenant governor. For the unexpired Senate seat it would be Allan Ellender, speaker of the Louisiana House of Representatives. As their authority, Weiss and Maestri remembered that Huey had chosen Leche to be the next governor. The Kingfish had merely not taken the time to communicate it to all the members of the alliance before he died.[6]

And that was that.

The Noe-Smith alliance was out of business just as suddenly as it started. Smith promptly dropped Noe to join the source of real power, causing Noe to threaten to beat him to a pulp if the evangelist ever showed up near him. But Smith found no welcome in the Maestri-Weiss camp. He had made some formidable enemies in that direction.

His precipitous action in stating that he would assume the leadership of the Share Our Wealth movement provoked the wrath of Earle Christenberry, secretary of the late senator, who reminded that he had all the files, names and documents and was not about to part with any of them. Weiss, under indictment by the Feds, was nervous about the strong remarks being broached about by Smith, who was demanding that Roosevelt investigate the conspiracy responsible for Long's death. But even more terrifying were the anti-Semitic statements being made by Smith about what would be done to Weiss and "his kind" (that is, Jews) once Smith and "his kind" (that is, bigots) took over.

In January, 1936, the elections went as planned. Leche was elected in a landslide, along with his lieutenant governor, Earl Long. Jimmy Noe, demoted from gubernatorial candidate, ran for re-election to his state Senate seat and won. Allen won the unexpired term of the Kingfish.

There was near panic shortly after the election when the 55-year old Allen, apparently in perfect health, mysteriously died within an hour after being stricken with a cerebral hemorrhage. This boosted Noe into the governorship, since the lieutenant governor, John Fournet, had been elected to the supreme court and Noe, as president pro tem of the Senate, was next in the line of succession. The organization worried that he would use the three and a half months of his remaining term to cause some mischief as revenge for his shoddy treatment, but, except for making a few inconsequential waves, he behaved himself.

As it turned out, there were three survivors who would inherit Huey's kingdom. Others would share in certain scraps of the inheritance, but there would be no mistaking who was in charge.

The two strong men in the Long organization, Seymour Weiss and Robert Maestri, gathered unto their bosoms the newly elected governor, Richard Leche. This troika governed the state of Louisiana until the federal government intervened in 1939, sending Weiss and Leche, along with a thundering herd of other baddies, to the federal penitentiary.

B.E. Sackett, Special Agent in Charge of the FBI New Orleans office, described the operation of this formidable trio this way in 1939, shortly before indictments were handed down:

> "The City of New Orleans is rather wide
> open as far as prostitution and gambling is concer-
> ned...the 'syndicate'...is composed of the Mayor of
> New Orleans (Maestri), the Governor of the State
> of Louisiana (Leche) (and) the Superintendent of
> the New Orleans Police Department, Seymour
> Weiss, who is chairman of the Police Board."[7]

Maestri, a man of limited education, was the son of an Italian poultry dealer who later acquired a furniture store on the outskirts of the red light district in New Orleans. The younger Maestri eventually assumed the proprietorship of the store.

He spoke in measured, direct language that sometimes offended and oftentimes shocked his listeners. One writer felt that Maestri could have been a creation of Damon Runyon.[8]

According to Hamilton Basso, a group of New Orleans grand dames called upon Maestri when he was mayor, asking that the planned Municipal Auditorium be designed in the shape of a Greek theater. The mayor refused the request, saying that he felt there were not enough Greeks in the city to support the project.[9]

He was a man of immense wealth, which came from the furniture store and later from real estate investments. His detractors claimed that much of his money was accumulated by selling furniture on installments to whorehouse madams. When the premises were raided, Maestri's firm would repossess the furniture and resell it.

In 1939, in a Bureau memorandum, FBI Director J. Edgar Hoover gave this rather unflattering description of Maestri to the U.S. Attorney General:

"Possessing a natural shrewdness, he was able with his inheritance, which consisted of control of the leading houses of prostitution in New Orleans, to make a great deal of money and in turn to acquire tremendous power in the state ...Maestri is alleged to be in control of the entire political ring which covers vice, gambling and innumerable shakedown and grafting activities, including the smuggling and sale of narcotics and the smuggling of aliens."[10]

Maestri was a friend of Frank Costello's and was reputed to have strong ties to syndicated crime figures, including Lucky Luciano and Owney "The Killer" Madden.

The record is unclear about the circumstances under which Long and Maestri made contact. Perhaps Maestri was a political groupie who saw in Long the prospects of greatness and simply wanted to be a spectator of the action. Perhaps he, himself, had political ambitions.

(He would become mayor of New Orleans after the anti-Long incumbent was brought to his knees and resigned. Even so, Maestri didn't face the voters. His opponent for the unexpired term withdrew, giving the office to Maestri. Four years later he was unopposed. In the only election where he was opposed, he was defeated. This was in 1946, when reformer deLesseps S. Morrison was a successful candidate for the office.)

But, regardless of the reasons, he was a valued supporter of Huey Long who enjoyed a special position with the Kingfish.

As host-mayor of one of the largest cities in the nation, Maestri was seated next to President Franklin Roosevelt in 1937, when the chief executive visited New Orleans. In the grand style, the presidential party was being treated to luncheon at Antoine's, the flagship of New Orleans restaurants and *de rigeur* for visiting celebrities.

The garrulous Roosevelt and the taciturn Maestri were an odd couple indeed. Unaccustomed to the art of addressing presidents, Maestri said nothing to Roosevelt until the President had finished his Oysters Rockefeller, most famous of all New Orleans dishes in the most famous of all New Orleans restaurants.

In an effort to make conversation, Maestri inquired, in the patois that is uniquely New Orleans, "How'd ya like dem ersters?"

Roosevelt, anxious to give the local yokels their due, launched into a paean of praise of the oysters, comparing the bivalves with the finest of foods he had ever encountered. Maestri, listening impassively until the President concluded his filibuster, responded witlessly, "Ya liked 'em, huh?"

Two hours later, when the meal was concluded, host Maestri, feeling compelled to open the conversation once more, invited another oration from Roosevelt by asking, "How'd ya like the meal?" He suffered the Roosevelt rhetoric and again responded lumpishly, "You liked it." At the table was New Orleans newsman (later U.S. congressman) F. Edward Hebert, who later asked the mayor, "Say, Bob, how did you like the President?" To which Maestri gave this earthy reply, "Say, that guy's full of bullshit, ain't he?"[11]

But there was a lot behind the bullshit that escaped Maestri's eyes and the eyes of the other Louisiana peacemakers. As he joked and lavished his charm upon his hosts, Roosevelt was getting perverse pleasure at the spectacle of Long's survivors playing up to him even as they were the subjects of continuing investigations by the IRS. Elliott Roosevelt has written:

> "It made for a certain piquancy to sit at dinner in Antoine's under the glazed stare of the dead Kingfish, whose photographs hung on the walls. Father enjoyed his first taste of Oysters Rockefeller, but the pleasure did not compare with twitting such notables as the Governor of Louisiana, the Mayor of New Orleans and Seymour Weiss...on the hazards implicit in undiluted political power."[12]

The unsuccessful efforts of the federal government to nab Maestri provided at least one amusing incident that offers a comic insight into the policies of the Federal Bureau of Investigation.

J. Edgar Hoover publicly professed an aversion to wiretapping. However, an exchange of memos in the Bureau's files questions whether that was a genuine policy or a cosmetic cover-up.

A memo from R.A. Guerin, Night Supervisor at FBI Washington headquarters, to E.A. Tamm, chief assistant to Hoover, dated July 26, 1939, reported that Assistant Attorney General John Rogge, charged with prosecuting members of the Long machine suspected of illegal dealings, had repeated an earlier request for a wiretap of Maestri's home to find out more about income tax and other violations. Tamm took no action on the request. A memorandum for the file written later that day says that Tamm pointed out to Rogge that "other agencies also are equipped for wiretapping," probably meaning that Rogge should take his business elsewhere, rather than involve the Bureau.

But this admission that the FBI actually did tap telephones was quickly clarified by Tamm in another memo for the file that same day, leading us to suspect that he had probably talked the matter over with Hoover:

> "I called Agent Dunker (in New Orleans) with regard to Rogge's request that the Bureau place a telephone tap on the home of Maestri...I told Dunker this was out of the question; that we do not tap telephones."[13]

But despite Maestri's shortcomings and regardless of his standing in the community, he had proved himself to Huey Long. When Long was on hard times, struggling desperately to avoid impeachment, it was Maestri who came forward and made available the money for printing to take the Long message to the people.

Long recalls, in his autobiography:

> "My friend Robert Maestri came to my room in Baton Rouge.
> "'Do you need some money?' he asked.
> "'All the silver in India and all the tea in China,' I replied.
> "'How fast do you need it?' he inquired.
> "'Just as fast as a printing office can turn out circulars and the government can sell stamps.'
> "'I will take care of that,' he said."

Long felt that his handbills had managed to counteract the bad publicity generated by the newspapers of the state and he gave full credit to Maestri—or, more precisely, Maestri's money. Maestri, according to Huey, was "the greatest of all friends in foul weather."[14]

When Long died, Maestri sent the word that Costello's slots would not be able to operate in New Orleans. However, after a visit to Hot Springs, Arkansas to meet with Madden, Costello, Lansky, Kastel and other underworld figures, the problems were ironed out and Costello was operating bigger than ever.

In contrast to Maestri was Seymour Weiss, easily the most intriguing member of the Long organization. He was the perfect complement to Maestri. Maestri was swarthy, direct, awkward, inarticulate and graceless; Weiss was polished, stylish, urbane and suave to the point of oiliness. This is not to say that Maestri was devoid of any talent at all, because he had a shrewdness and a grasp of situations that allowed him to run the city of New Orleans in a creditable fashion as mayor.

Also, we must remember that Weiss went to the penitentiary and Maestri did not.

Weiss was the standout personality in the Long hierarchy. His is a fascinating story.

His versatility was truly remarkable. He was a man for all seasons and all factions. He had the absolute trust of Huey Long, yet he enjoyed a long standing close personal relationship with the chief lobbyist of Standard Oil Company, Long's bitterest enemy, whom many believe to be more than casually involved in Long's demise.

Weiss served time at the federal penitentiary in Atlanta, but was a friend of FBI chief J. Edgar Hoover, identified in FBI files as being on Hoover's special correspondents' list and "known to the Director on a first name basis." Shortly before his indictment was handed down, Weiss hosted United States Attorney General Frank Murphy and Hoover at his Roosevelt Hotel in New Orleans. Years after he had served his prison term, Weiss was asked if Hoover could have helped with his problems. He answered that Hoover's hands were tied but that at least the FBI did not investigate the case.[15]

Weiss was head of the Police Board in New Orleans but he associated freely and openly with Phil Kastel, Frank Costello and others in the underworld.

Truly, Weiss had the capacity for a wide range of associations.

He was uneducated, born from poor parents and with few material resources. Yet he rose from shoe clerk to manager and, later, owner of the prestigious Roosevelt Hotel (now the Fairmont) in New Orleans. Eventually he owned not only the Roosevelt, but the New Orleans Hotel as well and the New Yorker in New York City.

When he died in 1969, his estate was valued at almost $7 million.[16]

His rise to fame and fortune was a testimonial to his ability and intelligence, although his association with Huey Long certainly didn't hurt. Some were disturbed about rumors that part of his success was attributed to a working relationship with the underworld.

Weiss was born in 1896, three years after Huey. His birthplace was a small agricultural trading community in central Louisiana named Bunkie. Obituaries and biographies published about Weiss do not agree on facts. The differences are minor and they relate to his very early years. (One account says he left Bunkie at age three to move to Abbeville, an Acadian-French community about 60 miles south of Bunkie. Another account fixes the age at eight.) His education was limited, probably consisting of three years of elementary school.

Some crime writers have not hesitated to label Seymor Weiss a member of the underworld. It is possible that the writers have confused Seymour with Hymie and Mendy Weiss, torpedoes from Chicago and New York during the 20s. However, there was a curious relationship between Weiss and the Mob which will be dealt with later.

As a hotelman, Weiss was quick to seize upon the potential of being close to a rising star like Huey Long. He taught Huey golf, gave sartorial advice and accompanied the Kingfish during some of his early excursions in pub-crawling. He arranged for Huey and his entourage to have a complimentary suite at the Roosevelt and from this command post Huey called the shots for his 1928 governor's campaign.

Huey valued Weiss' loyalty, intelligence and resourcefulness. Later he would emerge as the intimate confidant, the trusted advisor, the complete companion, the chief engineer for the Long railroad and the fiscal agent for the machine.

He would demonstrate his loyalty and his staying power during Huey's impeachment, the same trying period when Robert Maestri proved his own mettle.

One of the impeachment charges involved mishandling of state funds to entertain the national conference of governors when that body met in New Orleans in 1928. Long had obtained $6,000 from the State Board of Liquidation, a funding mechanism for unanticipated expenses of government between legislative sessions. The money was to be used to entertain visiting governors, a reasonable and understandable request which was readily granted.

However, when the full $6,000 was withdrawn all at one time in $20 bills—300 of them—eyebrows arched. This transaction surfaced during the impeachment proceedings and it was soon learned that the Roosevelt Hotel, site of the conference, had been paid $3500, but no record could be found of the remaining $2500. The impeachers got in touch with Seymour and had him meet with them.

Weiss was his usual polite self to the committee, but he gave them absolutely no information. What answers he gave simply gave rise to additional questions. Where was the money spent? Entertainment. What kind of entertainment? Various kinds. On whose instructions? Governor Long had instructed the hotelman to do for the visitors anything "they wanted me to do for them." But specifically? Specifically, the money was spent "on a party of such a nature that I would hesitate to give details."

Later Weiss would confide to an interviewer that the money had been used "on a big drunken spree" and few of the questioners were willing to press the matter for fear of the consequences of *en masse* embarrassment of chief executives of most of the United States. Weiss knew how far the inquisitors would go and feigned discretion and diplomacy to evade giving substantive answers. The wily fox knew the hunters would abandon the chase long before he had tired.

Weiss' performance before the committee proved his loyalty; his ability would solidify the relationship between himself and his newly acquired patron. In years to come, Long would lean more and more heavily upon the slick innkeeper and he would eventually emerge as the number one follower in the organization, second only to the Kingfish himself.

Weiss became the official treasurer of the Long organization. All dealings were in cash. No records were kept. Only Seymour knew details about transactions and you had to take his word for it.

In 1933, a Senate investigating committee questioned him about his peculiar bookkeeping habits. Weiss was not as courteous as he was to the impeachment panel four years before. Asked if there was any reason why he kept no records, Weiss blandly replied, "First, I did not want to and second, it was too much trouble." When his interrogator asked about the existence of bank accounts, Weiss snapped, "That's none of your business." It was a tart, contemptuous answer that was repeated to each new inquiry.

Syndicated newspaper columnist Westbrook Pegler claimed that Weiss had boasted that he "practically ran the U.S. Senate out of town." During a heated exchange between Weiss and Committee Counsel Ansell, Huey mischievously suggested to Weiss that Ansell might "invite you outside." Weiss haughtily responded, "No, he has much better sense than to do that."[17]

So much for the United States Senate!

Years later, after Long's passing, Weiss would express regrets that he had ever gotten involved in politics. He should have stuck to the hotel business, he moaned. He should have let politics alone. But these misgivings came only after he was sent to federal prison from which he was released after 16 months of a 4-year term. In truth, Weiss would, no doubt, have been a moderate success without Huey Long, given the hotelman's intelligence and ability.

However, it is doubtful that he would have left a $7 million estate when he died and even that figure probably represented far less than his actual worth. A single piece of property owned by Weiss, the Roosevelt Hotel, had been valued at $15 million six years before his death.

In December, 1934, about nine months before Long was assassinated, Weiss was indicted by the federal government. He was charged with having received, over the preceding five years, an income of $232,000, but having reported only $55,000. The government alleged that he had drawn a large part of his income from a kickback scheme involving the state's highway contractors, who were forced to obtain performance bonds from an insurance company which, in turn, returned 20 percent of the bond premium to him.[18]

Weiss' indictment was the opening gun in the campaign of the federal government to nail Huey Long. It also turned out to be the tip of the iceberg as far as Weiss' earnings were concerned.

As treasurer of the Long organization, Weiss had principal access to the de-duct box, mentioned earlier. He also administered funds derived from kick-backs paid by contractors, suppliers and others fortunate enough to obtain state business through the benevolence of Huey Long.

The amount of money that passed through Seymour Weiss' hands is incalculable. He shared in the proceeds from the slot machines after Huey's death, having gone to Hot Springs with Leche and Maestri to confer with Frank Costello and other racketeering figures. He was named by the FBI as an owner in a gambling establishment across the street from his Roosevelt Hotel. According to the FBI, the gambling joint enjoyed a monopoly in the city of New Orleans on "the more popular forms of gambling, such as dice and roulette."

Writing in the *New Republic* four months after Long's death, Hamilton Basso commented sadly:

> "I charge, simply, that the state of Louisiana is now being milked by a gang of venal and corrupt politicians for all they can possibly get: that the city of New Orleans has been turned into a vast gambling hall; that all forms of so-called vice have been organized to bring the greatest possible financial returns; that graft is the accepted order of the day; that the next election will be either bought or stolen; and that—which is possibly the gravest charge of all—nobody seems to care."[19]

The avarice and gluttony of Weiss and his associates were appalling. Anything that would yield a dishonest dollar was undertaken. Nothing was too small for these ravenous creatures. In addition to the big ticket items, such as rakeoffs from the slots, from gambling and from prostitution, the Syndicate acquired real estate, a candy company, a cab company, a dairy, a bakery and the local baseball team.[20]

The Syndicate owned a race track which the FBI asserted was reputed to be the most crooked in the country, with at least one race a day being fixed for the benefit of insiders.

Weiss was president of the Dock Board, which administered the affairs of the Port of New Orleans. The FBI has charged that he forced foreign flag vessels to dock as far away from public transportation as possible, to utilize the services of his Yellow Cab Company.

Another communique reported that all city employees were given a half day off on the opening day of the baseball season to attend the first game and root for the Syndicate's ball team.

Even the candy company was promoted with strong-arm tactics for the aggrandizement of Weiss and his cohorts. Special Agent in Charge J.A. Smith, Jr. reported to FBI headquarters in Washington:

> "Rumor has it that local merchants who are handling Whitman's and Hollingsworth and other well known brands of candy are visited by Jacobs Candy Company salesmen and are forcibly high-pressured into discontinuing of sales of other brands."

While Weiss had a tremendous capacity for a wide variety of activities, there is one association by him that stands out.

FBI files uncovered a continuing liaison and rapport, not to mention business relationship, between Weiss and the chief lobbyist for Standard Oil, Louis LeSage. In 1939, both were indicted for using the mails to defraud. The scheme involved another of Weiss' properties, the Bienville Hotel in New Orleans, which was sold, complete with furnishings, to the state of Louisiana. The furnishings were later resold to the state.

LeSage was paid $25,000 on the sale of the hotel, allegedly for his influence in bringing about the transaction. However, when he was questioned by FBI agents, he could recall very little that he had done to earn the commission. The following question and answer session is contained in FBI files:

> Special IRS Agent George A. Lambert asked:
>
> "Did you contact anyone in connection with the sale of the equipment?'
>
> LeSage: "Not a soul. No one."
>
> Lambert persisted: "Did you perform any services whatsoever in connection with the sale of the equipment to the Louisiana State University?"
>
> LeSage: "None that I can think of."

LeSage paid taxes on the $25,000 and then gave $16,500 to Seymour Weiss in the form of a "loan." The government didn't buy it and indicted the pair. LeSage, in a lower tax bracket than Weiss, obviously was being used by Weiss as a conduit to launder Weiss' money, thus evading a large share of taxes due.

The disturbing thing about this whole transaction is the fact that Weiss, top man in the Long organization, enjoyed a continuing relationship with LeSage, big in the Standard Oil group, throughout the entire confrontation between the corporation and Huey Long. In 1929, Long was impeached by the House of Representatives and there is little doubt that the impeachment sprang from attempts to pass the oil tax bill. Long charged that the Standard used bribes to defeat the tax bill, referring to LeSage and his associates as "financial agents, you henchmen of the Standard Oil Company."

LeSage, at the time, lived in the Roosevelt Hotel in New Orleans through the generosity of Seymour Weiss. Two years later he would occupy permanent quarters there, the beneficiary of a sweetheart arrangement with Weiss.

Weiss told the IRS that he had three brothers. LeSage, he told them, "is like my fourth brother. I love them all and would do anything within my power for any of them. There is nothing I would not do for Louis and there is nothing he would not do for me....He could not ask me for anything that I would not give him. It is a friendship of a lifetime."

Weiss intimated that LeSage had been especially helpful to him while Huey was alive. He remembered that LeSage had "always been very kind and kind at the time when I had my back up against the wall—during Huey P. Long's lifetime and things were so stormy."

For LeSage's part, he had reason to be grateful to his lifetime chum. His hotel room cost him $50 monthly, about a dollar and a half a day at an establishment which ballyhooed itself as "the Pride of the South."

Weiss wept to the FBI that he was chronically hard up for money, drawing only a modest salary from the Roosevelt. This arrangement, according to him, helped shore up the property against the landslide of debts that he had taken over when he assumed the mortgages on the hotel.

To explain his commission on the sale of the Bienville Hotel (his property) to the state and his subsequent resale of the furniture, Weiss offered this curious bit of reasoning:

> "I was entitled to something. For your information, I draw a very small salary. I do that deliberately, because I am interested in increasing my equity with Metropolitan (Metropolitan Life Insurance Company, holder of the mortgage on the Roosevelt). Seymour Weiss does not own anything. When I don't pay Metropolitan, I don't own any hotel. However, they have been very nice. They have said that if they make foreclosure, they want me to operate the hotel for them."

But Weiss' breastbeating and his pauper's mouthings just don't wash.

He figured in the Win or Lose bonanza, which grabbed the richest oil fields in the state of Louisiana. These fields are principally responsible for establishing the Texas Company as the largest oil producer in the state of Louisiana.

In 1925, Weiss was a simple shoe salesman. In 1935, he was the principal owner of four hotels. We can presume that he was a person of some means.

Under Weiss, Maestri, Leche and the other amoral wolves of the surviving Long machine, Louisiana descended into a morass of depravity unequalled by any other state in any era since the birth of this nation. The criminality went beyond stealing and graft and placed the lives of Louisiana citizens in mortal danger. So great was the lust of these vultures for power and material riches that they were prepared to defy authority, steal, kill and maim in order to perpetuate their accursed way of life. And, until 1939, the federal government—especially the FBI—did nothing to head them off.

In February, 1936, files of a congressional committee investigating irregularities by the Long machine were ransacked during a weekend and reports on 1,500 cases of alleged fraud were destroyed.

Federal investigators seemed powerless to react. In August of that year, U.S. Attorney John Rogge, in the midst of prosecuting the scandalous behavior of members of the Long machine, claimed that his telephone was being tapped. A message reporting Rogge's statement was carried into FBI headquarters over the Bureau's teletype and given to Director Hoover. Hoover exploded, in a handwritten note at the bottom of the sheet:

"Oh, for heavens sake! This is terribly
cheap publicity. Be certain Sackett (Special Agent
in Charge of the New Orleans district office) is
doing nothing toward checking such allegations."

Doing nothing was the stock in trade of the Federal Bureau of Investigation.

In 1935, when the nation clamored for some kind of resolution of the Long killing, the FBI files were full of warnings from Washington to New Orleans to "refrain from involving the FBI."

George Garig, from Hope Villa, Louisiana, traveled to Washington to ask if some of the "high-up" government officials couldn't do something about the Louisiana situation. Officials in the FBI sent him packing, suggesting he take his complaint to the IRS.

About the same time, Mrs. J.S. Roussel, president of an anti-Long women's group, wrote that one of Long's plainclothes men had threatened to shoot her. Hoover thanked her for writing and told her it was not a matter for his department.

In January, 1936, when three Louisiana congressmen approached the New Orleans FBI office, asking if it would investigate evidence that the "Purple Gang," a vicious group of murderous thugs out of Detroit, were en route to Louisiana to do "dirty work" in connection with the statewide elections, the Special Agent in Charge dutifully explained that no federal law was involved and hence, the FBI was not involved.

It was the IRS and not the FBI that was principally responsible for making the cases during the Louisiana scandals in 1939. Whatever help offered by the FBI was minimal and given grudgingly.

Dr. James Shaw, Director of the Minerals Division of Louisiana's Conservation Commission, was involved in a hot oil case and had agreed to testify as a government witness against others involved. Shaw was injured in a suspicious automobile accident but he survived. However, on August 20, 1939, while a patient in a New Orleans hospital, he committed suicide by shooting himself.

Jimmy Noe, president pro tem of the state Senate, still smarting over the refusal of Long leaders to support him for governor in 1936, was actively encouraging the federal government's investigation of those who had turned their backs on him. He was also involved in a suspicious automobile accident.

Prosecutor Rogge's wife was involved in still another automobile accident in Texas, of the type experienced by Noe, probably caused by applying heat to a tire with a torch, causing a blowout.

New Orleans SAC Sackett asked Washington if he shouldn't do something. Hoover's chief deputy, E.A. Tamm, responded emphatically, "Absolutely not!"

The merchant marine crew of the SS Fletcher Farrell wrote, in October, 1935, that one of their members had been murdered. They charged, "The city of New Orleans...has had the reputation of being one of the most corrupt cities in the entire world. Not only politically corrupt, but morally as well." Tough toenails, Director Hoover responded. Not for our department. Don't put it on us!

In 1939, the crew of the U.S. Dredge Jadwin, operated by the U.S. Corps of Engineers (federal employees and federal property, Mister Hoover) wrote Hoover regarding "the corruptive political conditions" in New Orleans, including murders and beatings of union members apparently sanctioned or unnoticed by New Orleans law enforcement authorities. Same response.

It has seemed to me a special irony that one of the principal wrongdoers of the Long machine, Seymour Weiss, was on such friendly terms with J. Edgar Hoover, appearing on his "special correspondents" list and worthy of first name treatment. I do not imply that Hoover slackened his efforts because of his association or friendship with Weiss. I simply question the propriety of the relationship because of the relative positions and backgrounds of the two men.

The correspondence between these friends is flavored with sugary brown-nosing by Weiss which should not be read by anyone with diabetes, such as this saccharine missive:

> "Mr. Hoover, you have earned and deserve the magnificent reputation which you and your great organization enjoy and I can only hope that the good Lord will permit you to continue to enjoy good health so that you may carry on for many years to come....I feel that the entire population of our great country owes you and your fine

department a debt of gratitude....You are a great
American, Mr. Hoover, and I am particularly
proud of the privilege of being able to call you my
friend...."

For his part, Hoover acknowledged these compliments graciously, with
ever so slight an accent of majestic modesty: "...you may be sure my only desire
is to continue as Director as long as I can be of service to our country."

Weiss' last letter to Hoover contained this contrite reflection:

"I shall always recall a statement which
you made to me many, many years ago to the effect that we will never get rid of corruption as long
as we have corrupt officials and your statement
then certainly applies today."

Weiss died of a heart attack in September, 1969, in an ambulance
bound for Our Lady of the Lake Hospital in Baton Rouge, where Huey Long
breathed his last on a September morning 34 years before. He was pronounced
dead on arrival.

When Long died in 1935, with Weiss at his bedside, the hotelman's
principal concern was the location of the de-duct box which Weiss claims Huey
moved without disclosing the new site. When Weiss expired in 1969, those
around him expressed a similar interest to state officials making arrangements
for Weiss' burial in making sure that the set of keys always carried by Weiss was
accounted for.[21]

CHAPTER TEN

The Senator Has Been Shot!

No one clearly remembers the sequence of events when Huey Long was shot that Sunday night in September. It is doubtful that even the Kingfish himself could have given a coherent recital of the happenings.

In pain, dazed and frightened, Huey stumbled down the marbled corridor of the first floor of the state capitol, seeking to flee the bedlam behind him. The first escape route offered him was the stairwell leading to the basement. Weaving unsteadily, he began the tortuous descent, caroming off the wall and handrail on the way down.

A bodyguard, Joe Vitrano, followed his leader down the staircase:

"Long went down the stairs then. I didn't think he was hit. But when he got down to the last of the stairs he slipped and hit the wall and this split his lip."[1]

In the cafeteria on the basement floor when the shooting started was Jimmy O'Connor, a favorite of Long and successor to the Kingfish on the Public Service Commission. In the House, minutes before, Long had asked O'Connor to fetch some cigars from the tobacco stand in the cafeteria. Having done so, O'Connor left the cafeteria to return to the first floor. He reached the staircase just as Long was emerging. O'Connor thought the senator had been shot in the mouth:

"When I saw him, he was wobbling and weaving. I asked him what the matter was and he said, 'I'm shot!'

"Well, I thought he was shot in the mouth. He had run down those steps and he must have hit his mouth and split it open. When he said,

'I'm shot!' he spit blood all over me..."

O'Connor and an unidentified bodyguard assisted Long as he left the capitol. They helped him into an automobile. O'Connor and the auto's owner transported him to nearby Our Lady of the Lake Sanitarium, separated from the capitol by a lake but connected by a dike flanking the western wings of both buildings.

Patrolman Gene Kemp told the International News Service that a night watchman named Joe D'Amico commandeered a nearby car and D'Amico, O'-Connor, Long and two bodyguards all huddled together in the crowded car. Bodyguard Joe Fakier offered a version which had Fakier and O'Connor flanking Long in the back seat of Fakier's car while another man drove. Vitrano's version supports Fakier's, but most testimony corroborates the version attributed to O'Connor.

Years later, an aggravated O'Connor would dismiss other versions of the flight from the capitol as headline-grabbing:

> "Afterwards I found out that there must
> have been close to a hundred people in that car on
> the way to the hospital. Everybody wanted to say
> that they were in there trying to save him. But
> there was only myself and that man."

According to O'Connor, Long was silent throughout the trip. The press, however, would maintain that Long inquired, while riding to the hospital, "I wonder why he shot me?"

At 9:30 on a Sunday night, Our Lady of the Lake Sanitarium was quiet and secured. At the emergency room entrance there was a bell which anyone seeking admittance could use to summon help. O'Connor placed Long on a rolling stretcher and pounded on the hospital door, shouting to attract attention. O'-Connor remembers that the driver sped away as fast as possible after Long got out, leaving O'Connor to manage as best he could.[2]

An unattributed melodramatic version of the arrival had O'Connor and the driver ripping the door from the hinges and using this as a stretcher to carry the Kingfish.

A nurse on private duty at "the Lake" that night gives a version that incorporates elements of both stories.

Doris Carnes remembers that the emergency room door was broken from the hinges before Sister Michael, head nurse on duty that night, could respond to the persistent hammering of O'Connor and others who had run or driven across the dike from the capitol.

According to Miss Carnes:

> "...There was a tremendous banging on
> the door, shouting and yelling, 'Help, help,' and
> the door was broken from the hinges before Sister

Michael could get there. Politicians in the capitol
when the shooting took place ran across the dike
between the two buildings, following the private
car bringing Senator Long.

"The tremendous influx of politicians
and hangers-on completely overran the
hospital...the hoopla aroused every patient, of
course. You cannot believe the commotion."[3]

Miss Carnes remembers that all night long men ran up and down the
stairs, shouting to each other, "The senator is shot! The senator is shot!"

O'Connor's recollection is that Dr. Arthur Vidrine, along with two interns, was in the hospital room where Huey was taken. Long asked Sister
Michael to "pray for me" and the nun countered with the suggestion that she and
Long pray together. The Catholic nun began her prayers and Huey, a Baptist,
joined in.[4]

O'Connor recalls that the medical personnel present began to remove
Long's clothes with nail clippers. Fournet remembered it differently. "They were
talking about seeing where the bullet went and they were going to take his
clothes off. So they cut his clothes off with my knife." Fournet added
philosophically, "Which I lost. I never got it back."

Fournet remembered that Vidrine made the determination that a single
bullet entered Long's body below the right ribs and exited through the small of
the back. Fournet said, "It didn't look like anything but a little pin hole."[5]

It is worth noting that Fournet's description of the wound of exit as "a
little pin hole" is far from the jagged slash that invariably characterizes a wound
caused by a bullet after it leaves the body. The wound would be described by
others as "a small blue puncture" and one of the coroner's jury that examined
Long's corpse remarked that the wound would probably have never been noticed
by the jury if it had not been pointed out to them.

During Long's surgery, Vidrine would have reason to question his early
diagnosis and wonder if the "little pin hole" was, in fact, a penetration or simply
an indentation. Another point worth noting is that neither Fournet nor O'Connor
mentioned anything about powder burns around Long's abdominal wound. In
1942, Fournet wrote a letter to a physician researching the Long shooting in
which he described the front wound as "a relatively small opening, which was
surrounded by powder burns." However, if the wound of entry was made by a
pistol pressed tightly against the abdomen, it could be expected that powder
burns would be massive and readily noticeable.[6]

While Long was being prepared for surgery, his supporters moved to
seal off the hospital. The single road connecting the building with Baton Rouge
to the south was closed. Only physicians, members of Long's political family
and reporters were allowed to use it.

Even pedestrian traffic was halted and residents in the immediate area of the hospital were forced to take circuitous alternate routes to reach their homes.

Uniformed and plainclothed state police barred entrance to the hospital itself, lining the half mile stretch of road between the capitol and the hospital which Long had traveled minutes before.

After Long's clothes had been cut from his body and Vidrine, assisted by interns, had checked pulse and pressure, the patient was wheeled into a room that was reserved by the hospital for Catholic bishops. Nurse Carnes remembers that the furniture was "not hospital in style." Beautiful hand embroidered sheets tailored by the nuns for the exclusive use of the bishops would soon receive the ailing body of Louisiana's Kingfish. It was in this setting that Long rested and discussed with Vidrine the operation that both knew was inevitable.

From the hospital, calls went out to physicians throughout the state.

Asked by Vidrine if he had a choice of a surgeon to perform the operation, Huey asked the physician to summon Urban Maes, prominent New Orleans surgeon and professor of surgery at LSU Medical School.

Maes was known to Vidrine and there is evidence that some friction existed between the two doctors.

Vidrine, a young surgeon from the southwest Louisiana rural French community of Ville Platte, was not held in high esteem by many members of the New Orleans medical establishment. Instead, he was considered by them to be, purely and simply, a political appointee who had reached a level of great prestige in medical circles only through the largesse of the Kingfish.

This was far from the truth, but it is a fact that there existed a political relationship between Long and Vidrine. This relationship tended to obscure many of the talents and capabilities of Arthur Vidrine.

When Long seized control of the administration of Charity Hospital in New Orleans in 1929 ("Big Charity," as it is commonly referred to because its size dwarfs other hospitals in the state) he had the governing board remove the incumbent superintendent in favor of his own choice, Arthur Vidrine.

Vidrine's credentials were good. He was a Rhodes scholar and was considered to be a competent practitioner. However, Long's tactless and brutal maneuvering to take command of Charity placed a cloud over Vidrine's head which would keep him forever in disfavor with many of his colleagues in New Orleans.

A year after he took over Charity Hospital, Long went even further to alienate the New Orleans medical community and to debase Vidrine in their eyes. He disclosed plans to establish a medical school in New Orleans under the sponsorship of LSU.

This news was viewed as an attempt to strike back at Tulane University (which operated the only medical school in the state) for its refusal to grant

Long an honorary doctorate, an honor later bestowed on the Kingfish by Loyola University, a Catholic institution in New Orleans. Vidrine was chosen by Long to be dean of the new school. The young rural surgeon had now become, thanks to Long's kindness, one of the most influential physicians in the state, since he not only headed its largest hospital, but also the newest medical school.

About the same time, an incident involving a Tulane Medical School faculty member further eroded the relationship between Tulane and the Kingfish and, in the bargain, Vidrine.

Dr. Edward William Alton Ochsner, head of the prestigious Tulane department of surgery, had written a letter to a colleague criticizing the political climate in Louisiana. The letter read, in part:

> "I feel that the outlook at Tulane as far as building up a department is concerned is absolutely hopeless. The University is dependent upon Charity Hospital, which is a state institution and which is in the control of politics. The University is merely tolerated in the Hospital and there is no cooperation at all. The house staff is appointed by the Hospital and the University has no control whatever over it....Under the present system...it is impossible to train men as surgeons."[7]

The letter was stolen from Ochsner's coat as it hung on a coat rack at Charity Hospital. It was given to Vidrine who, in turn, showed it to Long. Long flew into a rage and, at a meeting of the board of administrators of the hospital on September 13, 1930, Ochsner was bumped from the Charity staff as senior visiting surgeon.

Things got worse between Tulane and Charity and, as a result, between Vidrine and the New Orleans medical fraternity. Vidrine would not answer telephone calls from the dean of the medical school. The eye, ear, nose and throat department (where Carl Weiss had received his training) was put on temporary appointment. Prior to the opening of the LSU School of Medicine, Vidrine was raiding the ranks of the Tulane faculty for doctors. One doctor who declined an appointment to the LSU Med School was denied his scheduled appointment as senior house surgeon at Charity because he had been "disloyal" to Huey Long.

These actions combined to convince many physicians in the city that what was originally a purely political power grab to control jobs at Charity Hospital had become a vendetta against the professional staff of the hospital and the New Orleans medical fraternity. This suspicion was strengthened when physicians known to be anti-Long experienced difficulty in obtaining "visiting doctor" privileges at the reorganized Charity Hospital.

It was generally believed in New Orleans that Urban Maes was the original choice of Long to head the new medical school. But Maes was pes-

"I was elected in 1928 and they impeached me in 1929!" Long was fond of relating the perils he faced from enemies during his political career. He is shown here in May, 1928 as he delivered his inaugural address as governor. Two years later he was elected to the U.S. Senate. He took the oath of office two years later, in 1932, having been fearful of leaving the state in the hands of a hostile lieutenant governor. Less than four years later he was dead. *(Courtesy William B. Wisdom Collection, Tulane University Library)*

The Kingfish as a young man. A high school dropout, Huey Long tried his hand at various modes of employment, including that of a "drummer," or traveling salesman. He peddled Cottolene, a vegetable shortening, and staged bake-offs wherein contestants vied for prizes for the tastiest cakes. It was at one of these

bake-offs that he met Rose McConnell, whom he later wed. It was she, along with his older brother, Julius, who convinced Huey that he should attend college and become a lawyer. *(Courtesy Louisiana State Library)*

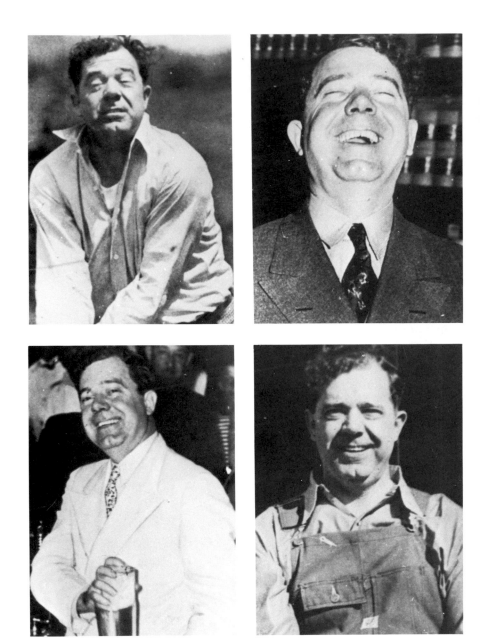

The many faces of the Kingfish. Huey Long, except for Franklin Roosevelt, was the most photographed, most publicized and most characterized man of his time. His features lent themselves easily to caricature and cartoonists took advantage of this. Here he is shown, clockwise from top left, digging divots on the golf course; enjoying a hearty laugh; relaxing between wood-chopping exercises; and teaching a New York bartender how to concoct a Ramos gin fizz. (*Courtesy Louisiana State Library*)

This bucolic scene of Huey Long eating watermelon was, according to older brother Julius, staged so that Huey could "show that he was a man who loved his father." Julius commented acidly, "Huey took a photographer with him, visited our father, cut a watermelon raised by (brother) Earl and had his picture taken with our father eating Earl's watermelon on Earl's farm." *(Courtesy Hermann Deutsch Collection, Tulane University)*

Music! Music! Music! Despite Huey Long's tone deaf musical ear, he loved music. His music man and co-composer of "Every Man A King" remembered that Huey would listen to orchestral music for hours at a time. In the top photo he leads the LSU band. In the bottom picture he tries serenading a group of attractive young women, despite his inability to play the guitar. *(Top photo courtesy Louisiana State Library, bottom courtesy William B. Wisdom Collection, Tulane University Library)*

Some maintain that Huey Long's final words were, "What will happen to my boys and girls at LSU?" While there is some doubt that he actually said those words, his feelings for Louisiana's flagship university and its students were deep and genuine. He saw that the university was adequately financed and took a special interest in the university's football team. In the top photo, he leads a contingent of students on the way to an out-of-state game and in the lower photo he gives advice to game officials. *(Top photo courtesy Louisiana State Library, bottom photo courtesy Louisiana State Museum)*

Democratic party chief James Farley shares a rare moment of peace with the Kingfish (top photo). Farley enlisted Long's aid in electing Franklin Roosevelt President in 1932 and lived to regret it. *(Courtesy Louisiana State Library)*

John F. "Honey Boy" Fitzgerald, grandfather of President John F. Kennedy, cozies up to the Kingfish in Boston when Fitzgerald was head of the Boston Port Authority in 1935. Long was considered the *enfant terrible* of the Democratic party and leaders went out of their way to avoid ruffling his feathers. *(Courtesy UPI Bettmann Newsphotos)*

"How'd ya like them ersters?" New Orleans Mayor Robert S. Maestri asked Franklin Roosevelt during the President's 1937 visit to the Crescent City. Maestri is on the right and Louisiana Governor Richard Leche on the left. *(Courtesy Associated Press/Wide World Photos)*

Heads we win, tails we lose. The Kingfish meets with political associate James Noe. Noe was an incorporator in Win or Lose Oil, a venture that reaped great dividends for insiders within the Long administrations. It was incorporated in November, 1934 with $200 paid-in cash and 100 shares. Less than a year later the company paid dividends of $2,000 a share. *(Courtesy LSU-Shreveport Archives)*

The Huey Long years were punctuated by one violent act after another. Fearful of assassination, Long was constantly surrounded by his cadre of bodyguards and national guardsmen. In New Orleans (top photo) he attended meetings buffered by half a dozen national guardsmen and additional bodyguards. In Baton Rouge, citizens occupied the courthouse and were later ambushed at the downtown airport where an anti-Long citizen was shot and a Long supporter badly beaten. *(Top photo courtesy William B. Wisdom Collection, Tulane University Library; bottom photo courtesy Louisiana State Museum)*

These remarkable character studies give an indication of the intense feelings that Carl Weiss, top, and Huey Long were capable of. At issue in determining the guilt or innocence of Weiss is his record of service as a compassionate and capable physician. Some, however, have alluded to a darker side that could have influenced his actions during his confrontation with Long. On the other hand, there was no veneer covering the emotions of the Kingfish. The bottom photo was taken in 1933 during a senatorial investigation alleging fraud in the election of Senator John H. Overton. *(Carl Weiss photos courtesy of Louisiana State Library, Long photo courtesy AP/Wide World Photos)*

Two artists give their interpretations of the shooting of Huey Long. The sketch at left was done by John Chase, editorial cartoonist who traveled to Baton Rouge hours after Long was shot. The painting at right was done by artist John McCrady, who conducted an art school in the French Quarter in New Orleans. Chase's version was based principally upon the recollection of Charles "Chick" Frampton, New Orleans *Item* reporter. There are significant differences between the two versions, prompting the suspicion that perhaps McCrady had other sources of information. However, both versions place Carl Weiss between the

armed bodyguards and Huey Long. An initial shot missed Weiss and struck Long or, perhaps, traveled through Weiss' body and lodged in Long's abdomen, accounting for the frontal wound. McCrady's painting shows clearly the possibility that a ricochet from the bodyguards' guns could have struck Long in the back, accounting for the second wound. *(Chase photo from the New Orleans Item, September 9, 1935; McCrady painting from the collection of Keith Marshall)*

The Kingfish is laid to rest. Huey Long's funeral was one of the biggest events ever in Louisiana's capital. Thousands of people came to pay their last respects and guards had difficulty restraining those who plucked at the flowers covering the bier. Newsreel cameras clicked while airplanes circled overhead to record the scene for posterity.

His ceremony less ostentatious than the funeral of the Kingfish, Carl Weiss was nevertheless laid to rest amid profuse outpourings of sympathy from the citizens of Baton Rouge. Virtually the entire membership of the East Baton Rouge Parish Medical Society stood in ankle-deep rain as he was lowered into his grave. Bottom photo shows the duplex where Weiss, his wife and three-month-old son lived, a stone's throw from the state capitol where he met his end. *(Top photo courtesy Louisiana State Museum, bottom courtesy Louisiana State Library)*

The Eternal Kingfish
(Courtesy Louisiana State Library)

simistic about the prospects for survival of the proposed institution, feeling that it would not receive necessary accreditation. He declined the honor.

However, the opinion of Maes and others to the contrary, the doors of the new school were opened in 1931 to provide medical training to 109 students. By 1935, there were over 900 students enrolled.

Long's continuing interference in the affairs of the school threatened its rating by the Association of Southern Universities. Advised that the rating would be safe if a competent surgeon like Urban Maes were installed as head of the department of surgery, Long hastily complied. Thus Maes, who had in haste turned down the top position at the school, was appointed to the staff in a subordinate position to Vidrine.

When Maes was advised of Long's wish that he perform the surgery, he contacted an associate, Dr. James Rives. The Long hierarchy had made plans for them to fly from New Orleans to Baton Rouge but they decided to drive instead, believing that travel to and from airports in both cities would wipe out any savings in time effected by the faster flying aircraft.

But fate stepped in.

Just beyond the New Orleans city line, in the adjacent Jefferson Parish community of Metairie, an oncoming car with glaring headlights caused Rives to swerve in order to avoid a head-on collision. His car snagged its undercarriage on a mound at the side of the winding road, disabling it for further travel. A tow truck was called. The physicians had little choice but to wait while precious minutes ticked away.[8]

Maes and Rives were not the only physicians being summoned. There were dozens of others contacted by Long, Vidrine and many of Long's political associates. Jimmy O'Connor, commenting upon the mass of medical talent at "the Lake," observed tartly, "Everybody had a doctor that was a bigshot up there!"[9]

In Baton Rouge, Long leaders attempted to contact Dr. Clarence Lorio, prominent local physician and Long leader. Lorio, exhausted by 13 straight hours of work, was at home with his telephone receiver off the cradle while he tried to get some badly needed rest. He was finally aroused by neighbors who thought it odd that his car was still parked in front of his house while the radio and newspaper extras heralded the news of Long's impending surgery. They pounded on his door until the sleeping Lorio awoke and joined the assemblage at the hospital.

His brother Cecil, a pediatrician, had been notified of the shooting earlier and was one of the first physicians to reach the hospital.

Also in Baton Rouge, Vidrine asked Sister Michael to notify Baton Rouge surgeon William Cook. Cook had been house surgeon at New Orleans Charity Hospital several years before and was known to Vidrine as one who had a great deal of experience with gunshot wounds of the abdomen.

In Shreveport, Huey's personal friend and appointee to the superintendency of Shreveport Charity Hospital, E.L. Sanderson, was contacted.

At Long's request, New Orleans surgeon Russell Stone was also called.

Vidrine drained the staff of New Orleans Charity. A physician in training at the hospital at the time recalled that the residents ("We were what you'd call super interns") were pressed into service, joining the fight to save Long's life.

Dr. Reichard Kahle, one of the "super interns," remembered, "They split the staff. Half were left at Charity and the other half were rushed up to take care of him."

Vidrine personally called one of the residents whom he held in high esteem, Felix Plaunche, and told him to contact three other residents whom Vidrine wanted in Baton Rouge. They were Edgar Hull, Willard Ellender (brother of Long's speaker of the house) and Roy Theriot.[10]

There were others.

The hospital strained under the weight of medical men and politicians elbowing each other aside to be part of this great moment in history. The institution was transformed into a political-medical caucus that one physician described as "nothing short of chaotic."

The description was offered by Dr. Rives, the traveling companion of Dr. Maes, who arrived in Baton Rouge after the operation had been completed. Here is how he remembers it:

> "Several physicians seemed to be on hand and in the case of a critically injured patient, when no one of the attending doctors is actually in command and giving the orders of the crew of which he is the captain...well, all I can say is that even during the four hours or so when I was there between about 1:00 a.m. and the time I started back to New Orleans, which I reached at daybreak, the situation was nothing short of chaotic."[11]

A nurse assisting at the operation reached the same conclusion:

> "Too many people were giving orders and I think this was said at that time by different people—nurses and so on. There were so many doctors in there and each one giving different opinions and different orders...There was so much controversy...I heard there were conflicts.
>
> "One doctor would say, 'Let's do this' and maybe another doctor would have another opinion."[12]

Time slipped away while Vidrine waited for Urban Maes, Long's choice for the surgery, to arrive. A steady stream of interns, physicians, nurses and politicians wandered in and out of Long's room.

Dr. Cecil Lorio checked pulse and blood pressure every 15 minutes. A pattern had been established. The pulse rate continued to increase and the blood pressure continued to fall. Long asked about the readings and, when advised what they were, speculated that there probably was internal bleeding. Lorio conceded this possibility, although he reasoned that the cause of the readings could be the result of shock, rather than loss of blood.

In Long's case, the systolic blood pressure dropped from an estimated 130 down to 90; the pulse rate increased from an estimated 75 beats per minute to 110. The heart was desperately attempting to supply blood to the system but it was a losing battle. Apparently the blood fluid was escaping from the circulatory system and leaking into an anatomical space, possibly the abdominal cavity or the area to the rear, the retroperitoneal cavity, which houses the kidneys.

Some accounts have it that Long made the decision to operate. Told of pulse and pressure readings, he said, "Come on, let's go be operated on!"

Another version holds that it was Dr. Vidrine who realized that the time had come when surgery could be postponed no longer. He advised Long of this. Long asked him who would perform the operation. Told it would be Vidrine and asked by Vidrine if he had objections, Long answered, "No."

But there is yet another version of the manner in which the decision was made and this comes from the ubiquitous Seymour Weiss, who drove at breakneck speed from New Orleans to be at the bedside of the Kingfish, ruining the engine of a new Cadillac automobile in the effort.

Weiss said that the decision to perform surgery without waiting for Maes to appear was made by "all of us." The phrase "all of us," used by Weiss, would seem clearly to include the assembled politicans at the hospital. In an interview he said, "Dr. Vidrine insisted that any further delay was progressively lessening the senator's chances. The other physicians present agreed that the outlook was not hopeful. Vidrine was the physician in charge and the rest of us were laymen."

Further, Weiss explains that the decision was made even in advance of receiving the intelligence that the surgeon whom Huey had chosen, Dr. Maes, had been involved in the highway mishap. Weiss explains, "The time came when we either had to agree to let the operation be performed at once or take upon ourselves the risk of endangering the man's life...In view of the medical opinions, the rest of us—all being individuals who were closed to Huey—were just about unanimous in agreeing that the doctors would proceed.[13]

And proceed they did, in one of the most bizarre and unreal operating room settings that one could possibly imagine. Spectators, bodyguards and medical professionals elbowed each other for space in the operating room.

Nurse Melinda Bandiera (now Delage), preoccupied with the task at hand, did not at first notice the spectators assembling in the operating room:

"I looked up when they were suturing him and I couldn't believe my eyes! And I thought, 'The nerve!' Sister Michael ruled with an iron hand and she was very staunch and Irish and determined but she couldn't control them."[14]

Cecil Lorio summed it up: "It was a vaudeville show."

Thus was one of the most celebrated operations in history begun. Dr. Arthur Vidrine, second choice for the task, required to obtain the blessings of politicians and political cronies of the Kingfish, was forced to perform under the watchful eye of the Long hierarchy and intimidated by the presence of police, bodyguards and henchmen.

Before the ether cap descended over his face, Long gave his instructions: "Nobody is to say anything about this. I'll do all the talking."[15]

CHAPTER ELEVEN

The Operation

Little is known about what actually happened in the operating room of Our Lady of the Lake Sanitarium on the night of September 8, 1935. Charged by Long to remain silent, everyone involved in the surgery has, even until now, steadfastly refused to release any information or divulge any details.

What is known is generally not believed.

This curtain of secrecy has made it all but impossible to determine with any degree of certainty the details of the operation performed upon Senator Huey Long. This is unfortunate, because it forces us to make judgments based on other available evidence, which is clearly incomplete and fragmentary.

Some feel that the medical care afforded Long borrowed extra time for the patient and was the best that could have been hoped for; others believe the treatment hastened his demise, that there was a direct cause-and-effect relationship between the quality of care he received and his death. Perhaps there were very good reasons why things happened as they did, but these reasons are not readily apparent and those who participated in the operation stubbornly refused to reveal them.

All of the surgeons who were directly involved in the operation are now dead. While they lived, all refused to be interviewed. Requests for interviews were met with rejection out of hand.

The Long family spokesman is United States Senator Russell B. Long, eldest son of the Kingfish. The two other children, Catherine and Palmer, defer to Russell's judgment in this matter. The physicians I spoke with concerning Long's death made it clear they would not speak without the authorization of Russell. For his part, Russell has consistently refused to be interviewed or to extend cooperation of any kind, maintaining that he is satisfied with the "official" investigation and that any "unofficial" investigation would serve no useful purpose.

Given this unbending attitude toward release of any information, any attempt to reconstruct the chronology of the period from September 8, 1935 (when Long entered the hospital) to September 10, 1935 (when he died) is difficult, if not impossible.

Medical records are sealed. Our Lady of the Lake Sanitarium (now Our Lady of the Lake Medical Center) will not make them available without permission of the family of Senator Long. But even if such permission were to be forthcoming, there is grave doubt if information could be obtained that would shed light on the mystery that still surrounds Long's death.

The medical records have been expurgated, stripped of vital information that could help explain causes of Long's death.

I was rebuffed in every attempt I made to obtain the hospital records. The fact that I eventually gained access to them reflects no credit on the hospital or the Long family. It was through the good offices of Dr. Hypolite Landry, coroner of East Baton Rouge Parish, that I finally laid my hands on them. In his official capacity, Dr. Landry asked for and received these records and copied them for me.

In an initial contact, I spoke to an official of the hospital who explained that permission from the Long family would have to be forthcoming if the records were to be released. The official confidentially told me of her dilemma, upon joining the staff of Our Lady of the Lake, in finding the paucity of information contained in the records of the hospital's most famous case. She had assumed that there was additional material kept under lock and key but was told by Sister Michael, the head nurse on duty the night Long was admitted, that the incomplete documents were all that remained.

It would seem that an assassination as celebrated as that of Huey Long would have been the subject of many serious studies. It is possible that there have been efforts in this direction that were discouraged by the stonewall attitude of those who, possessing vital knowledge, could have assisted. But, regardless of the reason, the body of knowledge about Long's medical care is meager indeed.

There is a single medical work extant, one produced by New Orleans surgeon Frank L. Loria, entitled "Historical Aspects of Penetrating Wounds of the Abdomen" and published in the December, 1948 issue of *International Abstracts of Surgery*. In his monograph, Dr. Loria notes of the Long case that "nothing on the case's surgical history has been published, except the incomplete and unreliable newspaper medical accounts of this tragedy."

But even as professional and credentialed a researcher as Dr. Loria was, it proved to be no cakewalk to obtain the necessary information to include Long's shooting in Loria's definitive work on penetrating wounds of the abdomen. The hospital refused him access to the records. One writer said Dr. Vidrine was reluctant to talk to Dr. Loria. Loria says this is not the case.

However, he was at least able to prevail upon the hospital to fill out a questionnaire and he pieced together some of the facts.

He also contacted Doctors William Cook and Cecil Lorio, who were likewise sparing in the information given. He notes that he was given "brief accounts of the surgical facts in the case."[1]

If we are to reach a judgment concerning the type of medical attention received by Long during the last 30 hours of his life, we must rely on the sparse information that is available, grudgingly given and pockmarked by wide gaps in continuity. It is inescapable that a judgment is not flattering to those responsible for the medical care.

When Huey Long entered the hospital that Sunday night, his symptoms seemed to indicate that he was bleeding internally. His pulse was rapid; his blood pressure was low; he repeatedly called for ice. These are the classic symptoms of internal hemorrhage. However, it should be remembered that these are also the classic symptoms of shock.

He was placed in room 314 of the hospital. The foot of his bed was elevated to increase circulation to the brain, a technique designed to avoid brain ischemia—loss of oxygen to the brain. This was another indication that he may have been suffering from internal bleeding.

When Long was examined by Vidrine, it was noted that he had a wound in the abdomen just below the right rib cage and another wound, smaller in size, in the back to the right of the spine. Dr. Loria explained:

> "...the bullet that struck Senator Long
> entered just below the border of the right ribs an-
> teriorly, somewhat lateral to the midclavicular
> line. The missile perforated it just below the ribs
> on the right side posteriorly and to the inner side
> of the midscapular line..."

"Midscapular" and "midclavicular" both refer to the middle of the right side of the body, the clavicle being the collar bone and the scapula being a large bone that helps make up the shoulder.

Given these coordinates and assuming that the bullet passed completely through the body, it would have been impossible for the bullet not to have hit the kidney. Dr. Loria remarked, "Shortly after the victim's arrival in the hospital, he went into profound shock and presented clinical evidence of internal hemorrhage." Once again, this evidence could also indicate the effect of shock.[2]

Good medical procedure would have called for tests to verify this clinical evidence. Even in 1935, techniques for testing for the possible presence of blood in the urine included catheterization and testing for blood in the intestinal tract by digital or proctoscopic examination of the rectum.

But, in the face of overwhelming evidence that the kidney could have been—in fact, certainly had been—injured, some have charged that Long was not checked for bleeding before he underwent surgery. Nor does it seem that Long was x-rayed. There is no guarantee that an x-ray would have determined if Long was suffering internal bleeding unless the hemorrhage was truly of monumental proportions. However, it would have certainly disclosed the existence of a bullet or bullets in Long's body. Use of x-rays was standard operating procedure in 1935. Its omission would have constituted a gross error on the part of attending doctors.

Did Vidrine conduct the examinations to which Dr. Loria refers? Some say yes. Others say no.

It is unbelievable that a surgeon with his credentials could omit such a basic procedure. Although Long's hospital care has cast a pall upon Vidrine's abilities, it is hard to believe that he was even remotely capable of the malpractice implied by such a stupid mistake.

Vidrine was no quack. He was a skilled and competent surgeon. This is well attested to by his record.

He was born in Ville Platte, in southwest Louisiana. He graduated from Tulane School of Medicine in 1921 at the age of 25. His qualifications were such that he was chosen to be a Rhodes scholar. His impatience with classroom study and his fascination with the actual practice of medicine caused him to be chastised by an Oxford official who wrote him, "You spend most of your time going to London for clinical work."

After interning at Charity Hospital in New Orleans from 1922 to 1924, he returned to southwest Louisiana to become chief surgeon and administrator at the Eunice Sanitarium. This small hospital boasted that, in 1926, under Vidrine's guidance, the sanitarium had undertaken 220 major operations and had experienced only six deaths.

Four years later the New Orleans press reported that Charity Hospital at New Orleans, under the leadership of Vidrine, had cut its death rate in half. The press also featured several striking examples of Vidrine's surgery: a delicate operation on a child who shot himself in the head with a homemade gun and successful surgery to remove a toy frying pan from the stomach of a three-year-old boy.[3]

Moreover, as superintendent of Charity Hospital, Vidrine was the overseer of the greatest training ground in the world for the treatment of penetrating wounds of the abdomen. Dr. Loria scarcely conceals his admiration for the hospital staff's expertise, pointing out that it admitted an average of 65 cases of penetrating gunshot and stab wounds to the abdomen every year during the period 1900-1948. Loria quotes a World War I surgeon as having "jokingly suggested that the students in the Army Medical School should come to Charity Hospital for part of their military training."[4]

Armed with this expertise and carrying the finest of credentials, is it possible that Arthur Vidrine allowed Long to be wheeled into the operating room with no preoperative treatment other than periodic pulse and pressure checks? Strange! Very strange!

Shortly before surgery, Long was given a blood transfusion, the first of four he would receive before his death. The donor was Senate President Pro Tem Jimmy Noe, who was a partner with the Kingfish in the Win or Lose Oil Company formed the year before. Noe and Long lay side by side as the vital fluid was transferred from Noe's veins to Huey's. Caught up in the drama of that moment of history, Noe brushed aside the cautions of medical personnel that he rest before leaving the transfusion site. He bounded from the stretcher, strode toward the door—and fell flat on his face. He was revived from his faint in less than a minute. [5]

No one has ever given a clear picture of Long's surgery. The exact roles of the physicians attending Long in the operating room are unclear. The hospital records list Vidrine as surgeon and Cook, Cecil Lorio and Clarence Lorio as assistants. However, two of the nurses present do not remember it exactly that way.

Theoda Carriere, a nurse interviewed by Hermann Deutsch, recalled that at one point in the proceedings Cook looked up and announced, "Well, my relief has arrived," after which he left the operating room, to be replaced by a Dr. Ben Chamberlain.[6]

I interviewed a second nurse present at the operation, Melinda Delage. Ms. Delage has signed an affidavit and vividly recalls that Dr. Cook was replaced, but she does not mention Dr. Chamberlain. She remembers, "Upon near completion of the surgery, Dr. Clarence Lorio arrived and replaced the surgeon, Dr. Cook. Dr. Cook stepped aside." This version is supported by others.[7]

A third source, Baton Rouge physician Ashton Robins, was at Our Lady of the Lake that night and saw Long enter the hospital. It is not clear to me whether Dr. Robins saw the surgery or whether his version was obtained from someone who did, but he told me:

"Billy Cook started the surgery. When Clarence Lorio came in, Billy stepped back...he changed from the assistants' side of the table and ran the tray. The nurse who was running the tray then became the scrub nurse and she kept her gloves and her mask and everything on and she began to circulate and take instruments that were brought in from the sterilizer and handed them to the operating team."[8]

The only detailed description of the surgery was given by Dr. Loria in his 1948 monograph. It follows:

"Under ether anesthesia the abdomen

was opened by an upper right rectus muscle-split-
ting incision. Very little blood was found in the
peritoneal cavity. The liver, gall bladder and
stomach were free of injury. A small hematoma,
about the size of a silver dollar, was found in the
mesentery of the small intestine. The only in-
traperitoneal damage found was a 'small' perforation of the hepatic flexure, which accounted for a
slight amount of soiling of the peritoneum. Both
the wounds of entrance and exit in the colon were
sutured and further spillage was stopped...."

There is a question about the amount of blood found in Long's
peritoneal cavity. In Dr. Loria's monograph, quoted above, he reported "very
little blood was found." Obviously he received this information from one of the
three doctors he interviewed: Cook, Vidrine or Cecil Lorio.

This description of Long's abdomen was published in 1948. However,
in 1971, writing for the *Louisiana Historical Quarterly,* Loria reproduced a
medical bulletin that was posted by Dr. Vidrine at 5:15 a.m. Monday morning
following the surgery in which "...considerable hemorrhage from the mesentery
and omentum" was observed. Dr. Loria says this is "the one and only bulletin"
posted by Dr. Vidrine, although a bulletin had been issued earlier at 2:00 a.m.[9]

Following surgery, the abdomen was closed in layers, the incision was
sutured and the operation was concluded. According to Judge Fournet, who inquired of Vidrine about Long's chances of survival, Vidrine answered, "It was
nothing. It was just a perforation of the intestines."[10]

Following the operation, rumors began to circulate that a bullet had
been retrieved from Long's body, although none of the official pronouncements
from the hospital even alluded to such a development. Physicians and Long
spokesmen doggedly clung to their story that there had been a single bullet that
made its way through Long's body, exiting from his back.

But many doubted that explanation.

One of the earliest dispatches filed, a story in an extra edition of the
New Orleans *Item,* took note of the fact that, immediately following the shooting, "Wild confusion then prevailed and persons gathered in groups all over the
building, hearing rumors that Long had been twice wounded...."[11]

The *Literary Digest,* in its September 14 issue, which must have been
prepared shortly after the shooting, considering the state of the printing art at the
time, reported that chief bodyguard Murphy Roden was distraught about the
episode. "He was inconsolable, despite the fact that he had almost saved the
senator from being hit by the two bullets which ploughed through his body."[12]

Special Agent in Charge Magee wired FBI Director J. Edgar Hoover at
10:35 p.m. Sunday night (almost an hour before Long's operation) that Long had

been shot twice.[13]

Those who were in the operating room that night obviously had heard the news about the purported second bullet. Dr. Cecil Lorio recalled that, as the surgery progressed, Long's supporters would call out, "How's he doing, Doc? Did you find the bullet?"[14]

At one tense moment during the operation there was extracted from Long's body a small dark object which could have resembled a spent bullet. It was placed on a gauze pad and passed among the assembled doctors. One by one, they quietly studied the specimen and then passed it along. Finally one physician, perhaps more observant than the others, lifted the gauze pad to his nose for an olfactory examination.

He wrinkled his nose, looked intently at his colleagues and soberly described the item: "Shit."[15]

Was there a bullet removed from Long at the hospital? Was he shot once or twice, as many were beginning to insist?

Ms. Delage, who was closest to the surgeons attending Long, doubts that any bullet was found, although she concedes that she was engrossed in her principal duty of passing instruments to the doctors. She feels that if Dr. Cook had found a bullet, "He would have taken a pair of hemostats, under sterile precautions, and picked it up and he would have put it on this table (demonstrating) right here." However, Ms. Delage's conclusion seems to be prompted more by her regard for Dr. Cook's impeccable ethics than by any sharp-eyed observations in the operating room.[16]

There are those in Baton Rouge who claim that attending physicians confided to them that a bullet was removed from Long at the hospital. An acquaintance of Dr. Cook says that the physician told him of the bullet's removal the morning following the surgery. Cook also told a patient the same story.[17]

Dr. Clarence Lorio told a young acquaintance the morning after the surgery that "a small caliber bullet" had been removed during surgery.[18]

Another physician, not on the operating team, told a colleague many years later that he had seen Dr. Vidrine find "a flat lead slug imbedded in the adrenal gland just above the kidney."[19]

This same bullet is mentioned in notes made by author T. Harry Williams during his interviews. On October 3, 1960, a Mr. J.C. Broussard, who was the owner of a bar and grill in 1935, was interviewed by Williams. Dr. Williams' notes concerning the interview with Broussard read:

> "After Huey was shot, Broussard talked
> to Dr. V. (Vidrine), who told him that Huey had
> two bullets in him, one a .38. Broussard believes
> that Messina shot Huey because according to B.,
> Messina had a .38."[20]

(Actually, bodyguard Joe Messina carried a .45; it was Murphy Roden who was armed with the .38.)

According to a member of the Vidrine family, Arthur Vidrine gave a bullet to a cousin with the explanation, "This is the bullet taken out of Huey." My source is L. Coleman Vidrine, Jr., who is the son of Arthur's cousin, L. Coleman Vidrine, Sr., the one to whom Arthur gave the bullet. Coleman has been left with the impression that Arthur was concerned about his own safety and gave the bullet to Coleman's father as a kind of life insurance.[21]

Coleman, like J.B. Broussard, identifies the bullet as a .38 caliber, the size of the weapon carried by Murphy Roden. (Weiss was carrying a .32.) Coleman recently retired from the Louisiana State Police after having risen through the ranks to the position of captain. It must be presumed that he has a good knowledge of firearms and ballistics.

The bullet is one of at least two mysteries of the operating room. The second is the decision to conclude the operation following the repair of the wounds to the colon. If this is the complete record of the surgery, it paints all the surgeons involved as absolute dolts, altogether devoid of the slimmest understanding of human anatomy.

All concerned conceded the strong possibility that Long was bleeding internally. The pulse and blood pressure readings indicated this. Yet, when the abdominal cavity was opened, there was very little blood. There was a small blood clot and a slight amount of soiling of the peritoneum. Or was there?

Now, if the pulse and pressure readings, in the words of Dr. Frank Loria, "presented clinical evidence of internal hemorrhage" and there was very little blood in the peritoneum, then obviously the blood had to be elsewhere. That elsewhere had to be another important area or compartment in the trunk of the body, the retroperitoneal space, which houses the kidneys. This space is immediately to the rear of the frontal cavity, separated by fleshy folds known as the mesentery and omentum and the peritoneal lining.

If the path of the bullet had been traced, it would have led unmistakably to the kidney and with this revelation, prudent surgical procedure would have demanded another operation to arrest the kidney hemorrhage.

But this was not done. Why not? Even if we assume that Vidrine had suddenly forgotten every single thing he had ever learned about human anatomy, what of the other physicians participating? What of Doctors Lorio, Cook, Chamberlain and others who were in attendance? Certainly Vidrine was not operating in a vacuum. Others must have been aware that elementary medical procedure was being violated.

There is something missing from this scenario. It cannot be possible that distinguished and qualified medical practitioners would allow a thing like this to happen. But this is what the record shows and during the intervening 50 years, no one has broken a consensus of silence to come forward and explain exactly what happened in surgery on September 8, 1935.

Thus the surgeon who established a record for saving lives in the Eunice Clinic and who slashed the death rate at New Orleans Charity in half suddenly abandoned all surgical judgment and condemns to death his leader, his friend, his benefactor and the most important patient the Rhodes scholar would ever treat.

It is incredible. Perhaps unbelievable. But, as ridiculous as it seems, this is the version that history has recorded as gospel and it is part and parcel of the "official" record.

Perhaps the confusion in the operating room made it impossible to hold the type of conference that would match opinions and conclusions of participating physicians so as to arrive at a consensus. Perhaps Cook was intimidated by Lorio, the Long leader in Baton Rouge; perhaps Lorio was intimidated by Vidrine; perhaps Vidrine was intimidated by Seymour Weiss, O.K. Allen, the Criminal Bureau of Investigation and the rest of Long's entourage who breathed down his gowned neck.

The "official" record makes no sense at all. It indicts Vidrine, Cook, the brothers Lorio and the Lord only knows how many other physicians who were in the operating room that night.

As we shall see later, the discovery of a bullet in Long's body during surgery answers many perplexing questions. Its existence was not only possible but also very probable—even necessary—if any logic is to be found in the sequence of events at the hospital.

But all were wedded to the "one man, one gun, one bullet" charade and it would continue to be played out to its tragic conclusion.

CHAPTER TWELVE

Death Of
A Kingfish

At 12:25 on Monday morning, about one hour after the operation of Long was begun, it was pronounced completed.

The patient was returned to room 314. Some have charged that his life's blood was draining inexorably from his kidney into the retroperitoneal space. T. Harry Williams wrote, "A renal duct to the kidney had obviously been hit by the bullet and Vidrine had not discovered this."[1]

Dr. Loria's monograph stated that catherization was not done until after the operation and the urine was found to contain much blood. Hermann Deutsch said that catheterization was not attempted until one of the visiting physicians from New Orleans suggested it and hospital records showed that it was not performed until 6:45 a.m. Monday, almost nine hours after the shooting.

The continued repetition of these charges by succeeding writers has led to an accepted conclusion that Long died because of inadequate medical treatment. There is some validity in this charge, but it is far from the entire truth, as we shall see farther along.

There was nothing but optimism in the communiques issued from the hospital by attending physicians. At 2:00 a.m. a bulletin was issued:

> "Senator Long was wounded by one bullet entering the upper right side, emerging from the back. The colon was punctured in two places. The first blood transfusion has been given the Senator with good results. The condition of Senator Long is thoroughly satisfactory. It will be 72 to 90 hours before further developments can be expected."[2]

Another bulletin, handwritten on Our Lady of the Lake Sanitarium stationery, was issued at 5:15 a.m. For the most part, it restated what was said in the first communique. It read:

> "Senator Long was shot through the right upper quadrant of the abdomen, the bullet going through the body.
>
> "There were two penetrations of the transverse colon and considerable hemorrhage from the mesentry and omentum.
>
> "The patient's condition is satisfactory and no important information will be available for about 72 hours."

It was attributed to "Dr. Arthur Vidrine, Surgeon in Charge, By: Earle J. Christenberry, Secty. to Sen. Long." (Note the reference to "considerable hemorrhage from the mesentery and omentum.")[3]

About 1:00 a.m., Dr. Maes, accompanied by Dr. Rives, arrived on the scene. A little later another specialist, Dr. Russell Stone, also summoned by Long, arrived.

It was reported that Stone was shocked when he learned the limited nature of the surgery, with no attention being given to the right kidney. After learning details of the shooting, Stone was certain that the kidney had been in the path of the single bullet which Vidrine said had entered the abdomen and exited from the back. It had to be.

There were harsh words exchanged between Stone and Vidrine. Stone later reported to friends in New Orleans that Vidrine had said that Long's kidney was bleeding, and that he (Vidrine) had made no effort to check the kidney or to stop the hemorrhage. According to Dr. Loria's monograph, Stone cautioned against another operation because of the certain prospect of death if additional surgery was performed.

According to others, Stone berated Vidrine for failing to check the kidney and he suggested that there should have been some examination of the retroperitoneal area to determine if the kidney had been harmed.

The story goes that Dr. Vidrine suggested to Dr. Stone that he (Stone) might perform the required operation, to which Stone was supposed to have replied, "This isn't my case and he isn't my patient. And besides, I don't operate on dead men."[4]

This strange episode is another curious incident in the strange death of Huey Long. Here we have learned medical men faced with the possibility that the operation had been a failure because a proper check of the kidney had been omitted in preoperative preparations (although Vidrine did not entirely ignore the kidney). Certainly Stone could chastise Vidrine for this oversight and there was little defense that Vidrine could offer.

But regardless of how well deserved Stone's censure was, it did nothing at all to improve the situation that faced the assembled physicians: a patient was dying before their eyes and they were apparently doing nothing to prevent it.

This is a fine kettle of fish! A medical catch-22. A patient is dying because of an injured kidney. Well, then, repair or remove the kidney! No. You can't! Why not? Because if the kidney is removed, it is possible that the patient will die!

On the other hand, there was always the slim prospect that additional surgery might succeed in arresting the flow of blood from the kidney.

I interviewed Dr. Ashton Robins, long time Baton Rouge physician and contemporary, as well as close friend, of Carl Weiss. Dr. Robins was at the Lady of the Lake that night. He quarrels with the decision not to operate further. He feels that any chance was worth taking, since death was certain to follow if nothing was done. He told me, "I have seen pregnant women with a hemorrhage and, when you clipped the kidney, you could see the color flowing into their cheeks immediately."[5]

It should be noted that the diagnosis of internal bleeding having been responsible for Long's eventual demise is not universally accepted. Later statements by Dr. Edgar Hull, one of the young residents of Charity Hospital summoned by Vidrine to provide postoperative care, questions if kidney damage was the cause of death. He offers an entirely different cause.

Hull tells us, "All this stuff about Maes telling Vidrine that Huey was bleeding internally—it couldn't have been. If Huey was bleeding, you know you ought to go back in right now and stop the bleeding. It just couldn't have been the case."

Moreover, Hull insists that all necessary pre- and postoperative care was afforded Long.

"We were catheterizing Huey from time to time and, in one specimen, there was some blood. Not a lot, but some. I personally thought and still think that it was trauma from the catheter. But anyhow, that brought up the question of whether he had been bleeding into his urinary tract."

Hull maintains that, when Dr. T. Jorda Kahle, who was head of the Urology Department of Charity and who was summoned by Vidrine, arrived, he "actually inserted needles into both perirenal spaces." Hull insists, "I was there when he did it."

According to Hull, Dr. Kahle said, "There is no bleeding around his kidneys or from his kidneys, you can forget that."[6]

However, Loria's monograph tells us:

> "(Dr. Kahle) aspirated the right perirenal
> area and upon withdrawing pure blood very easily,
> concluded that there was a massive retroperitoneal
> hemorrhage."[7]

I spoke to Dr. Reichard Kahle, son of Jorda Kahle, and was privileged to receive a family anecdote that corroborates Loria's version of the finding of the New Orleans urologist.

The story goes that, years after Long's death, Dr. Jorda Kahle was visited by an FBI man who had been assigned the job of tracing the origin of a quantity of paper money that had taken on a coloration strikingly different from the money placed into circulation by the government. There was no question that the money was genuine, but the normal dark green and black colors had been transformed into pastel, faded versions of the original hues.

Confronted by the G-man with a suitcase full of the faded currency, Kahle readily admitted to the government agent that the money had passed through his hands and was acquired by him from patients in payment for his fees.

As a urologist, a portion of Kahle's clientele came to him because of problems with their genito-urinary tracts. Many of these problems stemmed from venereal disease. The caseload included foreign seamen who visited New Orleans as a port of call. In need of medical attention, the sailors turned to Kahle, who treated them.

However, Kahle was fearful that the money they offered in payment for his services was germ-ridden and he was reluctant to handle it. He would ask his patients to place the required fee on a table and his nurse would use forceps to drop the money into the sterilizer. After such a treatment, the money was certainly germ free, but it had lost much of its coloring in the process.

Amused, the FBI agent suggested that Kahle find another way to cleanse the money without defacing it, something the urologist readily agreed to do.

Kahle was impressed with the ingenuity and efficiency of the government in being able to trace the money to his practice. He told the agent this. The agent responded, "Doctor, we know a lot more about you than you think!" When Kahle asked him to elaborate, the agent reminded Kahle that on September 9, 1935, when he catheterized Long in room 314 of Our Lady of the Lake Hospital in Baton Rouge, Kahle, outside of earshot of the patient, gave this one sentence prognosis of the patient's condition: "This son-of-a-bitch is gonna die!"[8]

Dr. Hull dismisses entirely the contention that Long died as a result of internal bleeding. He insists that the cause was fulminating peritonitis. "Fulminating" refers to an infection running a speedy course, with rapidly worsening results. Toxic shock syndrome can be compared to fulminating infection.

Hull's recollection is startling, since there is no mention of peritonitis in any of the reports from Our Lady of the Lake, although newspapers mentioned this possibility.

When Long was wounded, there was an Associated Press story filed from New York that read, "Huey Long faces only one major peril in his abdominal bullet wound and that is peritonitis. Other possible complications are numerous but all of them minor, and unpredictable."

This opinion was elicited by the Associated Press from surgeons and physicians who were shown the "official description of the wound issued by the senator's physicians after they had operated." However, the opinion of the physicians seemed to be based less on insight into Long's condition than a knowledge of routine perils from peritonitis whenever the abdomen is penetrated.[9]

There was also a reference to the prospect of Long's succumbing to peritonitis in a short-lived publication entitled *Louisiana Authors Journal,* which speculated that Long would die within 30 days because, "The world's greatest medical authorities say that when a bullet punctures the intestines, the victim, even though he doesn't die soon, is almost sure to die within a month's time of peritonitis."

The body of medical opinion of the day and even now seems to hold that peritonitis has a more insidious effect than the internal hemorrhage that characterized Long's injuries. Had peritonitis been the cause of death, he would have lived much longer than the day and a half following the shooting.

Obviously Long had some peritonitis, as there was spillage of a small amount of fecal material from the two wounds in the colon that were found at surgery. The surrounding area would have been exposed to infection and peritonitis.

However, for peritonitis to have caused his death, it would have had to be massive and would have followed massive fecal spillage with soiling of the abdominal cavity. There would have had to be a sufficient incubation period for bacteria to grow and for the tissue reaction of inflammation to occur. This could hardly have happened within the 30 or so hours between Long's wounding and death.

I am reluctant to dismiss Dr. Hull's position out of hand because I keep reminding myself that Hull, who went to his death maintaining his contention that peritonitis was the cause of Long's death, was there and others were not. However, physicians I have consulted about the possibility of peritonitis being the culprit have generally dismissed it, although they point out occasionally new ailments such as toxic shock syndrome appear and perhaps something was present which might make Dr. Hull's theory plausible. If hospital records were intact and available, it is possible that they would help clear up some of the confusion. But it is sad that some party or parties saw fit to mutilate and destroy such vital records and that, half a century after his death, there is still a sharp difference of opinion about the cause.

When Long was returned to his hospital room, physicians and associates who were willing to be quoted were optimistic, at least outwardly so, that he would recover. Soon there would be long faces and hints that the condition was more serious than pictured, but on Monday morning everyone was publicly optimistic.

Almost everyone, that is. Justice Fournet felt, on that Monday morning, that the future of the Kingfish was out of the hands of the physicians and only intervention from Divine Providence could save Long. In a 1975 interview he recalled that three of the physicians in attendance were alarmed because they had been giving Long "one transfusion after another but it just went right through."

Fournet's memory is faulty on this point. He says it was on Monday morning that he became alarmed at Long's chances of survival. It was probably Monday night, since, up until noon Monday, Long had had only a single transfusion, that given by Jimmy Noe shortly before surgery.

The matter of blood transfusions is another area which demonstrates the incompleteness of the hospital records. According to Hermann Deutsch, the hospital records show only one transfusion, administered at 8:15 Monday night. There were, in fact, four transfusions completed and a fifth attempted, but never completed.

Fournet said of Doctors Maes, Stone and Ellender:

"...(They) diagnosed that he (Long) had been shot through the kidney and Vidrine had not probed the bullet beyond the intestines and that if they operated at this time the shock would kill him immediately.

"The only thing they could do was hope for a miracle that somehow the wound would heal with a bloodclot or something. And when I saw him I knew it was only a question of time—he looked like a dying man."[10]

Dr. Loria reports that doctors had just about abandoned hope for Long after the catheterization by Kahle, commenting, "....the patient was practically moribund and any further surgery was deemed most inadvisable." This would have been some time Tuesday morning.[11]

But the day before, the official reports were upbeat. At 6:00 a.m. Monday, a little more than eight hours following the shooting, Earle Christenberry, the senator's secretary, emerged from Long's room pronouncing, "He has improved more in the last 15 minutes than during all of last night."[12]

At 8:30 Monday night the hospital announced that Long was gaining strength, although reports began to surface that his condition was deteriorating rapidly. Newspapers disclosed that a second blood transfusion was made, some giving the time as noon and others placing it at around 2:00 p.m. Hospital records showed no such transfusion and one physician flatly denied it, explaining that it was simply a matter "for watchful waiting hour by hour."[13]

C.P. Liter, reporter for the Baton Rouge *Morning Advocate,* learned from a nurse that Long was passing blood in his urine, reinforcing the belief that massive bleeding was continuing within the patient's body. The New Orleans *Item* reported, "It was learned reliably that Senator Huey P. Long took a turn for the worse around noon today. He was reported as passing blood with an increased pulse and a second transfusion was given. Callers at his room turned away with grave faces and general concern was felt in the hospital over his condition."[14]

(C.P. Liter later became managing editor of the Baton Rouge *State-Times,* the afternoon daily. During his tour of duty, the shooting and death of Huey Long was never referred to in print as an "assassination." He kept close watch on the activities of Long's bodyguards and whenever one seemed close to death, he told reporters to be on the lookout for some kind of deathbed confession that would unravel the mystery of the shooting.)[15]

Monday afternoon the news media began to take exception to the reports that had been issued. The *Times-Picayune* challenged a statement by Dr. Vidrine that Long was "holding his own." The journal charged:

"The physician's statement was in sharp conflict with unofficial reports emanating throughout the day from OLOL (Our Lady of the Lake Sanitarium) where Senator Long has been under treatment since Sunday night for a bullet wound in the abdomen. The unofficial reports are to the effect that there has been a decided change for the worse in the senator's condition, that a hemorrhage which started immediately after he was shot has not been checked."[16]

Monday afternoon at 3:00, oxygen was brought to the senator's room— a bad sign. But still, those charged with issuing news to the world about Long's condition effused optimism. Pollyanna was doing all the talking.

Universal Service reporter Opal Beasley reported about that time, "I was permitted this afternoon to go upstairs to the corridor outside Senator Long's hospital room....The physician said, 'Senator Long is progressing nicely. He has a good chance to recover. He is nevertheless a very seriously ill man but he is at least showing improvement.'"[17]

At 8:15 p.m. Monday, Long received a second transfusion. Following the transfusion, the senator's blood pressure was taken and was reported to be 114 over 84. The pulse rate was more than double a normal rate, "170-plus."

Late Monday evening the wraps were off. The hospital's head nurse was responding to inquiries of Long's condition, "There is little hope." The *Item* reported, "High state officials abandon hope for senator's recovery."[18]

At midnight a third transfusion was completed. Two hours later still another one was given. Physicians issued a prescription for ephedrine, a drug that would constrict blood vessels and speed up flow of blood to the brain. At 2:00 a.m. Tuesday, pharmacist Redfield Bryan was awakened by a pounding on the door of his pharmacy, which also contained his living quarters. Sleepily, Bryan read the prescription for the brand new drug and advised his callers he did not have it in stock. He did, however, direct them to a pharmacy managed by an anti-Long pharmacist who nevertheless filled the prescription.[19]

A fifth transfusion was later attempted but never completed. At 3:00 a.m., Dr. E.L. Sanderson, Long's appointee as superintendent of Charity Hospital at Shreveport, concluded, "Senator Long is dying."

At 4:10 a.m. Tuesday morning the spirit left Long and returned to its Maker.

The miracle had not happened.

It is possible that there was no way that Long would have survived, given the condition he was in. Probably, however, his fate was sealed when attending physicians decided not to make an incision in the anterior wall of the peritoneal cavity to inspect the kidney visually, instead of simply observing its outline. According to an eyewitness, special attention was given to the "black eye" or hematoma that had formed on the anterior wall. The clot seemed to have stabilized the kidney and there was no hemorrhage. Weighing the dangers of additional surgery against the prospects of letting well enough alone, the operating room decided to leave things be.

However, what probably happened is that the improving condition of Long, ironically, caused his death. As he recovered from shock, his heartbeat improved, sending the newly-acquired blood coursing through the system. The "black eye," capable of containing a slackened flow of blood, could not cope with the increased pressure and burst, much as a temporary plug in a punctured garden hose might give way when the water is turned on. This probably happened late Monday morning and accounts for the sudden turn of events following surgery and before additional transfusions were attempted Monday afternoon.

When Long died, his bodyguards released their surveillance and reporters were allowed to roam throughout the hospital. One reporter had been attempting to gain access to the clothes worn by the Kingfish when he was slain.

Private duty nurse Theoda Carriere was hard-pressed to keep the newsman from spiriting the clothes away with him. She finally hid them and they were turned over to law enforcement authorities. Ms. Carriere has no idea why he was so interested in the clothes. However, it would seem that the existence or non-existence of powder burns and the relative condition of the clothing around the area of the two punctures in Long's body might have yielded interesting insights into the nature of the wounds.[20]

Larger than life even when he lived, Huey Long grew to immense proportions in death. His place in history was assured by the spectacular and colorful activity of less than 18 years in public life—14 years in statewide service and a little more than three years on the national scene. He had changed the course of history and his passing left unsatisfied what had become a national preoccupation with his future.

As befits a legend, Huey's deathbed words were recorded for posterity. There would eventually be a consensus of a sort that Long's last thoughts were of the students at LSU and that his dying words were, "What will my poor boys at LSU do without me?" Some felt that he had died saying, "God, don't let me die. I have so much to do."

Perhaps Long said these words, perhaps he didn't. As with any public figure and especially one who commanded the respect and loyalty of so many, there would be an understandable temptation to record distinctive, pungent and dramatic utterances to inspire and enlighten generations to come, even if the required *bon mots* might have to be forced a little. The final words of the Kingfish, as reported by those who say they were with him at the time of his death, reflect a little of this manipulation.

Some, including Dr. Cecil Lorio, were of the opinion that Long was delirious when he recovered from the operation and did not regain full consciousness again. Any words he spoke, Lorio felt, were not rational expressions. This view was shared by Jimmy O'Connor, who maintained, "I don't recall him saying anything on his death bed. I didn't hear him say anything about his boys at LSU. That man was in a deep coma."

Dr. Hull, one of the young residents at Big Charity in New Orleans who was summoned by Arthur Vidrine, felt that Long was rational for about the first 20 hours, during which he was heard to say, "Now they'll know why I had a bodyguard" and, when his wife arrived, "There's my darling!" Hull was in and out of the room during Long's unsuccessful fight for life and heard no other remarks.

The Reverend Gerald L.K. Smith would later hastily don the mantle of Long's Share Our Wealth clubs and he would offer his own quote, "Oh God, don't let me die. I have a few things more to do." Smith added, "I was with him when he died. I said, 'Amen' as he breathed his last." It should be obvious to the reader that there is a certain self-serving value in Smith's version of the final words.

Dr. Clarence Lorio agreed with Smith and added his own embellishments, "Oh God, if only it were not Your will that I die. My work for America is not finished. And what will my university boys do without me?"

On the morning that Long died, Seymour Weiss told the Baton Rouge *Advocate* that Long had been unconscious from midnight Monday until 4:10 a.m. Tuesday, when he died. He said he could not remember the last thing the senator said while he was conscious.

Standing nearby, Governor Allen broke in to correct Weiss, "Oh, yes. The last thing he said when he was still conscious was, 'I wonder what will happen to my poor university boys.'" Loyal to a legend, Weiss would later jog his memory and remember that Long did, indeed, think of his youngsters at LSU and wonder aloud what would happen to them.

Theoda Carriere, Long's special duty nurse, was at Long's side until he drew his last breath. Her recollection is different from most. "About the only thing he wanted was to get up and go to the bathroom," she recalled.

However, Weiss would tell others that Long's final words were in response to Weiss' questioning about a matter close to everyone's heart: the location of the "de-ducts" box that Long had recently moved from its resting place in the Riggs National Bank in Washington to an as yet unrevealed hiding place.

"Huey, you've got to tell me. Where is the de-ducts box?" Huey replied weakly, "Later, Seymour, later."[21]

But there was no later and the de-ducts box, like Huey Long, belongs to the ages. That is, if Seymour Weiss is to be believed.

Some chose not to believe him. In the FBI files there is a note from an anonymous tipster who charged, on September 19, 1939, following indictments rendered against Weiss, that Weiss left New Orleans to meet a New York hotelman named Ralph Hitz, who the informer claimed "has helped Weiss either dispose of the property stolen from the Huey Long trust box or conceal it." Weiss was reported to have used the de-ducts box money to buy into a chain of hotels controlled by Hitz.[22]

CHAPTER THIRTEEN

The Wild Bullet

For almost 24 hours following his wounding, Huey Long was conscious and, according to Dr. Edgar Hull, perfectly lucid.

Later he would slip in and out of consciousness, occasionally speaking in a rational manner. But, for the most part, he was in a deep coma. Then, shortly before he died, according to Dr. Cecil Lorio, "the dying man thrashed wildly about the oxygen tent that had been put over him. A little after four in the morning his breathing stopped."[1]

Conscious of the historical importance of the moment, Doctors Hull and Plaunche, two of the young physicians drafted from New Orleans Charity Hospital by Vidrine, concluded that it would be wise to perform an autopsy.

Disturbed that none of the senior physicians had suggested it, Hull recalls, "I said to Felix Plaunche—Felix and I were close—I said, 'Felix, there ought to be an autopsy because there is going to be all kinds of talk about what killed him.'" (I have been told by the family of Plaunche, now deceased, that he was convinced that there was a bullet in Long's body when it left the hospital on its way to the mortuary.)

Plaunche was noncommittal, preferring to leave the decision to Dr. Vidrine. They approached Vidrine in the room that had been set aside for him at the hospital and suggested, "We think there ought to be a post (mortem)."

Actually, Vidrine was far ahead of the young doctors, having summoned Dr. Rigney D'Aunoy, Charity Hospital pathologist, to Baton Rouge for the purpose of an autopsy when it seemed certain that Long would die. Vidrine told the young physicians that he was in agreement, but felt that Long's widow should be consulted. "Let's go ask Rose," he said.

As the trio filed out of Vidrine's room, Dr. Sanderson, the Long family's physician from Shreveport, met them and Vidrine told him what they were about. Sanderson objected. His objections were hardly scientific or professional in nature. According to Hull, Sanderson scotched the whole idea by protesting, "Oh, no, we must not violate his sacred body!"[2]

Incredibly, this single statement was enough to scuttle the entire idea of an autopsy. It serves also to help establish the relative positions of both Sanderson and Vidrine. Despite all testimony that Vidrine was in charge at the hospital and Long was considered to be his patient, it must be remembered that it was Sanderson and not Vidrine who delivered the climactic news that Long was dead. A single objection from Sanderson sufficed to block the attempt to determine conclusively the cause of Long's death.

Dr. Loria reports that it was Mrs. Long who objected to an autopsy, "despite the fact that a New Orleans pathologist was on the scene and ready at the time of Long's death." However, there is no evidence that the widow was even consulted.[3]

Hull said:

> "Those were Sanderson's words and I said to myself, 'Oh, hell!' But I didn't speak up. I was a coward. But there was Sanderson and he was 20 or 30 years older than I was; he had a beard and I was a youngster, so I kept my mouth shut....I'll say I was intimidated, yes. But at least I was the one who suggested the autopsy in the first place and Vidrine did not demur."[4]

Present Louisiana law is clear regarding the performance of autopsies. Article 102 of the Code of Criminal Procedure requires that the coroner shall perform an autopsy when there is a "reasonable probability that a criminal statute has been violated."

However, Louisiana Revised Statutes in effect in 1935 allowed for a great deal of leeway by the coroner. Article 15, Section 28, provided that when the coroner:

> "...shall have just cause to believe that the deceased person came to his or her death by means of poison or violence, or in consequence of any criminal act and that a post mortem examination of the body is necessary or will materially aid in the prosecution of any person charged or who may be charged with any criminal act resulting in the death of such person, it shall be the duty of the coroner to...remove the body...for the purpose of holding an inquest over the same."

LSU Professor of Law Dr. Raymond Lamonica, a leading authority on Louisiana criminal law, interprets the above statute as meaning that a coroner "would have been justified in concluding, based upon testimony presented at the inquest, that the autopsy was not necessary or would not materially aid in prosecution." He adds, "Of course, an autopsy would have dispelled the lingering questions of the actual cause of death, but the statutory duty is couched only in terms of criminal prosecutions need."[5]

Around 5:00 a.m., funeral director Merle Welsh's telephone rang. He left for the hospital, just as he had left for the state capitol some 30 hours before, to pick up a corpse. This morning he was being summoned to pick up the body of Huey Long. He left with an attendant in an ambulance. At the hospital he proceeded to Long's room where he met Dr. Cecil Lorio. The trio loaded Long's remains on a rolling stretcher and returned to the mortuary.

There was little conversation between them as they drove to the mortuary along the streets of Baton Rouge, still wet and shiny following the downpour of the previous night. Welsh would remember that Lorio showed a keen and heartfelt sense of personal loss, remarking, "Never before have we had such a brilliant man among us." Lorio speculated soulfully that the silent passenger was "the brainiest man you'll ever have in one of your ambulances."

Three or four miles and ten minutes later, the journey was over. Long was taken to the embalming room of the mortuary.

It was here that Merle Welsh made a discovery that he was to keep to himself and live with for almost half a century. In inspecting the body it became all too clear to him that the diagnosis that had been fed to the public regarding Long's injury was false. The diagnosis held that he had been shot only once and a single bullet entered the abdomen, traveling through the abdomen and retroperitoneal space, exiting from the back.

Welsh, familiar with gunshot wounds because of his calling, which involved close observation of such injuries, concluded that the two wounds in Long's body were not wounds of entry and exit, respectively, but instead were both wounds of entry.

He maintains:

> "I know there were two bullet holes in the senator's body, the one in the abdomen where they made the incision and, I understand, recovered the bullet (during the surgery) that entered the abdomen.
>
> "I also know that a bullet...entered the back alongside the spine. The reason I think that was an entry was because of it being such a clean cut, small hole, not one torn or ruptured by a bullet coming out. Now that's the only bullet hole—the second one, the one I referred to as being on the side of the spine, in the lumbar region—that I

could observe. It was a clean, tiny little bullet hole."[6]

The seemingly innocent appearance of the wound to Long's back was also noted by one of the members of the coroner's jury examining the body. Tom Davis remembered that the coroner, Dr. Bird, raised the right side of Long's body so the jury could see the puncture. Davis remarked, "It was so small I doubt we'd have even seen it had it not been pointed out to us. But they never did let us feel around to see could we get out another bullet." Davis compared this with the thorough examination of the coroner's jury that fixed the cause of death of Carl Weiss. He recalled that they were crowded around the body and were able to touch and feel the body. With Long the jury was kept about 12 feet from the body.

Welsh makes no judgment about the wound caused by the bullet which entered the abdomen because of the incision made by operating physicians through the wound, which made it impossible to study the opening. However, he is firm in his conclusion that the wound in the back was definitely a wound of entry and not exit.

He would soon see positive proof of his judgment when one of the attending physicians, Dr. Clarence Lorio, would make his appearance at the funeral parlor. Welsh remembers:

> "It was daylight then and before I had an opportunity to begin preparations to start my work, Dr. Clarence Lorio entered. I had things to tend to, since it was my responsibility and everything was on my shoulders at that time—I had to see about a few things.
>
> "And in the meantime, Dr. Clarence Lorio came and said he wanted to go in and see the senator. So I went in with him and he just kind of probed around—"

Whereupon Welsh proceeds to relate a story which rewrites the entire accepted "official" version of the assassination of Huey Long. He remembered that Lorio undid the sutures placed in Long's body the previous Sunday night and inserted a hand into the senator's abdominal cavity ("he kept exploring with his hand") until the physician located a bullet. Asked whether the location of the bullet, according to the placement of Lorio's hand, was in the abdominal cavity or the retroperitoneal space, Welsh replied that it was "to the rear, to the back part of the cavity." Having removed the bullet, Lorio placed it on the table in full view of Welsh and his assistant, Jack Unbehagen.

This episode was known to many of the medical personnel at the hospital. I talked to one doctor who witnessed the surgery, commenting that there was no autopsy on Long. I was corrected: "Oh, yes there was. Dr. Clarence conducted his own autopsy at the funeral parlor to find the bullet."

And the size of the bullet? Welsh remembers that vividly. Ignorant of measurements and calibers and never having owned a gun himself, he cast about for a frame of reference to indicate size: "About the end of the first joint on my index finger," pressing his thumb to the first joint of that finger on his right hand to illustrate.

There are four sizes of bullets involved in Huey Long's shooting. Weiss' weapon was a .32. (Calibers are measured by percentages of an inch. Hence, a .32 caliber bullet is 32/100 or about one-third of an inch). Roden used a .38 "special," a .38 caliber barrel mounted on a .45 frame. Other bodyguards had .44 and .45 caliber weapons, almost equal in size.

A .32 caliber bullet is about the size of an ordinary pencil eraser. If Welsh had used the little finger as a guide, this would have more correctly approximated the diameter of a .32. His choice of the index finger could only have indicated what, to his mind, was an extremely large bullet.

Welsh remembers that it was his assistant, Jack Unbehagen, who took possession of the bullet. I attempted to trace the bullet to find if it was still in existence and also to verify Welsh's story. I believe my efforts have confirmed, independently of him, that the bullet existed and perhaps still exists, although its whereabouts are not known to me.

I called the half dozen or so "Unbehagens" in the Baton Rouge telephone directory and found, surprisingly enough, that none of those with whom I spoke was related to Jack Unbehagen. One man had some knowledge but he told me apprehensively that he "didn't want to get involved." However, one lady told me that she and her family had traveled through Galveston, Texas the previous summer and were surprised to learn that the mayor of that city was named Unbehagen, although there was no relationship between the families.

I followed this lead, contacting the mayor's office and found that, sure enough, the mayor was the nephew of Jack. I talked with several members of the family and was rewarded with the information that all of the Unbehagen family was familiar with "Uncle Jack," who was a collector of pistols, handcuffs and other law enforcement hardware, a heritage from Jack's service with the sheriff's office of East Baton Rouge Parish after he left the funeral parlor and Merle Welsh.

Jack had the bullet fashioned into a piece of jewelry which he displayed on a chain from his vest pocket. He was quick to relate, when showing off the souvenir, "This is the bullet that came from Huey!" I asked one of his nephews to recollect the size of the bullet and suggested that it might have been a .32 caliber, the size of the weapon used by Carl Weiss. Professing to be unfamiliar with firearms, O.C. Unbehagen nevertheless was quick to reply that it was "too big to be a .32," ruling out the possibility that the bullet came from Carl Weiss' gun.

This accounts for one bullet. There were two wounds of entry and no wound of exit. What about the second bullet? The second bullet was removed in the operating room at the hospital. As stated before, Doctors Cook and Lorio had mentioned such a bullet.

One of the biggest skeptics concerning the "official" theory of the shooting was the man in charge of the inquest, Baton Rouge Coroner Thomas Bird. Dr. Bird, visiting a friend following the shooting of Long, confided to him, "I am being prevailed upon to say that the bullet that killed Huey Long came from Carl Weiss' gun, but I don't think I want to say that."[8]

When Clarence Lorio had accomplished the mission that brought him to the funeral parlor, Merle Welsh returned to the task of preparing Long's body for viewing. Welsh was a true professional. He was manager of the parlor, embalmer and funeral director. At the age of 33, he had already accumulated 13 years of experience in his chosen field. He was well aware of the historical significance of the events of the previous four days and he understood that he had been placed smack in the middle of them.

Monday he had handled the arrangements for Carl Weiss. On that day he correctly concluded that Long would soon follow Weiss into eternity and he had prudently arranged a suitable coffin for the senator that would be in keeping with the deceased's exalted station in life. Some felt that ordering a casket in advance was an indication that Long's death had been carefully orchestrated. But this was not the case. It was simply a knowledgeable and experienced embalmer being able to read between the lines and surmise what the surgeons already knew: that Long could not survive.

Welsh admits that he had "used a little precaution there to be prepared." He called his regular supplier, Orleans Manufacturing Company in New Orleans, and arranged for the shipment of a copper-lined casket. The truck from New Orleans was met by one of Welsh's vehicles halfway and the casket was transferred. Welsh called Monday to order the casket and recalls that it reached the funeral home either late Monday afternoon or Tuesday morning.

The arrangements for Long in death were handled by the advisor and confidant who took care of his affairs in life, the omnipresent Seymour Weiss. It was Weiss and Governor Allen who negotiated with Welsh, although the governor obviously was a silent partner in the dealings. Long's widow was never a party to the arrangements and Welsh was left to speculate that perhaps she was relaying information to Weiss, although a more realistic interpretation would have Weiss calling the shots and the widow simply concurring.

Security was tight around the funeral home. State police were stationed at every entrance and no one except mortuary personnel and approved members of the Long organization was allowed in. Welsh remembers that his wife left the funeral home to do her grocery shopping and she was accosted by the guards as she took her car from the garage. She was allowed to leave but, when she returned, had difficulty re-entering the funeral home.

The reason for the tight security is unclear. Welsh maintains that there were no telephoned threats nor were there any attempts on the part of the citizens of Baton Rouge to mass around the funeral home. No one seemed concerned about the possibility of attempts to vandalize or steal the remains of the senator. Perhaps old habits die hard and, just as Long lived surrounded by a cordon of bodyguards, it would seem appropriate to carry the protection to the graveside.

The following day, Long's family arrived at the funeral home for a private viewing of the deceased. That afternoon, the remains were taken to the state capitol where Long's tuxedo-clad body (that's right, the Redneck Messiah was dressed in a tuxedo, for some inexplicable reason), protected by a window of glass, lay in state.

Baton Rouge, as well as Louisiana, had never seen anything like the Kingfish's funeral. But the Long machine, organized and oiled during Huey's life, carried off arrangements to perfection.

Even Welsh was impressed by it:

"There was nothing to equal it in any respect. It surpassed anything else I had ever been connected with. It was a stupendous undertaking, if I may put that in the vernacular.

"There were so many different things that had to be correlated that I had to see that they were done. Ordinarily I'd just call up the man at the cemetery and tell him the family was coming out there, to tell them what to do and show them where to do it.

"In this case, I had to see that somebody did it. I went to Mr. Weiss and said, 'Someone's got to see that this grave gets properly prepared and located.' He said, 'Mr. Stewart of the Highway Department will do that for you. You tell him what you want. You give him dimensions. You tell him how you want it done.' Well, that was very simple for me."

Everybody pitched in, even the Golden Band from Tigerland, the 200-odd strong marching LSU band, Huey's pride and joy. Welsh remembers that the flowers that arrived as final tributes from all parts of the world threatened to create a crisis by their sheer mass. They extended from the House of Representatives to the Senate chamber. "Solid with flowers," Welsh said:

"I told Mr. Weiss, 'We're going to have to get some help to get these flowers into the sunken garden.' He said, 'The band boys will do that for you.' So the band boys did that. All I had to do was just stand there and direct them, point to where they'd put some of those things. I had that help there. It was an easy operation in spite of the fact that it was as tremendous as it was in interest and attendance.

"And it had to be right. It had to go right all the time."

And it did go right.

Before Long's body was lowered into the grave, an estimated 100,000 persons filed past the bier as it lay in the rotunda of the capitol. The Airline Highway leading to New Orleans was jammed with bumper-to-bumper traffic. In New Orleans, city government was shut down for the day and an estimated 4500 persons journeyed to the state capitol by train. Five chartered buses carried 185 prominent New Orleanians and all traffic in the city's business district was halted for one minute at 4:00 p.m., the time scheduled for his funeral.

A group of United States senators selected by Vice-president Garner, including Senator Hattie Caraway of Arkansas, arrived in Baton Rouge for the services.

The mood of the crowd ranged from deep sorrow to carnival spirit. Long's body was carried down the steps of the state capitol to the accompaniment of a special composition by the Kingfish's music man, Castro Carazo. Carazo, in less than 48 hours, had rescored "Every Man A King," campaign song composed by himself and Long, transposing it into a minor key which transformed that upbeat melody into a mournful dirge that was unique if it was anything at all.[9]

Seymour Weiss had chosen Reverend Gerald L.K. Smith to deliver the graveside eulogy, sidestepping the sticky choice of having to favor Catholic over Protestant, or vice versa.

Smith was one of the most controversial members of the Long organization. Being a mid-Westerner, he never quite fit into the machine. Moreover, his relationship was never with the business of government, so to speak. It was, instead, with Long's Share Our Wealth movement and his influence never went beyond that.

He was an imposing figure, tall, heavyset, a strong nose softened by a handsome, boyish face made to look innocent by flashing blue eyes. He professed a fierce loyalty to Huey Long which came across to many as bootlicking.

He was pastor of a Shreveport Protestant church, leaving to join Huey with, some say, the blessing of many of his congregation who felt they could not handle this dynamic live wire, who seemed to possess a darkly evil current flowing through his imposing and disarming exterior. One writer described the reverend this way:

>"He is an opportunist; complete, firm
>only in self advantage, his consuming passion for
>power and more power. Dressed up in a uniform,
>Reverend Smith would look like a beefy New
>York cop or Goering. He has massive drive, is a
>bit bull-like, stolid, determined, shifty, but wearing
>the gauze of idealism, social adventure and kindli-
>ness."[10]

Weiss would later regret the choice when Smith attempted to usurp the leadership of the Share Our Wealth movement, using the funeral oration as a wedge in that direction. Smith and Long secretary Earle Christenberry would lock horns in a jurisdictional dispute for proprietary ownership of the movement and Christenberry would win out. Eventually, Smith would leave the state and establish a Nazi-type pseudo-religious organization heavily flavored with anti-Semitism.

But for the moment, he was the voice of the Long machine and what a voice it was! He sounded the clarion call for "a new order." He salted the sermon with sanguine metaphors: "This blood which dropped upon this soul shall seal our hearts together...he died for us...his spirit shall never rest as long as hungry bodies cry for food, as long as lean human frames stand naked...."

At one point, the mourners seemed to take on the makings of a mob as they surged toward the grave, intent on gathering some of the floral tributes as memorabilia. The *Times-Picayune* reported:

>"Breaking its silence, the throng of spec-
>tators on the west side of the lawn broke through
>police lines and surged forward as the casket was
>placed in position to be lowered into the grave.
>The crowd was not checked until it was within a
>few feet of the graveside.
>
>"On the opposite side of the garden, a
>crowd previously had fought its way past the
>guard, only to be driven back."[11]

The *Times-Picayune* reported that at least 50 men and women "were taken in a faint from the crowd." *Time* magazine estimated that there were 200 who keeled over during the wake.

Airplanes carrying the press of the world circled and buzzed the capitol; newsreel cameras dotted the capitol steps and grounds and the whirring of their machinery counterpointed the dirge that accompanied the funeral procession down the steps and onto the sunken gardens of the capitol grounds.

The event represented an economic bonanza of sorts to Baton Rouge merchants. The New York *World Telegram* remarked that the "little capital city of 40,000 was in a holiday mood....The walks of Third St.—Baton Rouge's main street—were crowded from buildings to curb. Men in galluses and men in white linen, women in gingham and women in silk, children dragging along beside their parents and babes-in-arms moved slowly toward the capitol."[12]

Huey Long was in the cold, cold ground, reposing in eternal sleep. It was the final, supreme irony that he was laid to rest in the bosom of Baton Rouge, the community he had failed to tame, losing his life in the bargain.

He would await the judgment day in a concrete vault and copper-lined casket, a prisoner unto eternity of the city and its citizens.

CHAPTER FOURTEEN

Doctor Jekyl And Mister Weiss

With the Kingfish dead and buried, attention began to focus on the man named as his assassin. Who was he? Why did he do it? A thousand questions. No answers.

History has never provided us with an assassin who even remotely resembles Carl Austin Weiss. If Weiss was, in fact, the killer of Huey Long, then he was, like Long, "sui generis"—one of a kind.

He was the firstborn son of Carl Adam Weiss, first generation American of a Bavarian family. The younger Weiss' grandfather was a musician and family members believe it was he who stimulated in Carl's father a desire to become a professional person.

Carl's father received a degree in pharmacy after having been apprenticed to a druggist in New Orleans. He received a certificate as a registered pharmacist and, at the time, this was enough to gain admission into Tulane University School of Medicine. He graduated from Tulane in 1900 and began the practice of general medicine.

He moved to Lobdell, a small farming community across the Mississippi from Baton Rouge. He was a "plantation doctor," tending to the medical needs of workers on a sugar plantation. He married Viola Maine of Baton Rouge in the beginning of 1905 and in December of that year his first son, Carl, was born.

Why Carl Adam Weiss chose to name his son "Carl Austin" is lost to history. Family members have no knowledge of the reason. There has been speculation that the senior Weiss had been teased as a child with mutilations of his name ("A-damn") and he did not want his son to undergo this ridicule. There is also speculation that the elder Weiss had a physician friend named Austin and he chose the name to honor him. No one knows for sure.

178

The similarity of names between father and son has led to some confusion and, on occasion, the incorrect identification of Carl as "Carl A. Weiss, Jr.," and his son as "Carl A. Weiss, III."

Two years after Carl was born, he was followed by a second child, Olga Marie; 10 years later a second son was born, Thomas Edward, shortened by the family to "Tom Ed."

It was after the birth of Olga Marie that the elder Dr. Weiss decided to specialize. He moved his family to New Orleans to study the specialty of eye, ear, nose and throat medicine.

Eight years later, in 1916, he moved again, opening an office in downtown Baton Rouge.

It was about this time that Carl enrolled in LSU in an engineering course. Midway through his course of study at the school, he abandoned engineering and decided to enter medicine.

Carl Weiss was slight of build. His death certificate states that he was five feet nine inches tall and weighed 130 pounds. Most of those who remember him comment upon the aura of tenderness and delicateness that he carried with him.

Mercedes Garig, who taught him in his freshman year at LSU, described him this way:

> "A dark, serious face—the kind of face
> with which one bargains for a smile and feels the
> gainer when a smile appears...eyes that meet your
> own and generously accept you at your own valua-
> tion; a slight frame; hands of extreme delicacy."[1]

The eyes and hands were apparently among the most striking features of Carl Weiss. A friend and patient during the time Carl interned at Bellevue Hospital in New York gave this appraisal:

> "Weiss' eyes were remarkable....He was
> moderately handsome and although only average
> in height and weight he had a vital appearance.
> His chin was cleft, his nose delicate and his eyes
> remarkably expressive. They were jet black and in
> moments of emotion they flashed brilliantly even
> through his faintly tinted octagonal-shaped glas-
> ses. If any one of Huey Long's bodyguards had
> known Carl Weiss personally, he would have seen
> death stalking in his eyes as he stepped into the
> corridor of the Louisiana statehouse that Sunday
> night....
>
> "He could probe a nostril as eptly as an
> old-fashioned   seamstress   used   to   thread   a

needle."[2]

Not a lot is known about Carl's early years and what we do know is reported through the eyes of his younger brother. Thomas Edward followed in Carl's footsteps and became a physician. (He has just recently retired from active practice as a rheumatologist in the world-renowned Ochsner Clinic outside New Orleans.)

Because of the difference in ages, the two boys were never close as youngsters, but there was genuine affection between them and, on Tom's part, a certain amount of hero worship and envy of his accomplished older brother.

Tom recalls, "There was a generation gap. I remember Carl being involved in things I knew some day I would be involved in."

From his earliest days, there was nothing about Carl that was queer or quirky, or even eccentric. Ms. Garig described him as being "one of the quietest, most retiring personalities I ever knew." She added, "He rejoiced in a keen sense of humor and, though a thinker and an idealist, there was no trace of the morbid or erratic in his personality."[3]

He was an avid reader, possessing an inquiring mind, but he was not a loner or a recluse. He had a circle of friends and participated in peer activity. Oftentimes his interest in toys and things of childhood went beyond simple amusement and into the realm of their inner workings. He was an inquisitive and curious child. There was nothing that did not have some interest for him.

Carl became knowledgeable about many things, in particular, electricity and electronics. In his teens, he pieced together a radio which his brother Tom believes was the first of its kind ever assembled in Baton Rouge. Starting with a crystal set, Carl added additional pieces until, Tom remembers, "When he got through it had cost many a dollar. There was a room about the size of an average bedroom and it was just filled with batteries." Carl and a companion would begin heating the batteries early in the morning and they were able to bring in Philadelphia and other far-off stations in the evening.

Tom considered Carl a "crackerjack carpenter—a true craftsman." On a visit to New Orleans, Carl observed a screened porch gracing one of the homes. When he returned to Baton Rouge he screened in the porch of his own family home, allowing the Weisses to enjoy the cool breezes of the evening.

Music had a special attraction for Carl. He would open a practice book and play for hours, ignoring his mother's announcements that dinner was ready. He played mostly lighter classical music and those practice exercises that contained runs and complicated passages. When family critics asked why he didn't play more familiar and more melodic compositions, Carl would respond that he was playing for himself. He would then return to the piano, alone and lost in a world of music.

A freshman teacher at LSU noticed this ability to lose himself. She wrote:

"One's dominant impression of him was
of the singular quietness which enveloped his personality, as though somewhere along his pathway
he had discovered a secret zone of calm in which
he moved serenely and cheerfully through a turbulent world...."[4]

Smitten with the urge to travel, Carl applied for a position with a band.
The bandleader asked what position he played and Carl responded by asking
what positions were open. There was an opening for a clarinet player, prompting
Carl to journey to New Orleans to study for a few days under his grandfather.

Soon the band got a new clarinetist.

There was much of the clown in Carl. Tom remembers that he indulged
in "a lot of foolishness." The elder Weiss was conservative, part of his Bavarian
makeup. Mrs. Weiss also was very reserved.

Carl delighted in enlivening this sober bourgeois atmosphere, injecting
his humor and bringing pleasure and lightness into the circle by his good natured
teasing of siblings and parents alike.

He labeled Tom with the nickname "Butz," meaning "little brother" in
German. Tom recollects:

"He always had something new or dif-
ferent to bring to the table by way of conversation,
something stimulating. I never knew him to bring
grief, nor was he a pessimist. I'~ had a very
wholesome outlook on life."

As a teenager, Carl lived a full life, as he would later during his college
years. He ran errands for the family, helped around the house and even did
chores for neighbors. He was a Boy Scout.

In addition to his music, his carpentry and his electronics, the young
man sketched, wrote and still had time for fishing, tennis and sailing along the
languid Louisiana bayous.

He was skilled at fencing and had a knowledge of swords. He told a
fencing companion who had completed his internship at Bellevue and was then
living in New Orleans that he had been shown two swords and was asked if they
might be valuable. One he dismissed as worthless. The other he suggested the
owner take to a gallery for appraisal. He wrote that the sword was "an excellent
steel of possible Crusade date, a weapon they would not know where to dupli-
cate." The gallery suggested the owner take it to the Metropolitan Museum of
Art and Carl bragged, "That's naming 'em, eh?"[5]

He took photographs and processed his own film. He was a wood
sculptor and had on his desk the bust of a friend which he himself had carved.
He mastered soft-point etching and was passably good at portrait work.

He spoke French and German fluently. He was fond of the theater. But he also attended prize fights and wrestling matches at Madison Square Garden in New York City. He followed the Tulane University football team and occasionally placed bets on the outcome of his alma mater's matches. While at the Tulane School of Medicine, he and classmate Edgar Hull attended Saturday afternoon matinees at the St. Charles Theater in New Orleans where, according to Hull, "There was a good stock company and you could see a good stage play for 50 cents."[6]

A friend would later describe his hobbies as "those of a clever and cultured man."[7]

He graduated from St. Vincent's Academy, a Catholic school in Baton Rouge, in 1921 and was chosen valedictorian.

Throughout his teens, Carl Austin Weiss was a winner, far removed from the assassin's profile which typically causes one "to drift through early childhood, never completing anything they start...blaming failure after failure on an unjust system, perfidious friends or unseen demons."

In 1923, he transferred from LSU to Tulane, since LSU was without a medical school and would not have one until Huey Long established one in 1931. In 1925, he received his bachelor of science degree, continuing in graduate school for two more years. He was awarded a two-year internship at Touro Infirmary in New Orleans. In 1927, at the age of 21, he received his M.D. degree.

Carl's college days were an extension of his teens. He was a well-rounded, well-adapted young man.

College friend Ashton Robins described him as an intellectual and "extremely well trained...the equal of anything in the larger cities in this area." Robins and Weiss were not very close in medical school, because "Carl worked like hell." When both had finished their internship, Carl became ear, nose and throat consultant to Robins' pediatric practice. Robins remembers Carl as a physician "attentive to his patients and an excellent companion to be with, to go out to dinner or somewhere."

Carl joined a fraternity at Tulane. He had enough friends to be elected secretary-treasurer of his class. He continued to play music and became a member of the Tulane band.

He stayed on at Touro for a year after he received his medical degree and was rewarded, because of his scholarship, with prized internships at the American Hospital at Neuilly, on the outskirts of Paris, and at the University of Vienna. The latter scholarship was obtained by Dr. Rudolph Matas, who taught Carl at Tulane and who was regarded as one of the world's great teachers and surgeons. Matas was instrumental in developing a cure for yellow fever and made the first large scale photomicrographs of the blood of yellow fever patients.

Carl Weiss would later establish a reputation for microscopic photography, no doubt a result of the tutoring of Matas.

He sailed to Europe and, before taking up residency in Paris, went to Vienna to take postgraduate courses in treatment of the ear, nose and throat. His knowledge of German, learned from his grandfather, was sufficient to allow him to follow the lectures.

Vienna provided Carl with political, as well as medical, knowledge.

Europe, like the United States, was crushed by a depression. Weary, disillusioned and impoverished citizens of central Europe were casting about for messiahs who would lead them out of the economic quagmire and into prosperous times. And, just as in the United States, leaders did, in fact, materialize with their messages of hope.

Germany had Hitler, poised to seize power; Italy had Mussolini, the elder statesman of the dictators who had, almost ten years prior to Carl's arrival in Europe, assumed control of the country; Austria had Engelbert Dollfuss, disminutive chancellor (he stood less than five feet tall) but a forceful and persuasive leader who exploited the Austrian republic's political and economic woes while trying to fend off a takeover by archenemy Hitler on the border.

Carl Weiss saw at point-blank range the workings of dictatorship. His travels on side trips took him to Italy, where he was elbowed off the sidewalk by the Blackshirts, members of Mussolini's militia. He lived under the tyranny of Dollfuss, observing the confrontations between the tiny dictator's forces and the Austrian Nazi Party, Hitler's subversives who were working toward unification with Germany. Austria, a prize being contested by competing tyrants, was a troubled and unhappy nation.[8]

He traveled frequently to Germany where the roots of the Weiss family were planted, 200 miles away in Bavaria.

In central Europe, Carl Weiss would have had little reason to reflect upon the similarities between that region and the growing concern in Louisiana with the activities of Huey Long. Weiss had left the state in the late summer of 1928 and, although Long was elected in that year, he had not yet fallen into the role of dictator that would eventually give him control of Louisiana.

But the parallels would emerge later and it is highly likely that he would reflect upon the resemblance when he returned to America, especially in the light of the assassination of Dollfuss in 1934.

In June of 1929, Carl traveled to Paris and began his internship at the American Hospital. He enjoyed himself immensely. So much impressed with the City of Light was he that he suggested to the family that his younger sister, Olga, join him. She agreed and spent some time in Paris, finding a job as a telephone operator at the American Hospital in Paris.

Carl and his sister fell in love with Paris. Later, while interning at Bellevue Hospital, he wrote a New Orleans colleague, "...Life here is just about the last extreme from that at the American Hospital. The contrast is a pleasure, tho' I'd rather, I confess, begin again now that other contrast in Paris."[9]

While in Paris, he traveled to Belgium, visiting the Fabrique Nationale d'Armes de Guerre, which manufactured weapons for the European market under a licensure agreement with the Browning Company of the U.S. Carl had received a letter from his father, asking if he would arrange to find a Browning automatic shotgun. Apparently this was the principal reason for the trip but Carl, always fond of guns, picked up a .32 caliber pistol for himself, the weapon that he carried the night of Long's shooting.

On May 19, 1930, slightly more than a year and a half after his departure from the U.S., Carl Weiss returned. His customs declaration listed $247 worth of merchandise purchased in Europe: surgical instruments, a camera, fencing equipment, antique swords and an $8 Browning pistol, made in Belgium.[10]

Upon his arrival in America, he went immediately to work at Bellevue Hospital in New York in the ear, nose and throat division. He took to life in the Big Apple just as readily as he did in the sophisticated capitals of the Continent. He wrote from Bellevue, "This perennial interning is not so bad...it is a pleasant debauching experience...am getting exactly what I sought: practical work and the application of the work I took in Vienna...."[11]

The years he spent in New York were joyful years. He renewed acquaintances with a number of Tulane alumni who passed through the hospital. He developed the reputation of a clown and on the name plate of his room door, some friend had added the letters "guy" so that the name read, "Dr. Carl A. Weissguy." Carl never bothered to change the nameplate. His friends felt he enjoyed a joke as well as the next person.[12]

While in New York he kept up with the political shenanigans of Huey Long in Louisiana. He received copies of the Long weekly *Louisiana Progress,* sent to him by a friend in Louisiana. He would read these papers aloud, interrupting himself to make caustic and penetrating criticisms. A friend who knew him during this period commented sadly after his death, "Sometimes after reflecting on the 'rag,' as he termed it, his amusement turned to chagrin. It is now apparent that what he found bearable in New York he found unbearable in Baton Rouge."[13]

He spent a little more than two years in New York and, in July of 1932, he returned to Louisiana.

He had reservations about returning to Baton Rouge and Louisiana. To a Louisiana colleague he commented, in a letter from Bellevue, "Can't deny there is life here and it is bad to grow accustomed to it, you miss it so. That's what I fear in Baton Rouge...I can get too busy to think of other things."[14]

The Carl Weiss who returned to Baton Rouge in 1932 was a vastly different person from the one who had left the city four years earlier and embarked for Europe on the steamer *George Washington* at the Hoboken, New York, docks.

He had visited Baton Rouge on occasion during the time he was enrolled at Tulane and interning at Touro. But except for these infrequent visits to Baton Rouge, Carl would be absent from the capital city for nine years.

How much Weiss had changed can never be measured. We can speculate on the extent the influence of the big city atmosphere of New York and Continental capitals of Paris and Vienna had on him, but that there was a change is obvious. He wrote to a member of the medical staff at Bellevue:

"Wish I could see all the new things—
even in Bellevue—Radio City. The new theater
must be a marvel to visit—and here there isn't a
single legitimate stage in town excepting Huey's
nauseous clowning which is reflected in his puppet
show in the capitol."[15]

His friends felt he had changed greatly. He seemed more in tune with Europe than with America and certainly more European than Baton Rougean, possibly with a touch of snobbishness about the level of sophistication in his home town compared to the glitter of the Continent. This should not really surprise anyone who reflects that the adult years of his life, from 21 upward, had been spent away from his birthplace. Moreover, they had been spent in an environment of sophistication and glamour far removed from the small, unhurried pace of the town of Baton Rouge.

Brother Tom observed:

"He was most knowledgeable about a lot
of things just brought up in casual conversation. I
guess I used to be annoyed at the ease with which
he played the piano. This was after he came back
from New York and was in practice....

"I recall he used to visit us during the
days of Prohibition and Dad prided himself on the
fact that he had altar wine. Carl said he had tasted
better wines in Europe."

Just as Carl had changed, so had Baton Rouge and Louisiana changed. By 1932, Huey Long had established himself as the dictator of the state and the feeling in Baton Rouge ran high against him. This feeling had obviously been communicated to Carl when he was outside the state.

An undated and unattributed newspaper clipping received by the Weiss family after Long's death quoted a close friend of Carl's, Dr. William H. Dick, who had interned at Bellevue with him, as saying, "He hated Long vehemently. He had the belief fixed in his mind that Louisiana politics were the worst of any state's. He was always a strong-willed and determined man, and on this point he could not be shaken."

A slightly different approximation of Weiss' feelings toward Long is gained from another news report in the New York *Herald Tribune* following Long's wounding in the state capitol. Once again, Dr. Dick is the source, and it is possible that the same interview contained the raw material for differing interpretations. "He felt as a great many people do, that things were being badly managed down there," Dick was quoted as saying. "He certainly was no admirer of Huey Long, but there was nothing to indicate any deep feeling on his part...."[16]

Carl himself apparently had doubts about his ability to blend into the Baton Rouge community after returning from Europe and New York. Here is brother Tom's recollection:

> "When he came back to Baton Rouge I think he was not sure if he could find the right atmosphere and be comfortable. He picked up several doctors as friends and they had more than just medicine in common. He picked up a few professors from LSU as friends. He frequently would go back and pay visits to his old English teachers, the Garig sisters."

One of the most revealing insights into his character is provided us by Carl Weiss himself, in a letter written to Tom Ed on the latter's 15th birthday. Carl had returned to Baton Rouge for a brief visit prior to establishing his residency at Bellevue and apparently he noticed what he considered to be a personality change in his younger brother. The letter communicates Carl's wishes for "all manner of good things," and then confesses to a "particular sincerity, an almost egotistical interest in my wishes for your future."

What follows seems to amount to an expression that Carl labels "this semblance of a sermon." It embodies what Tom had diagnosed as a "generation gap," but it also seems to reveal a certain dissatisfaction of Carl with himself and points to a hidden, deeper and perhaps darker nature that few had sensed in him:

> "...in you, Butz, are my hopes for all the ambitions I never realized, all the goals I never attained, all the pleasures I rushed past, all things desirable that diffidence, timidity, too sensitive pride can rob one of."

Strange words, these, from a man who had the world by the tail, returning to his native land following rewarding, enriching experiences on the Continent, standing poised to crown these with a two-year tour of duty in one of the nation's busiest and most prestigious hopsitals.

Carl continues to say that he notices in Tom "evidence of traits that I have, traits I try hard to banish...not actually evil, but unfortunate, and productive of regrets, destructive of pleasures, and more, of highly valuable associations that would ripen through life."

He warns: "These traits will form a barrier, shutting you off from other people, making it ever more difficult to bring yourself to enjoy the interests of your fellows."

In the summer of 1932, Carl Weiss began the practice of medicine in Baton Rouge, associating with his father. He was listed on the directory of the Reymond Building in downtown Baton Rouge as "C. Austin Weiss." His father, sharing the same office, was listed as "Carl A. Weiss." Some have read into this an effort by Carl to avoid capitalizing on the elder Weiss' prominence and a desire to make it on his own. More probable is the need to clarify the identity of the two doctors without using the middle names of "Adam" (which the elder Weiss apparently preferred to bury) and "Austin."

The Weiss practice was a Baton Rouge institution. Indigent patients were forgiven their debts and the Doctors Weiss shared in their patients' joys and adversities. Carl's former teacher reminisces:

> "Here is a woman who says, 'After my husband died, Dr. Weiss (the elder) sent me a receipted statement for all that I owed him. He wrote me a beautiful letter'—she broke down and wept uncontrollably—'and told me that it would be his pleasure to treat me whenever I wished. And when I went to his office and thanked him, he shed tears for my sorrow.'"[17]

In the fall of 1932, a strikingly beautiful young coed from LSU was treated by the elder Dr. Weiss. She was Louise Yvonne Pavy, daughter of a district court judge in the parish of St. Landry. Both the judge, Benjamin Henry Pavy, and the parish as a whole were diehard opponents of Huey Long. Both father and daughter were addressed by middle names by family members, she, "Yvonne" and he, "Henry."

In 1932, St. Landry Parish was the fourth most populous parish in Louisiana and it was independent of Huey Long to the same degree that East Baton Rouge and Caddo (of which Shreveport is the parish seat) were, although not for the same reasons. St. Landry followed in the mold of New Orleans, where an established political machine resisted Long and his own machine. The St. Landry machine was headed by two popular elected officials, one of whom was Henry Pavy. Three years later, at the urging of his supporters in St. Landry Parish, Long would attempt to unseat Pavy by gerrymandering his district in such a manner that it would be impossible for him to be re-elected.

Yvonne was one of eight children born to Henry Pavy. She had received an exemplary education, which included study at exclusive Newcomb College in New Orleans, the girls' affiliate of Tulane. She majored in French at Newcomb at the same time that Carl Weiss studied medicine at Tulane, although their paths never crossed. She graduated with honors and decided to teach, a profession that was becoming a tradition in her family.

She taught French from 1929 to 1932 in the lovely south Louisiana town of St. Martinville, famous as the reunion site of star-crossed lovers Gabriel and Evangeline in Longfellow's epic poem "Evangeline." She traveled to France in the late '20s as part of a contingent of young women sponsored by Dudley J. LeBlanc. LeBlanc was a colorful, long-time Louisiana Acadian politician and medicine man who launched a patent medicine called HaDaCol (HAppy DAyCOmpany) which made millions for him and drained a like amount from an eastern drug concern which had the poor judgment to purchase the company from him.

Yvonne later won a scholarship and went to France a second time in 1931, after Carl had returned to America.

Carl and Yvonne were married in Opelousas, parish seat of St. Landry, on December 27, 1933. On June 7, 1935, the couple became parents of a boy whom they named Carl Austin Weiss, Jr.

Both Carl and his father were held in high esteem in Baton Rouge and in Louisiana. In 1933, the elder Weiss was elected president of the state medical society. Carl himself was developing a reputation as a competent and caring professional.

When news was broadcast that it was Carl who encountered and shot Huey Long in the state capitol on September 8, 1935, the general reception in Baton Rouge was that of disbelief. It is a feeling that persists to this day. The reputation of the young doctor was such that friends, associates and even casual acquaintances rejected the "official" version fostered by the Long machine.

Those who knew him regarded him as a man of great compassion. He was capable of a firm resolve that carried him through years of grinding medical education, but he exhibited none of the hardness that one might expect from one who had scaled heights, experiencing rigorous years of self-denial and discipline to become one of the most promising physicians in Louisiana at the time.

One of the last persons known to have spent time with Weiss is Dorothy Morgan, wife of one of the doctor's patients whom he visited shortly before entering the state capitol. Mrs. Morgan refuses to concede that Weiss shot Long:

> "You'll never convince me that he ever had any part of that, as far as deliberately planning to kill Long. You will never convince me of that. I feel just as sure, having known him. He was a magnificent man. Certainly he never showed anything but kindness. He was, we thought, just a magnificent person—his compassion, his kindness, his gentleness, all that goes to make up a real

gentleman, in my book."[18]

Carl's sister-in-law, Marie Pavy, expresses similar sentiments:

"Such a miscarriage of everything! You just can't conceive of it, that that brilliant young man with everything to live for could have wanted to go up there and sacrifice himself like that. I just don't think they could ever, ever—nobody could ever convince me. They could show me a moving picture, I could never believe that he could do it. You just have to know the gentleness of him."[19]

Perhaps one might conclude that these are the musings of those who loved the physician, colored by a desire to believe the best of a man who married a sister or who healed a husband. But they were echoed by others who had a less sentimental attachment and, perhaps, a more objective view of Weiss.

Carlos Spaht, a lawyer in Baton Rouge who has achieved prominence in law and in politics, was a neighbor of Weiss in the office building where both worked. Spaht was an avid Huey Long supporter. He would later be elected mayor of Baton Rouge and district judge in the 1940s. He was the choice of Huey's brother Earl to succeed himself as governor of Louisiana in 1952. Louisiana law, at the time, prohibited a governor from succeeding himself.

Weiss was Spaht's physician as well as his fellow tenant. They would frequently take coffee breaks together and the meetings were pleasant ones, as Spaht recalls, despite their political differences.

He says:

"We weren't as busy in those days as we are now and we had more chances to visit. I visited with Carl, had coffee with him in the Green Room at the Reymond Building. I got to know him quite well.

"He was a fine man. Very nice, courteous, pleasant, wonderful sort of personality. It was hard for me to visualize that that would have happened."[20]

However, lest anyone conclude that Carl Weiss was devoid of strong feelings, let it be understood that there are many instances besides the aforementioned quotation from Dr. Dick to make it clear that Weiss considered Huey Long a menace to the state of Louisiana and that something should be done to curb him.

Spaht used essentially those words in describing Weiss. After giving Carl credit for his sterling qualities, Spaht alluded to the rancor the physician held for Long:

"...He expressed a great deal of strong

feelings about Huey from time to time, because Huey had upset his family. He felt strongly that Huey was some menace to our democratic way of life and generally to the welfare of the state. I knew his feelings were strongly anti-Huey.

"He was very strong in his feelings that Huey was a very bad thing for Louisiana, that somebody ought to get rid of him in some way. That was his feeling."[21]

The feeling of hatred on the part of Carl Weiss for Huey Long deepened during 1935. In fact, following Long's shooting and Weiss' death, this feeling was noted in a report of the Baton Rouge *State-Times* following an interview with Carl's wife, Yvonne. The journal reported, "The belief of the family of Dr. Weiss, they (the family) said, is that his deed was not the result of any single act of legislation, but an accumulation of the acts of the Long dictatorship."[22]

Weiss did not hide his loathing of Long. He confessed it to a fellow member of the Young Men's Business Club when the two arrived early for a meeting of the group in the Roumain Building. The member said, "Carl carried on something awful. He didn't like Long and didn't care who knew it."[23]

Long's son Russell told a reporter that a Long legislative floor leader from St. Landry Parish, a patient of Weiss, remembered, "All the man could talk about was what Huey Long was doing when he was seeing to it that Mrs. Weiss' father (Judge Henry Pavy of Opelousas) was to be gerrymandered out of office. According to Judge Guillory, he was like a man possessed when he spoke about that."[24]

Following the shooting in the state capitol, the New Orleans *Item* carried a story attributed to a "prominent Baton Rouge surgeon" who said:

"A number of us were sitting around one afternoon about ten days ago (story dated September 9, 1935) in the amphitheatre of a local hospital....Several of the doctors present...began panning Senator Long....The talk became heated....Suddenly I looked at Dr. Weiss. He said nothing but great big tears were rolling down his cheeks. He got up from the table and walked out of the room, still without saying a word."[25]

Some weeks before Long's shooting, Carl, Yvonne and the baby visited Yvonne's parents in Opelousas. Conversations centered on the recent dismissal of Yvonne's uncle, Paul Pavy, and her sister, Marie, from the St. Landry Parish school system. About Carl's reaction, a member of the family commented:

"He was distressed. I can remember the Sunday we went out there. Carl was asking Papa

(Judge Pavy) about politics in St. Landry Parish and what would happen. This was around August, a Sunday around the 21st. It must have just happened. He thought that was dreadful that people who had taught school since 1909 had just been dismissed."[26]

To Carl Weiss, the brutal hand of Huey Long seemed to be everywhere. His wife's uncle and his sister-in-law had suffered the weight of the despot's fist. The New Orleans *Item* added another incident, published a few days after the shooting:

"Another thing which is thought to have prayed (sic) on Dr. Weiss' mind concerned a young woman teacher who was a patient of his. This young woman supported a widowed mother, but she lost her job as a teacher through the political operations of the new school system. She is reported to have expressed her distress at Dr. Weiss' office."[27]

Some months before, Carl Weiss visited a young man who had developed complications in a tonsillectomy performed by the physician. The problem was minor and was soon remedied. The young man, anxious to be pronounced well enough to join the U.S. Navy, recalls, "The tonsillectomy started seeping blood and Dr. Weiss came out to take a look at it. After he had completed his examination, we talked."

The young man, son of a deputy sheriff in East Baton Rouge Parish, had seen many of the parish's citizens gather at his house and discuss the excesses of Huey Long. Although not allowed in the discussions when the men talked, he understood clearly that Long and his machine presented a problem. Seeking to make his own contribution to his conversation with the family physician, he offered:

"What's going to happen about this Huey Long mess?"

To which the young doctor replied, staring fixedly toward the floor, "All I know is, somebody's going to have to kill Huey Long."

And, after a slight pause, "It just might be me."[28]

The ensuing months would do little to lessen Weiss' bitterness. To the contrary, subsequent events would feed the gnawing anger until, in early September, it would foment to the point of overflowing.

CHAPTER FIFTEEN

The Motive

We will probably never know for certain what possessed Carl Weiss to journey to the state capitol on the night when Long was shot.

This is not because of any lack of motives offered for his actions. There are many, but none is based on solid evidence. Every theory is rooted in supposition and speculation. Some might be considered valid hypotheses. Others are based on rumor, gossip and, in one or two cases, pure fantasy.

Not a shred of testimony or fact was offered at the inquest—or since—to support any motive Weiss might have had to shoot Huey Long. In the previous chapter I have given evidence of Weiss' hatred for Long, a powerful enough motive in itself. However, most of this information is new, having been uncovered just recently. Those who have charged that Weiss was the assassin did not have this evidence to help them arrive at their conclusion.

This is another puzzling aspect of the case. The history of assassination shows that assassins are inclined to leave a trail that is easily traced.

Additionally, an oversight investigation usually reveals a mental imbalance and preoccupation with some slight, some affront, intentional or not, that causes the assassin to take offense.

This is not the case with Carl Weiss.

The days prior to September 8, 1935, were days of promise and hope for him. It is only during the last minutes of his life, when he showed up at the state capitol, that we get any inkling that he could possibly consider the course of violent action attributed to him that Sunday night. And even this insight is based on assumption and postulation and not hard evidence.

Those who maintain that Weiss did not plan in advance to kill Long and that, to the contrary, he could be the victim and not the perpetrator of the violence that exploded, point to his activities on the fateful day and during the previous week.

The week before the shooting, Carl confided to his brother his intention to build a combination office and residence on property owned by their mother on Capitol Lake. He planned to approach his mother and offer to buy the property.

He explained to Tom, "I want to talk to Mother about this property, but it is just as much yours as mine and I want you to know about it. If you have any objections, I want you to tell me about them."

Several days before the shooting, Carl had visited a heating and plumbing contractor to discuss having a floor furnace installed to replace the inefficient and dangerous space heaters in his home.

On Saturday he worked in his office in the morning. In the afternoon, he and Yvonne visited a local store to select new furniture. His receptionist recalls that it was a routine Saturday, so unspectacular that she cannot even remember which patients came in and out of the office.

There is a question about Carl Weiss' whereabouts Saturday night which will never be solved. This will be addressed later in this work. But there is no evidence that he did anything out of the ordinary at any time that Saturday. His brother remembers that he spent the previous night at home.

The next day, he and his wife went to church as was their Sunday habit, leaving their three-month old child with his grandparents. They returned from Mass and settled down to a standard Sunday dinner with Carl's father and mother.

At the dinner table there was conversation among the Weisses about Long's calling of a special session of the legislature which had convened the previous night.

When a special session is called in Louisiana today, it is necessary for the governor to give the legislature five days notice and to specify the items that will be considered. In 1935, there was no such requirement. Legislators learned what they would have to vote upon on Saturday night, when the session began. Ordinary citizens, for the most part, learned the content of the session the next morning when the Sunday paper was delivered.

Sunday was when the Weiss family learned that a bill had been introduced that would rearrange the district over which Judge Henry Pavy presided. As the district was constituted, the parish of St. Landry was the dominant one in a two-parish area. The proposed legislation would take St. Landry and move it into a district which had three parishes that were strongly pro-Long, insuring that the voting strength of St. Landry would be so diluted that Pavy could never hope to be re-elected.

The news of the legislation was carried in the Sunday *Morning Advocate* and was the central topic of conversation at the Weiss dinner table. It was the elder Dr. Weiss who was most incensed about the pending legislation.

Yvonne, whom Tom Weiss described as having "a wonderful way with Mom and Dad," attempted to assuage the feelings of the senior Weiss. She rationalized, "Don't worry about it. We're delighted. We've been trying to get him to quit for a long, long time. We've never been able to get him to retire, but now that he won't have any work to do, he can rest."

Carl took the cue, minimizing the impact of Long's action with a different brand of logic. He soothed his father, "Dad, don't worry about it. You're so foreign to those people. You don't act that way and it's not your way of life! So why get excited about it?"

Carl's father was irate. "That's the way with Long, the dirty rat." Tom felt that if there was a potential assassin at the dinner table that noontime he would have concluded that it was his father and not his brother.[1]

After dinner the grandparents, Carl, Yvonne and the baby rode to the family camp on the Amite River, a popular recreation spot for Baton Rougeans then and now. Carl and Yvonne swam and talked while the elder Weisses minded the child.

The camp was located near the village of Watson in the nearby parish of Livingston. It originally belonged to the father-in-law of Carl's physician friend, Ashton Robins. It was remotely located and consisted of three acres, accessible only by a rutted dirt road. Dr. Robins' brother-in-law, who had used the camp a great deal, died of rheumatic fever and the doctor's father-in-law had disposed of the camp because it rekindled memories of his dead son.

Carl Weiss used the camp frequently, even when it was owned by Robins' in-laws. This was one of the reasons why the Weiss family bought the property. Carl and Robins visited the camp often, carrying with them shotguns, rifles, pistols and targets. On occasion they would bring clay pigeons with them.[2]

The elder Mrs. Weiss told the press, "My son and his wife went in swimming while my husband and I stayed on the shore in the camp, playing with the baby. We stayed out there in the woods all day."[3]

On these outings, Carl usually carried with him the Browning pistol that he had bought while in Paris. He was teaching Yvonne to fire the pistol and it was a part of their routine at the camp that the pair would practice target shooting. Carl kept the gun in the bedroom dresser at home and took it with him on calls for protection. According to the elder Weiss, several intruders had recently been driven away from Carl's garage and the assumption was that they were after the drugs usually carried by physicians making their rounds.

Where Carl kept his pistol when making his rounds is unclear. It is possible that he kept it in the glove compartment of his car. It is also possible that he carried it in his bag, wrapped in a white sock to keep the oiled piece from staining other objects and to keep it from rusting. It is possible that he carried it on his person. Associates of Carl in New York remember that he carried the weapon on him on the streets of New York during his internship at Bellevue, a risky thing, in view of that state's strict regulation of firearms.[4]

Also unclear is whether Carl fired the gun that Sunday afternoon. There is some ambiguity on this point which seems to indicate a reluctance on the part of those with Carl at the river to state definitely that he fired the gun.

Yvonne did not remember if she and Carl used the gun that afternoon. The elder Mrs. Weiss was at first unsure if Carl used it but then was positive that he did not. The gun, she said, may have been in the glove compartment, but no one on the outing saw the weapon. However, Yvonne told a family member that the gun was used. One of her sisters recalls, "They did target shooting—they did target shooting in the water. Remember? They told us that!"[5]

Dr. Robins is also of the opinion that Carl fired the pistol that afternoon.

It is understandable that family members might tend to minimize the importance of the Browning pistol and even to forget the fondness that Carl had for firearms. All his life he used them, owning a .22 caliber Remington rifle as a boy and later owning a second pistol, in addition to the Browning he brought back from overseas.

Carl spent a lot of time with the Browning pistol.

A colleague who graduated from Tulane with him in 1927 and whose family boarded Carl for the last several years of his medical schooling, remembers the many outings the pair had, firing the Browning, after Carl had returned from Europe. The friend recalled:

> "He said he wanted to try it out. We went down to Barataria (a wilderness area south of New Orleans) where there were at that time a lot of alligators, turtles and snakes in the swamps.
>
> "He and I together fired about 100 rounds of ammunition at alligators, gars as they jumped, snakes and turtles. That little gun just felt so nice and comfortable in your hand. I liked it because it did not have any appreciable recoil. I had been using a .32 Luger that belonged to my father....That had a recoil that brought your hand upward, not just backward, when you fired.
>
> "Carl's gun had no appreciable recoil and that was why I liked it so much. That was how I got acquainted with the gun."[6]

If we are to reach any conclusion about the innocence or guilt of Carl Weiss, it is necessary for us to determine his itinerary when he returned to Baton Rouge from the Amite River and the actual time he returned to the city. There is some confusion about these points.

Carl's father told reporters that the group returned about 7:30 p.m., although the correct time was probably at least an hour and perhaps as much as an hour and a half sooner.

The time of Carl's arrival in Baton Rouge is important. If, upon his return, he accomplished his ordered tasks—eating dinner, feeding the dog, showering, changing clothes—and then went directly to the capitol where he confronted Long, then a strong case can be made for a cold, calculating, determined assassination attempt. If, on the other hand, he did these chores and then went about an established physician's routine Sunday evening, making professional calls, after which he visited the capitol, then the case is not so strong.

Before he left, Carl made a telephone call. His mother told reporters that Carl made the call to a patient at 8:30, "telling him to be at the hospital early Monday morning for a scheduled operation." Yvonne remembered that Carl placed a telephone call, but maintained that it was to Dr. J. Webb McGehee, anesthesiologist who was to assist Carl Monday morning in a tonsillectomy. Yvonne estimated the time at a little after 8:00 and said the purpose was to inform Dr. McGehee that the operation site had been changed from Our Lady of the Lake Sanitarium to the Baton Rouge General Hospital.

Dr. McGehee himself confirmed that he did, indeed, receive a telephone call from Carl Weiss. He splits the difference in time between the Weiss women, fixing the time of the telephone call at 8:15 p.m. However, Dr. McGehee gives two versions of the call.

He told Baton Rouge reporters on Friday, September 13, that Carl Weiss called his home the night of the shooting and spoke to Mrs. McGehee. He asked her to relay to Dr. McGehee the news that the locale for the operation had been changed to Baton Rouge General Hospital.

When he testified at the inquest eight days later, McGehee was still sure that the time was 8:15 p.m., but he remembered that it was he and not Mrs. McGehee who had the conversation with Carl. "I spoke to him on the telephone at 8:15 p.m. Sunday, a week ago. He asked me if I knew that the operation for the following day had been changed from Our Lady of the Lake Sanitarium to the (Baton Rouge) General Hospital. I told him I knew that."

During his testimony, Dr. McGehee also volunteered the information that he had talked with Carl personally on Friday, two days before the altercation in the state capitol. McGehee's office was in the Reymond Building, two floors below the Doctors Weiss. There is no information about when Carl Weiss learned about the change of the place of the operation, but it can be presumed that this occurred sometime during the ordinary Monday-Friday work week, rather than Saturday or Sunday. If this assumption is granted, then a logical question arises why Carl did not communicate the change on Friday when he talked to McGehee or, if the change was made later, to his Reymond Building neighbor before the close of business Friday, or during the half day of business on Saturday.

Dr. McGehee's recollection that his conversation with Carl took place at 8:15 p.m. roughly approximates the estimates of Yvonne and the elder Mrs. Weiss—a little after 8:00 p.m. and 8:30 p.m., respectively. But we do not know that these time estimates are all independent of each other. It is possible that Dr. McGehee and the senior Mrs. Weiss are reinforcing the recollection of Carl's widow.

Then, about 9:00, according to Yvonne, Carl "had to go out on a sick call." She confesses her bewilderment, "This is what I cannot understand. The capitol is only a stone's throw from his house. Maybe he went over there to look in, because we knew it would be in session last night. I don't know why he went in. None of us can understand it."

This is, indeed, a mystery, but it becomes less so if one determines that the Weiss family returned to Baton Rouge at 6:00 p.m.—which is one of the estimates given us—instead of 7:30 p.m.

One of Yvonne's sisters remembers that it was much sooner than 7:30 p.m. that the family returned. "What I recall from what Yvonne said, it was around 6:00—6:30. They got back before dark."[7]

Dr. F.O. Pavy, uncle of Yvonne and member of the House of Representatives from St. Landry Parish, was chosen by the family to be the spokesman in meetings with reporters. He recalls:

"On Sunday, while his parents sat on the beach of their camp with their baby grandchild, Carl and Yvonne sported about the water. When he returned home, he bade his wife an affectionate good-bye, as he left about 7:00 p.m. for a professional call."

So it could have been "about 7:00 p.m." that Carl left, according to the family spokesman, who, clouding the picture about the Monday operation even more, added, "He even phoned the Lady of the Lake Sanitarium to make an appointment for an operation Monday morning."

Dr. Ashton Robins remembers that Carl left his home to visit patients at the Baton Rouge General Hospital. According to Dr. Robins:

"He was my ear, nose and throat consultant at that time. I was doing everything. I was delivering lots of babies and treating children and he did most of my tonsillectomies and in fact, the night he supposedly killed Huey...he told his wife that he was going to the Baton Rouge General Hospital...to check on the two patients he had admitted that Sunday afternoon to operate on Monday morning."

It is not possible to determine from hospital records at Baton Rouge General Hospital if Carl Weiss, did, in fact, make a call there Sunday night. Because of the need to make room for additional records, all records prior to 1936 have been destroyed.

However, Carl Weiss' movements for much of the balance of that night, before he arrived at the state capitol, are documented by a witness.

Carl Weiss was the physician for the Morgan family—Elmore, Dorothy and their son Elmore, Jr. He had removed the tonsils and adenoids of Elmore, Jr. Elmore, Sr. had a throat infection—a "husky throat"—that defied diagnosis. One physician diagnosed tuberculosis, but all tests came out negative. Carl became the physician in charge and eventually Morgan recovered.[8]

Morgan was confined to his bed. He was a prisoner of his bedroom. According to Dorothy, "He was not to cross the street, couldn't speak, couldn't talk, couldn't see anybody except me and the family. He couldn't write letters, couldn't do anything but count the leaves on the trees."

Carl had arranged to have Morgan sent to a sanitarium near Prairieview, Texas. He would later be pronounced cured and the attending physician would inform him that he had spent two years longer in bed than he had to.

Mrs. Morgan recalls that Elmore, Sr. was quite a fisherman and this he had in common with Carl Weiss. She remembers, "If there was any one thing that broke my heart, it was when they told me he was never going to get well. He used to ask me on a sunny day, 'Please put these fishing flies out and air them out because I'll want to use them again.'"

Earlier in the week, Dorothy had visited Carl in his office and he promised her, "I'll be out to see Elmore as usual," which meant a Sunday night visit of 6:30 or 7:00 p.m. On this Sunday night, Carl returned a collection of flies loaned him by Morgan.

Dorothy remembers that it was an extended visit. "Some of the time he would spend an hour or so, maybe not that much, depending upon how much time he had. That particular Sunday, it seemed like a very leisurely visit. He didn't seem to be in any hurry at all. I had to believe that he must have gone straight from here—it seems to me— to the capitol."

Morgan received his news of the outside world from a crystal radio set. Forbidden to speak, he would knock on the wall of his bedroom to call to his wife. When she answered his knock, he would write out his requests or comments on a pad of paper.

"As I remember, Dr. Weiss hardly had time to get back to town when Elmore knocked on the wall," Mrs. Morgan tells. "He knocked on the wall to tell me what had happened, that Carl had just been killed. I said, 'That's impossible.' It does seem impossible. But that's true. And that was it."

It is important to determine just exactly how Carl Weiss spent the last hours of his life. If he left his home about 9:00 p.m., went to the state capitol and lay in wait for Huey Long, then it could be an assassination—a pure, cold-blooded attempt to kill.

If, however, Weiss spent two hours ministering to patients, then it hardly seems he had an assassination on his mind. His brother Tom seems to feel that Carl had never entered the capitol building until that night. If so, he can be presumed to have been ignorant of the legislative process, for if he had entered the capitol at 9:30 or 10:00 p.m., he would have found no Huey Long. The House of Representatives was in the process of adjourning when Long left to visit the governor's office and there would have been no reason for him to linger. This does not seem to reflect the type of planning we might associate with a person having an assassination on his mind.

If Carl Weiss did visit the Baton Rouge General Hospital and then travelled to the bedside of Elmore Morgan, then it was simply bad luck that he arrived in downtown Baton Rouge while the lights of the state capitol were still burning. A sudden impulse to visit the state capitol could have sprung up; a decision to confront Long could have prompted him to climb the steps. However, at the very worst, it was not the cold, calculated, premeditated action of a man who had concealed his true nature during a day of idyllic leisure with his family during his last day on earth.

This itinerary—that of Weiss attending to his chores as a healer and perhaps impulsively stopping by at the capitol—also lends credence to the version of the killing espoused by the Weiss family that Carl approached Long to remonstrate with him about his treatment of Yvonne's family. Insulted by Long, he struck the senator. Guns were drawn and, in the barrage that ensued, Weiss was killed and Long was wounded.

In which case, Carl Weiss was no assassin.

Something transpired between Carl and Yvonne Weiss on the night of September 8 to cause her to become concerned about Carl's intentions and to worry after he left home. None of her subsequent interviews allude to any concern she might have had, but others mention her misgivings following Carl's departure.

Carl's father testified at the inquest that his son occasionally carried a pistol. He had the pistol with him that night, according to Yvonne, as repeated by the Baton Rouge *State Times:*

> "Dr. Weiss left his home early in the evening telling Mrs. Weiss that he was going to make some calls and would stop by the hospital before his return. But, as Mrs. Weiss was putting their three-month old baby to bed, she missed the pistol and spent considerable time in making phone calls trying to locate her husband."

(Note the newspaper's reference to Carl leaving his home "early" in the evening. It seems doubtful that 9:00 p.m., which is the given time by Yvonne for her husband's departure, could be considered "early.")

Years later, Yvonne could not explain why she had suddenly gone to the dresser drawer where the pistol was kept and why she became concerned that it was missing.

Yvonne's concern is borne out in two stories in the September 17, 1935 edition of the *Times-Picayune*. In one story, Weiss' father is quoted as telling District Attorney Odom:

> "My son's wife telephoned me about ten minutes to ten o'clock that night and asked me if my son was at my home. She said that he had gone out to make a call."

The same edition also offers another version of the telephone calls:

> "Twice during the early evening, according to the witness (Dr. Carl Adam Weiss), the wife of the young Doctor Weiss called his home by telephone. Once Mrs. Weiss answered and the other time the doctor himself answered."

The picture we get is one of a distraught woman attempting to locate her husband. By Yvonne's own admission, it was the absence of the firearm from the dresser drawer that prompted this concern.

Although Tom Weiss believes that the night of September 8 was the first occasion on which his brother visited the state capitol, one of Huey Long's legislative supporters believed otherwise and felt that he saw Carl standing opposite the governor's office on Saturday night, the first night of the special session. (As stated earlier, the Weiss family remembers that Carl spent Saturday night at home.)

Henry Larcade, now dead, was one of the state senators who signed the "Round Robin" that saved Huey Long from conviction on impeachment charges. He was a political power in Opelousas and was anti-Pavy. Because of his pressure and that of others of his faction, Long consented to have introduced in the House the bill which gerrymandered Pavy out of his judicial district. Larcade is also blamed by the Pavy family for the loss of jobs by family members in the school system.

Senator Larcade arrived in Baton Rouge for the session Saturday evening and answered roll call when the Senate convened. All bills were introduced in the House of Representatives and the Senate had nothing to do until the bills were passed by the House and sent to the Senate. The Senate adjourned and Larcade left the chamber to go to the House. In the corridor, he noticed Carl Weiss standing in the recess opposite the governor's office, the same spot where he stood the following night.[9]

Because the special session was not advertised in advance there is some question as to whether Carl Weiss would have known such activity was planned for Saturday night and Larcade's recollections could be open to doubt. On the other hand, living as close to the capitol as he did, it would have been obvious to the doctor that something was going on in the statehouse and it would have been a simple matter to conclude that there was a session in the offing and that Long would be in attendance. The newspapers that week had speculated about the prospect of such a session.

However, if there is a doubt about Weiss' presence at the capitol on Saturday, there is no question that he was there Sunday night. His car was parked in front of the building, as close to the entrance as it is possible to get.

He was noticed standing between the pillars opposite the governor's office a half hour before the shooting by three young girls who were visiting. Patsy Odom was the 14-year-old daughter of Frank Odom, who knew Huey from the days when the two were travelling salesmen. Patsy was in the capitol with two girl friends. They were seeking the Kingfish's autograph.

Patsy (now Patsy Odom LeBlanc) remembers the trio roaming the halls in the state capitol in search of Long. Her family was strongly pro-Long. Earl Long, Huey's brother, was a regular visitor at the Odom household and it was here that he courted his future wife, Blanche Revere. During one of their passes through the corridor outside the governor's office, she and her friends saw Carl Weiss. Patsy met him for the first time.

She recollects:

"Frances and Mildred Sanchez lived in my neighborhood and Dr. Weiss was their doctor. And the thing I remember so well is that at least a half hour before the assassination they introduced me to him. It was in the area where Long was later assassinated."

The youngsters did not get Huey's autograph. They were about to pass the outer doors of the House of Representatives when shots rang out. Patsy recalls:

"I remember three very large men coming through the crowd and I was terrified because many people thought this was a gang war. I think he had gotten in Dutch with the Mafia in some sort of way. You've probably read something about that. And that's what I thought had happened. I thought there was going to be more shooting."[10]

It is highly likely that Huey Long was in the governor's office, a few yards from Carl Weiss, Patsy Odom and her friends, while they chatted in the corridor. Well over an hour before, Long had left his 24th floor penthouse apartment in the capitol after eating a meal that had been sent from the basement cafeteria. He went to the first floor and, appropriating Governor Allen's desk, he sent for the legislative leaders, one by one, explaining the strategy being used to pass his legislation and assigning tasks to each.[11]

No accounts of the shooting of Huey Long make any mention of any contact between him and Carl Weiss other than the single confrontation when the shooting took place. However, if Weiss was in place fully a half hour before the shooting and if Long had arrived at the first floor and the governor's office an hour before that time, the paths of the two must have crossed.

Long was a peripatetic politician, always on the move, except for those occasions when he was restrained from locomotion, such as the floor of the U.S. Senate. But even at these times, he vibrated in place, gesturing and shifting—a stallion in a starting gate, scarcely able to contain the pent-up energy inside.

That Sunday night Long had much to do and was leaving nothing to chance. His bills had been introduced the previous night in the House. Sunday morning they had been heard and reported favorably by the House Ways and Means Committee. They would be received by the complete House Sunday night and would be acted upon Monday morning. They would immediately be sent to the Senate, where they would be received and placed in line for a committee hearing Tuesday morning. They would all be finally passed on Wednesday morning, five legislative days—the legal minimum—for passage of legislation.

Long was mobile. A reporter describes his actions that night, during the hour and 20 minutes between the time the House went into session and the time the shooting took place:

> "When they (the legislature) met, Long was, as usual, everywhere at once, rushing from the Senate to the House and back, over to Governor Allen's office for a quick huddle with one or another of the floor leaders, up to the Speaker's rostrum, back to some doubtful member's desk— and everywhere he went he was followed by a nimbus of hurrying bodyguards."[12]

With such a restless hustling, with Long briskly moving from the House to the governor's office, trailing in his wake the assembled toughs and hangers-on that formed his entourage, it is unlikely that he would not have passed Weiss.

It is also highly unlikely that the group would not have noticed the doctor, and perhaps several other men, observed to be standing across from the governor's office. We have learned from the bodyguard's testimony that the guardians would ordinarily station themselves outside the governor's door while Huey tended to his business inside. Is it not fair to speculate that there would have been some curiosity about the slight, bespectacled physician across the way?

Those who talked to Long during the last week of his life were well aware that he considered his days to be numbered. The concern he had always had with assassination was intensified. He displayed an alarm that seemed to approach panic.

Justice Fournet recalled, "He knew he was going to get shot. Everybody told him that. I remember when he left the lobby of the Roosevelt Hotel the Wednesday or Thursday before he was shot to go to Baton Rouge ...Huey said he knew they were going to shoot him but he was going to go anyway."[13]

One of his bodyguards remembered that his wife pleaded with him at their Audubon Boulevard home Sunday morning not to go to Baton Rouge. He recalls that Long told Rose, "I may not come back, but I'll die fighting."[14]

When Long's motorcade left New Orleans to go to Baton Rouge Sunday morning it did not travel its usual route. There were detours. Long directed his driver to visit the site of the bridge that, at his direction, was being constructed over the Mississippi in neighboring Jefferson Parish. He left the car and walked as far as he could on the unfinished span. The bridge is now known as the Huey P. Long Bridge.

Also under construction was the Bonnet Carre Spillway, a federal project that would provide protection for New Orleans by diverting flood waters from the swollen Mississippi River into Lake Pontchartrain. Huey's Airline Highway crossed the spillway area and was yet to be opened to traffic. However, he and his entourage forsook the meandering and winding River Road, removed the barricades from the spillway construction and used the more direct route.

Bodyguards believed, retrospectively, that Long genuinely believed he would be killed and that he wished to view his latest works in progress before going to eternal rest.[15]

On Sunday night, unusual security precautions were taken in the capitol. Long's 24th floor apartment was well guarded. Judge Fournet remembers that he was stopped by a guard and questioned when he attempted to visit Long.

Virtually every state policeman who could be spared from highway duty was summoned to the capitol. The bodyguards had been warned to expect trouble. According to the New Orleans *Item,* "They had been told to expect 'almost anything.'"

State Trooper Joe Fakier remembers that there were over a hundred bodyguards on duty with Long that night, 50 of which were stationed in the House of Representatives. Others place the estimate of security forces on hand at several hundred.

There are three doors to the House and these were normally open to the public. Sunday night, state police closed two of the chamber doors and guarded the third, allowing only legislators and public officials to enter. The public was banned from the ground level of the chamber and was relegated to the balcony overlooking the assemblage.

Fakier said the security force had been told there would be a group of men from Opelousas who would attempt to storm the capitol. If there was any sign of hostility, visitors would be evicted from the building.

Fakier remembered:

> "It looked like something just had to happen...We escorted 25 people out of there. Put 'em out of the capitol building. They was raising so much hell, so much commotion..."

According to the trooper, "Spectators were yelling, 'Huey Long ain't worth a damn! You ought to run him out of the state!' And we'd take those people and throw them out of the capitol—get 'em out of there."[16]

But yet, in this charged atmosphere, with tension and suspicion crackling like lightning throughout the building, with the tightest security imaginable, it was possible for a single individual to approach Long, jam a weapon against his body and fire.

And this is what we are asked to believe. Is this believable?

Also, is it believable that on the numerous occasions that Long and his coterie passed the killer lying in wait outside the governor's office, bodyguards had no curiosity about him?

On his final pass through the corridor, Long outstripped his bodyguards and paused, ten feet from his assassin, to open the door to the governor's office. His back was to Weiss. He presented an ideal target, alone, unaware, with no bodyguard nearby. Moreover, after having done his job, the killer would have had an opportunity to flee down the same stairs that Huey would use a few moments later. But yet, Carl Weiss ignored this opportunity and chose to strike seconds later, when Long was surrounded by bodyguards and escape was impossible.

Is this believable?

No, it is not.

If, as Patsy Odom remembers, Weiss was standing opposite the governor's office as long as 30 minutes before the shooting began and if, as was Long's habit, he paced the distance between the House of Representatives and the office constantly, then Long and his retinue would have seen the physician. Some reports have it that Weiss was hiding behind a pillar in the hallway, but the pillar is hardly 18 inches in diameter, incapable of "hiding" anyone, considering the suspicious and alert contingent of bodyguards that surrounded Long.

But was there a witness to any contact between Long and Weiss or Weiss and the bodyguards before the climactic confrontation that left Weiss dead and bleeding on the marble floor of the capitol?

As a matter of fact, there was and the story he remembers differs substantially from the "official" version. His name is Douglas M. Linney.

And what follows is the Linney Hypothesis. It answers a lot of questions that have been unanswered until now.

CHAPTER SIXTEEN

The Linney
Hypothesis

If Carl Weiss did, in fact, shoot Huey Long, why did he do it?

And even if he did not shoot him, why was he at the state capitol that night, in a place where he should have known his presence would be misunderstood and misinterpreted?

Some have speculated that he saw the lights burning in the building after making his rounds and dropped in out of curiosity. His brother does not recall that Carl was ever in the capitol before that Sunday night.

He had returned to Baton Rouge from New York just about the time the new capitol was being put into use. Oscar K. Allen, successor to Huey Long, was inaugurated in May of 1932, which roughly coincides with the time that Carl arrived in the capital city. There had been eight legislative sessions held in the new capitol before the one that convened on September 7, 1935. Huey Long had attended all of them. If a curiosity in the building and an interest in observing Long were Weiss' reasons for appearing at the capitol that night, such an interest might easily have been satisfied much earlier.

There should be little doubt that the doctor's visit to the capitol was prompted by the events of the few days preceding. The fact that he was in possession of a gun would seem to indicate that he was acting from a destructive impulse. While one might speculate that he could have carried the weapon with him on his calls and simply had forgotten to divest himself of it before entering the capitol, this hardly would befit an intelligent man entering the camp of an enemy—an act fraught with woeful consequences.

It is impossible to believe that Weiss innocently entered the building to watch the show—or even to confront Long—without harboring a plan of violence if he encountered some kind of resistance or opposition from Long.

The question that remains yet to be answered is: Why? What prompted a young doctor, father of a three-month-old son, acknowledged to be one of the most promising physicians in the area, if not the state; a man who had none of the clinical characteristics of an assassin and who obviously was making plans for a future—what prompted him even to venture into the presence of Long, to invade the lair of the Kingfish?

Some have suggested insanity, a temporary mental imbalance, or perhaps the product of a darker side of Weiss' nature that was unleashed. There is little question that Carl Weiss was insane, at least to some degree, on that night, if he stalked and gunned down Long. If this accusation is correct, obviously he lacked the mental capacity that might have prevented him from entering an arena and precipitating an encounter from which nothing but tragedy could ensue.

But the question still nags: Why?

There are half a dozen theories about Weiss' reasons for entering the capitol and confronting Long. All of these are based on conjecture. Some can be rejected out of hand; some seem to be better founded than others. But after we discard the theories that are patently defective and those that rest on insufficient evidence and shaky premises, we still have several rather vaguely defined hypotheses.

Let us take each of these conjectures and examine them, starting with those which can be dismissed with little or no discussion.

The liberal journal *New Republic,* which had followed Long's career with a love-hate attraction from the time he burst on the national scene, offered its own theory. The publication, attracted to Long because of his anti-establishment and Populist views, was also repelled by his fascist and dictatorial ways. Here is the version the weekly propounded:

> "So far as can be learned at the moment of writing, Long's murder was not the work of an organized conspiracy among his political opponents. The young doctor who did the deed and paid for it with his life seems to have acted alone and without any contact with groups of persons hostile to Long. We learn from reliable private sources that his chief quarrel with the Senator was because the latter was attempting to destroy the Tulane University Medical School, in which Dr. Weiss was interested, by building up in opposition to it a medical school in New Orleans."[1]

We need not dwell on this theory for any length of time. While the creation of the LSU Medical School, in competition with Tulane, may have been prompted by spite and anger, there was no long-lived resentment on the part of the medical establishment toward its existence. The new medical school was established in 1930, almost five years before Long's shooting. While Carl Weiss no doubt had fond memories of his training at Tulane University, there is no evidence that he felt the LSU school would do any enduring harm to his alma mater.

Walter Winchell, radio and newspaper gossip and public affairs columnist, offered a theory of his own in an October, 1935 column. Winchell has a special place in the Huey Long shooting and his Sunday night radio program, "The Jergens Journal," figured prominently in reports of the episode.

Winchell's program aired between 9:00 and 9:30 p.m. on Sunday nights, Louisiana time. Announcer Ben Grauer would croon, "The Jergen's Journal, featuring Walter Winchell." Following this, Winchell would burst into living rooms throughout the nation breathlessly and urgently delivering a familiar salutation that caused Americans to stop what they were doing to listen: "Good evening, Mr. and Mrs. America and all the ships at sea. Let's go to press."

For half an hour Winchell, in his rapid fire machine gun, rat-a-tat delivery, would involve the nation in the doings of the political, social and criminal elite, blending words into a peculiar Winchellesque slang and heavily slanting his interpretation of events.

Toward the tail end of his program on September 8, 1935, some listeners recall there was an interruption to announce that Huey Long had been shot in the state capitol. To this day, many Baton Rougeans will swear that Walter Winchell first broke the news that Long had been killed and that Dr. Weiss was responsible, even before positive identification had been made in the capitol. This has promoted claims that a conspiracy was afoot that extended far beyond the state's boundaries. Otherwise, "How would Walter Winchell have known so soon?"

The written transcript of Winchell's program that Sunday night contains no mention of the Long assassination. And, given the fact that Weiss was not identified as the assassin until well after the close of Winchell's program, listeners probably heard a flash after the conclusion of his show and mistakenly attributed it to the popular commentator.

Winchell took a special interest in the shooting. The week following it, he gave the Weiss family version of the shooting, which involved Weiss' confrontation of Long as having been prompted by a desire to get Long to stop vilifying and persecuting his in-laws, the Pavys.

Here is Winchell's fanciful version, whose source is a "famed newspaper man" who, for his part, received the version from a "young physician in New Orleans." (Capitals and ellipses are Winchell's.)

> "Not only had Huey thrown Weiss' dad-
> in-law in the gutter because of political differences
> of opinion, but Huey had taken his two sisters

(instructors in Baton Rouge high schools) and had
them kicked out to show his authority. On top of
ALL THAT, Long issued an order prohibiting
young Dr. Weiss from operating in any hospital in
Baton Rouge or vicinity!...Thus ruining the whole
family and wrecking their lives...When he went to
the hospital that night, the surgeon-in-chief had
just gotten the order, and when he told Weiss, the
poor fellow just had about all he could endure,
naturally."

Winchell follows this revelation with a description of the shooting
wherein Long and Weiss argued, Weiss slipped and "whipped out the old pistol"
and fired. Always needing the boffo conclusion, Winchell tells us that Long was
wearing a bullet proof vest and only one spot on his body, about three inches
across, was vulnerable. This is the spot the bullet penetrated.[2]

A popular version of the shooting advanced by the Long organization
involved Weiss' participation in a "death conference" wherein one of those
present picked the black ball or the short straw which meant that he was chosen
to assassinate Long. Much of the reasoning for this theory stems from the meeting held in New Orleans at the DeSoto Hotel which was overheard by Long
supporters. Long had read from the transcript during a session of the U.S. Senate
and, in retrospect, it seemed the assassination was a fulfillment of the purpose of
that meeting.

The house organ of the Long machine, *The American Progress,* in its
December, 1935 edition, attempted to link Carl Weiss with other conspirators.
The front page of the journal carried a banner headline in 72 point type which
read, "AND THEY DARE ASK YOUR VOTE!" Below the headline were three
photographs. The first was of Carl Weiss, the second was the Browning pistol
recovered at the scene of Huey's shooting and the third was a scene of
pallbearers carrying Long's body to the grave. Cutlines were, respectively, "One
Man...One Gun...One Bullet."

Also reproduced in the publication was what was represented as a portion of the original transcript of proceedings at the DeSoto Hotel meeting. The
transcript was obtained by poking a microphone out the window of a room adjoining the one where the alleged conspirators met. At the end of this Rube
Goldberg contraption was Herbert Christenberry, court reporter who was known
in Long circles as the world's fastest stenographer. He was the brother of Earle
Christenberry, Huey Long's secretary, who had his own claim to fame as the
world's fastest typist. Everyone in the entourage of the Kingfish was world class.

The transcript read, "DR. WISE entered the room and was introduced."
This was interpreted by the Long people to be an account of Carl Weiss joining
the conspirators, his name being somewhat garbled in transcription. Long forces

even had an affidavit from a bellman at the DeSoto Hotel who swore he had seen Weiss at the meeting.

The bellman, D.F. Robichaux, said, "In this gathering affiant saw a man who very much resembled the picture of Dr. Carl A. Weiss which was published in the paper shortly after the shooting of Senator Long." However, Robichaux confessed that he could not "state the month of this meeting."

That there was such a meeting and that Long's death was discussed—perhaps even plotted—is a fact. However, there are three problems with this theory. The first is that Weiss did not attend any of the meetings at the DeSoto. He was elsewhere on both days. On one day he was in Opelousas at the house of Yvonne's family and the second day he and his father treated patients (including a relative of Long's) at the Weiss office.

The second problem is that there was no clearcut course of action decided upon at the meeting and no definite plans were laid for the assassination.

Finally, none of those who actively planned violence for Long seemed to have known Weiss. One author quotes the leader of the Minute Men, a paramilitary organization with a tilt toward violence, as having attended a death conference with Weiss and three others who drew straws to choose Long's assassin.[3]

One of those supposedly present was Fred Parker, former Baton Rouge deputy sheriff, who was accused by Long on the floor of the U.S. Senate of plotting his killing. While this book was being written, Parker suffered a stroke and could not communicate but I was told by Parker's son, Federal Judge John Parker, of the Baton Rouge district, that Parker and Weiss had never met.

The claim that Weiss was part of a cabal that conspired to kill Long had a certain utility for a machine looking for political cannon fodder in an election to be held four months hence. The opposition slate of candidates was labeled "the assassination ticket" and the entire campaign for the governorship and the other offices at stake rested on the single issue of Long's death.

That certain members of the opposition were prepared to assassinate Long is well founded. However, all attempts to link Weiss with the plotters fail.

There is the interesting and widely held version of Weiss' motive that involved a racial slur that Huey Long had made or was prepared to make involving the ancestry of Judge Henry Pavy. It was stated in perhaps its bluntest form by Justice John Fournet in a 1975 interview appearing in the *Times-Picayune*:

> "...They made Dr. Weiss believe that his son had Negro blood, that Huey said his son had Negro blood...but I never heard that and I know it's not true. But I believe they told that to that poor boy."[4]

In 1935, just as 50 years later in Louisiana, the possibility of miscegenation was very real. It did, and still does, provoke strong feelings. Louisiana law provides that ⅟₃₂ Negro blood is sufficient to qualify a person for classification as non-white. Whites and non-whites are still polarized today, perhaps not as sharply as half a century ago, but still polarized, nevertheless. As a rule, black candidates receive black votes and white candidates receive the votes of their own racial constituency. There have been exceptions to this in recent years but, for the most part, the rule holds.

Although there are few who would attribute racism to Huey Long, he was as insensitive to the feelings of Negroes during his political life as any other white politician in the South. Before the civil rights advances made in the '40s by Truman and followed by other national and local politicians, blacks, in general, were considered by even the most tolerant of public officials to be inferior, almost sub-human. However, progressive politicians like Long held that they were entitled to humane treatment, if not equality.

The Louisiana politician generally considered to have been most attentive to black needs, the late Earl Long, Huey's brother, carried black precincts in landslide proportions, even against such accredited liberals as New Orleans Mayor deLesseps S. "Chep" Morrison. But he was as unfeeling about black pride as anyone. When asked about black progress in Louisiana, Earl Long used this crude measure of their advances: "Fifty years ago they were eating each other."

Huey Long was no racist. However, his insights into black feelings were dulled by his redneck remoteness from their plight. An interview granted by the Kingfish to Roy Wilkins (in 1935, editor of the NAACP's publication *The Crisis*) illustrates this.

Wilkins reported, "In the first two minutes I found out Huey does all the talking and that he uses 'Nigger,' 'Nigra,' and occasionally 'colored,' but mostly 'Nigger.'"

He summed up what he considered to be the Kingfish's position on the race question this way:

> "My guess is that Huey is a hard, ambitious, practical politician. He is far shrewder than he is given credit for being. My further guess is that he wouldn't hesitate to throw Negroes to the wolves if it became necessary: neither would he hesitate to carry them along if the good they did him was greater than the harm."[5]

Although his ego was too large to allow him to harbor racial feelings, Huey didn't refrain from accusing political enemies of having "a little too much coffee in their cream" if it suited his purpose. He nicknamed opponents "Kinky" and "Shinola" with devastating results.[6]

Where the story began that Long planned to accuse Henry Pavy of possessing Negro blood, thereby casting a shadow upon the racial purity of Carl Weiss' son, is not clear. There is no record that he ever used the smear. Former St. Landry Parish Sheriff Adler LeDoux maintains that he grew up near the Pavys in Opelousas and never heard the slur. Others in St. Landry Parish remember the rumor that the Pavys had Negro blood, but it obviously did not affect the political future of Judge Pavy, who was re-elected time and time again.

I learned from the Pavy family the origin of the rumor. It seems that around the turn of the century, a politically prominent member of the Pavy clan deserted the Democratic party to support Republican candidates. Because of the lingering memory of the Reconstruction following the Civil War and the efforts of the Republicans to establish Carpetbag government in Louisiana with Negroes at the helm, the party had the label of the black man's party. Thus, when the renegade Pavy left the Democrats, he was promptly labeled "Nigger Pavy." The slur was used on occasion by political enemies but, for the most part, it was met with a certain amount of amusement by the Pavy family, which apparently could afford to be tolerant of the smear, since physical characteristics of the clan were far removed from Negroid features.

No one seems to offer hard evidence that the prospect of Long slandering his wife and son was known by Weiss, or, for that matter, that Long was even intending to use the canard. Despite its tenacious survival as a possible motive for the shooting episode, there is nothing to document it.

There is another scenario that was advanced by the Weiss family shortly after the incident.

Here it is.

Carl Weiss went to the state capitol because he was fed up with the actions of the Kingfish. He was unarmed. He intended to reason with Long, to ask him to stop persecuting the family of his wife. He approached Long. Long cursed him. He struck Long. At Long's order, the bodyguards cut Weiss down. In the fury of the shooting, Long was hit by one of the bullets, accidentally or intentionally, from the gun of a bodyguard.

Panicked, the bodyguards searched for a way out. They located Weiss' automobile, took his gun from it and threw it down on the floor next to his lifeless corpse. This is why Long commanded that no one comment on the matter. The truth, had it been known, would have obviously shown that Long had caused his own death in ordering the shooting of an unarmed man who approached him seeking only for himself and his family to be left alone.

This theory makes as much sense as the "official" theory but it has its own built-in flaws.

Like the "official" version, it presumes that a hostile person could pierce the tight security of the Kingfish, getting close enough to plant a fist on his jaw, or even shoot him. (But something like that did happen, didn't it?)

Secondly, if Carl Weiss was not identified for some minutes after his death (as few as 15—as many as 30), how was it possible to (1) identify him, (2) determine that his car was parked at the capitol, (3) locate the car, open it and remove the pistol and (4) plant the gun at Weiss' side?

However, it is not this easy to dismiss this theory.

No one really knows when Carl Weiss was identified. The coroner, Dr. Bird, made positive identification. Merle Welsh, summoned from the funeral parlor to pick up the body, knew at once that it was the body of Dr. Weiss, although we can't be sure that he arrived before or after the coroner. Weiss' brother, Tom, and his cousin found Carl's car locked and, peering through the window, saw that the medical bag on the passenger side had been rifled, with instruments sticking out of the bag. They felt it was contrary to Carl's habits to leave his bag in this kind of disarray.

Unable to open the car, they went home, returned with an extra set of keys and found the car had been moved to another part of the capitol building.

There is one final motive advanced by those who accuse Carl Weiss of shooting Huey Long.

This is actually a syndrome of motives to explain Weiss' appearance at the state capitol and, if an assassination or attempted assassination occured, offers us a logical explanation for his behavior that night.

This collection of reasons follows.

1. Carl Weiss was inherently an idealistic and sensitive man. He had seen the excesses of dictatorship in Europe where Dollfuss, Hitler and Mussolini were holding sway. Returning to America and to Louisiana, he sensed a quality of the Long system uneasily reminiscent of Central Europe.

2. Weiss was reacting to the latest attempt by Long to destroy the Pavys.

3. Weiss was unnerved by the experience of one of his patients, a young teacher who visited the doctor the week of the shooting. The sole support of a widowed mother, she had been fired from her job on Friday, two days before the shooting. The State Budget Committee, which screened teachers for service in the school system, had refused to approve one supervisor, six van drivers and 19 classroom teachers. She was one of the 19.

These three motives are all part of a larger motive and complement each other. Together, they combine synergistically, fueling Weiss with the blinding hatred that caused him to go to the capitol and seek Long out.

Carl Weiss was not a disinterested professional with no concern for politics. His colleagues at Bellevue recall his distress with the Louisiana situation. Others who came in contact with him in Baton Rouge have the same opinion.

He was surrounded daily by reports of the abuses of Long and his dictatorship. At home, his wife's family was being persecuted. Away from home, at his office, he was surrounded by one of the greatest concentrations of anti-Long sentiment in Baton Rouge. Although Weiss was not officially identified with any of the numerous plots and conspiracies springing up in Louisiana like toadstools after a rain, he was exposed to coffee break talk and social and professional chit-chat lamenting the dismal state of affairs in Louisiana because of Huey.

His social contacts were, for the most part, anti-Long. His family was anti-Long. And the roster of his fellow tenants in the Reymond Building read like a hit list for anyone ferreting out potential assassins of Huey Long.

Here is a partial list of tenants in the building:

J.Y. Sanders, Jr., attorney and Sixth District congressman accused by Long of involvement in a conspiracy to kill him; Shelby Taylor, former member of the Public Service Commission, ousted as chairman because of Long's efforts and defeated for re-election for the same reason; Ashton Robins, physician friend of Weiss, strongly anti-Long; William B. Chamberlain, anti-Long physician who was present when Long underwent surgery; Hewitt Bouanchaud, former lieutenant governor and anti-Long politician; Doctors Henry McKeown and J. Webb McGehee. McKeown was the anesthetist at Long's surgery and McGehee was one of the last persons to talk to Weiss.

Through that last year of his life, Carl Weiss saw close up a devil that would eventually have to be destroyed. The previous December it had brought Standard Oil to its knees, jeopardizing the livelihood of many of Weiss' patients; in January, martial law had been declared and it seemed that the Brownshirts of Germany and the Blackshirts of Italy had been transplanted to the capital city. In August, because of the devil, his sister-in-law and his wife's uncle had been fired from the St. Landry school system. On Friday, a patient related her personal suffering and on Sunday morning the evil had reached into his immediate family by threatening his wife's father.

It was too much. Carl Weiss was able to contain his anger until his journey home from his last call that weekend. But then it exploded. He parked his car in front of the capitol and ascended its steps into history.

These are the established theories of the shooting. There is one final theory that has never been discussed. That is because it is being revealed in these pages for the first time.

It is the Linney Hypothesis.

Douglas M. Linney was a Raffles-type character who was born in northeast Louisiana in 1900, one of six boys and girls in a decent, God-fearing and upright family. All the children went to college except Douglas, who finished the ninth grade. Douglas had a quick mind and made several fortunes during his lifetime.

At the age of 18, he became interested in the oil fields. He worked in the fields, helping to drill wells. He soon went beyond roughnecking and formed his own company. In the meantime, he had made contact with others trying to make it in the oil business, including Jimmy Noe, who would provide the oil exploration expertise to form Win Or Lose Oil Company, a goose that laid golden eggs for Noe, the Kingfish, Seymour Weiss and unnumbered generations that survived them.

At one time, Linney and Noe were in business. According to Linney's sister, Mrs. Ruth Mae McDermott, Noe had the capital, but Linney had the knowledge of the oil business, "drilling or whatever."[7]

Linney was possessed of a great personality. He was tall, slim, pleasant of manner, neat to the point of being spotlessly clean and given to wearing tailored, expensive-looking cowboy clothes which in the 1980s may not stand out but in the 1930s were eye-catching. When thinking of Linney, one conjures visions of Hank Williams, Tom T. Hall, Porter Waggoner or a dozen other loose-jointed country and western personalities.

There were other descriptions of Linney, not quite as flattering as the one above. When he was admitted into the Louisiana State Penitentiary, the description read, "Poor teeth; two gold uppers; large, irregular ears; large, sharp nose, wide nostrils; large mouth, average lips..."

Linney first ran afoul of the law on January 8, 1930, when he was arrested in Shreveport on suspicion. The arrest record does not specify what infraction was involved. In March of the same year he was arrested in Tallulah, in northeast Louisiana, for larceny. There are no court records extant for his trial but there is reason to believe it was as much a civil matter as a criminal one. It seemed to involve possession of some oil field equipment that Linney's family believes he had as much claim to as did the plaintiffs. He pleaded his own case, lost and was sentenced to serve from 16 to 24 months at the state penitentiary at Angola.

Linney went to the penitentiary with letters of recommendation from merchants and public officials that were so convincing that the manager of the prison sawmill recommended, on July 29, 1930 (about a month after he had been sentenced to the pen), that he be made a trusty. On September 4, he was made a trusty and on November 5 he was granted a full pardon and released.[8]

His sister tells us:

> "He was not a criminal. He was the type
> of man who was the envy of a lot of people. In-
> stead of serving time they gave him a job, if you'll
> look at the record. He wore plain clothes and
> would guard the inmates there. But he was only
> there a couple of months."

Linney stayed out of prison for almost three years and then he went back. His sister believes it was for a gambling violation. The record shows only the charge of "operating a confidence game." When he was sentenced, the court records showed his occupation as "oil field driller." He spent more time in prison the second time around, although he still received such tender loving care that the shock of recidivism was properly cushioned.

A few months after he arrived at Angola in 1933, he was cited for meritorious service. Two years later he was discharged from the prison's camp "E." Although no records have yet been found to determine where he went from that camp, it is highly likely that he was furloughed to duty with the governor's office as a chauffeur.

Lest anyone raise an eyebrow at the thought of a criminal associating with the state's most exalted officials and their families, let them understand that even today prisoners are detailed to duty in the governor's mansion and other areas in Louisiana. Murderers and other convicts routinely cook and perform domestic chores for the state's first family. At the end of the governor's term it is customary to commute their sentences and grant them freedom. One governor announced, following the annual Gridiron Show in Baton Rouge, that he was paroling the membership of an entire prison band upon his leaving office.

A writer of the era lamented:

> "Both the state pen and the Parole Board had been politicalized and exploited to the limit...There was a state-owned building in Baton Rouge where favored convicts lived. They dressed as citizens, drove state-owned cars, travelled about the state and held wild orgies in their residence..."[9]

Linney's sister remembers that he was at the capitol the night Long was shot. An attorney who met Linney in Monroe after he had been discharged from Angola, Brunswick Sholars, relates this story provided him by Linney himself:

> "Doug had been furloughed and he was given eating money and money to buy clothes and a place to stay. He stayed in downtown Baton Rouge—I think it was the Istrouma Hotel.
>
> "On the night in question the assignment he received was to work with (bodyguard) Joe Messina and others in Senator Long's party. They would walk from one end of the capitol to the other, from the Senate to the House of Representatives. They would stop en route quite often at the office of the governor.
>
> "They would move back and forth as Huey was very interested in keeping check on how the voting was going, although he was not then a state official.
>
> "On one of the trips from the House towards the Senate, as he came along the wall talking, there was a man in a white linen suit and a

Panama hat, quite small, standing on the left side of the passageway going toward the Senate. Not much attention was paid to him until he stepped out and said, 'Senator, I must speak to you!'

"When he said this, Huey was interrupted in his conversation and turned to the man and very pleasantly said, while waving his hand, kind of pushing the man away, 'I'll be glad to talk to you later,' and they walked right on by. The man in the linen suit was pushed back against the wall but not much attention was paid to him.

"Twice more as the group came along the passageway from one direction or another, the man in the white linen suit (who turned out to be Dr. Weiss) stepped forward and said, 'I must speak to you now.' Each time Huey said, 'Later,' and kept walking.

"Finally, on the last fateful pass he became more alerted to the man who forcefully stepped out into the middle of the passageway, and with his hands raised to his side, he said, 'Governor'—not 'Senator'—'I must speak to you now!'

"At this time Huey took both hands and made motions as if he was brushing the man away—not touching him—and said, 'I told you: not now. Later!'

"The group moved forward. This confused Dr. Weiss and he slipped and fell back on the floor and his hat fell off. When this happened, Doug said, the guards became alerted to a problem, with the man lying on the floor in front of the group. Their attention was directed—all of them—at the man on the floor.

"At which time the man on the floor, Dr. Weiss, pulled what appeared to be a small, non-professional pistol from his pocket and fired. When this happened, Doug and all of the other guards pulled their pistols and started shooting at Dr. Weiss."[10]

Linney didn't explain to Sholars whether Weiss hit Long with the shot he fired. If he was lying on the floor, it is doubtful that any penetration made by a bullet fired from that position would cause the type of wounds found on

Long's body.

A bodyguard, Joseph Vitrano, was at the scene of the shooting and he told me that Weiss fired and the bullet went into the ceiling. "It's still up there. You could probably find it, if you looked," he assured me.

Linney died in Albuquerque, New Mexico, in June, 1983. He was no bum. His family remembers him as smart, street-wise operator who remembered his mother and father. He had two broken marriages and finally wed a Mexican girl who was his companion when he died.

Sister Ruth Mae recalls:

> "He was always a jump ahead of the other fellow. You'd better be smart or not mix with him. I got along with him real good, but I never did understand him too good. He was so good to my mother and father. I know when my mother was on her death bed, he had his own airplane and pilot and flew in from Salt Lake City and when he left, just to make her happy (that was way back then in 1965) he laid a hundred dollar bill down and he went by the hospital and paid all the bills even though she had insurance and when he left he still laid one hundred dollars. After he got older he always was coming home and bringing something to my mother and father."

Linney died a comfortable man, if not actually wealthy, having made much money in a copper mine which he acquired in New Mexico. According to his sister, he was an aide de camp of the governor of New Mexico and was connected in New Mexico politics.

The Linney hypothesis is vulnerable. After all, it is now a thrice told tale, relying for its believability on recollections almost half a century old. But it is no more incredulous than the contradictory testimony of eyewitnesses who might, understandably, be tempted to reconstruct a bit of history to divert attention from the fact that they failed in the most important assignment of their collective lives: to keep the Kingfish alive.

CHAPTER SEVENTEEN

The Way It Really Was

Part One: The Medicine Men

In the preceding pages, I have attempted to document the flaws and deceptions contained in the "official" theory of the shooting and death of Huey Long. If I have not created serious doubt in the mind of the reader and, in the process, demolished the deception that has been fostered for some 50 years, it is not because I have not tried.

This fraud depends upon three supports for its survival. They are as follows:

1. Carl Weiss was the assassin, lying in wait in the corridor outside the governor's office Sunday night, September 8, 1935.

2. Long was shot once by Weiss, the bullet entering the right abdomen and exiting through the back about an inch to the right of the spine.

3. Long died because of the ineptness of Dr. Arthur Vidrine, who did not check the condition of Long's right renal space, which was bleeding massively from a wound to the kidney itself or to one of the vessels connected to it.

There are some things wrong with this sketch. Two of the assumptions are false in their entirety. The third has elements of truth in it but it must be qualified considerably.

First, Carl Weiss did not shoot Huey Long. Second, it was not "one man, one gun, one bullet." It was two bullets, fired by two men with two guns. Finally, the kidney was indeed studied and not overlooked, which would have been a monumental exercise in malpractice. A decision was made not to proceed with further surgery, a decision which turned out to be wrong. It was a judgment call and was made by everyone connected with the operation—including the doctors who assisted Vidrine and the assembled hierarchy of the Long organization. If Vidrine is to blame, others must share in that blame.

The quality of surgical care afforded Long by Vidrine and his team of physicians was probably as good as could have been provided, given the state of the art in 1935 and the unconventional circumstances under which the surgery was performed. Vidrine did not ignore the possibility of renal damage, as some have charged. He had Long catheterized, although there have been charges that this was not done. All of these attentions were in keeping with standard medical practice of the time.

It is true that serious errors of judgment were made and these will be recalled later in this chapter. Since Vidrine was the surgeon in charge, these errors can properly be laid at his feet.

Perhaps if the same operation was being performed in 1985, there would be some things done differently. Perhaps if it had been performed in a medical setting instead of a political arena, things would have turned out differently.

We must remember that Huey Long was a very sick man when he was delivered into Vidrine's hands. In 1935, a patient with a penetrating abdominal injury had no more than one chance out of two of recovering. There were no antibiotics then and no colon or rectal specialists. A wound to the colon invariably resulted in fecal spillage, which made it a very serious wound. When we add a second injury to the area of the kidney, we reduce the prospects of recovery.

It is highly likely that Long would not have survived under any circumstances.

In any event, granting that judgment errors were made, it is my point that Dr. Vidrine has been made a single scapegoat and is undeserving of the broad brush of guilt with which he has been painted and which has caused history to record his actions as quackery or worse.

Vidrine and those closest to him are, along with the families of Huey Long and Carl Weiss, the real tragedies in this historical drama.

For almost 50 years, Vidrine and his survivors have had to live with the shame associated with the charge that he was solely responsible for Long not surviving the operation that was performed on September 8, 1935.

The physicians, the Long machine and others were part of a consensus of silence that has maligned and vilified innocent people, causing them to suffer unjustly for half a century.

If men are silent when they should speak the truth, they make cowards of themselves and their silence makes liars of them.

To a great degree, the medical men are more deserving of censure than the lay individuals responsible for withholding information and writing a perjured page in American history that has been accepted by many as gospel for five decades.

Those who were scrambling to preserve their power and perpetuate the

Long machine had what were to them valid personal reasons to cover up the manner of their leader's death and to continue a calumny—the "one man, one gun, one bullet" premise fostered by them. It was self-serving, neatly removing blame from those closest to the Kingfish and placing it as far away as possible, clear into the remote reaches of the Long opposition. It saved the January elections for the gang and allowed them to make hay for another four years.

We may not condone their crass actions, but we can understand them. In fact, it would be surprising if such a collection of rogues had done anything else. It was survival, pure and simple.

But it is different with the physicians.

We expect much more from those in the learned professions whose entire *raison d'etre* is to minister to others and to serve the causes of reason and truth. What I will relate in the following pages was known to many of the several dozen physicians who were involved in the operation and subsequent medical treatment of Huey Long. But there has yet to come forth a single one who will say, "Enough! This is not the way it happened! Let the truth speak!"

It was a curious alliance of interests that allowed this twisted account of the Long surgery to survive for as long as it has. On the one hand, there were the politically amoral cohorts of the Kingfish whose only concern was to keep themselves in power. They were perfectly willing to sacrifice the reputation of a lone country doctor, altogether defenseless now that his patron, Huey Long, had joined the ages.

And there were the physicians. Some were prevailed upon to remain silent because of the "doctor-patient relationship." As patriotism is the last refuge of scoundrels, so is the "doctor-patient relationship" the magical incantation that forbids inquiry, limits debate and seals records.

Others—the younger physicians—were intimidated and discouraged by the awesome wisdom of their elders and the trappings of power that surrounded the Long dictatorship.

More than any other single factor, the animosity and jealousy of New Orleans physicians has continued what can only be labeled a vendetta against Arthur Vidrine. I was told by Dr. Frank Loria that Vidrine was hopeful that he would be accepted as a fellow in the American College of Surgeons but he was thwarted by his colleagues in New Orleans, who successfully blocked the appointment.

And it continues. In his biography of Huey Long, T. Harry Williams throws out this gratuitous shot, quoting an anonymous physician who evaluated Vidrine's capabilities thusly: "If I was going to be operated on, I would not have picked Vidrine."

This mixed bag of strange bedfellows has fostered a canard which holds that Arthur Vidrine failed in the greatest challenge of his promising professional career. We can second-guess Vidrine because his course of action failed but who is to say that another course would have not met the same end?

What follows is something I sincerely believe is a true and accurate account of what happened during those 30-odd hours in the life of Huey Long between 9:20 p.m. Sunday, September 8, when he was shot, and 4:10 a.m. Tuesday, September 10, when he gave up the ghost.

One crucial source is an eyewitness to the surgery who, while not part of the operating team, nevertheless was privy to most of the details of the surgery and knowledgeable about subsequent developments. So great is the apprehension that still exists among those with information about this episode, that it was only on the condition that I protect this person's identity that I was given the facts.

I have been successful in obtaining the hospital records, despite the censorship that has been clamped on them. Although they are pitifully incomplete, they nevertheless shed some light on the condition of Long during his final hours and I have relied heavily upon them.

The sources of the remaining information are clearly cited. They are hospital bulletins, newspaper accounts and interviews with those who had knowledge about the surgery and death of Huey Long. Attempts have been made to blend all of these sources to provide the reader with a kind of stereoscopic overview of the final days of the Kingfish.

The conclusions are mine alone. But given the information that supports them, I cannot see what other conclusions could possibly be warranted.

When Long was admitted to the hospital, he was examined by Vidrine. His condition was carefully monitored for blood pressure and pulse, in keeping with accepted medical procedures of that time and today as well, although today we have better monitoring and intravenous evaluation.

The admitting report was written on a plain sheet of unruled stationery. It is unsigned, as are most of the entries in the hospital records. This is unfortunate and once again reflects upon the professionalism of Dr. Vidrine who, after all, was in charge of the surgery. Accepted medical practice then and now requires the physician in charge to sign records. Probably most of the records were written by nurses but we can only guess at this. The hourly entries are written in a neat, legible hand, probably ruling out the indecipherable scribblings of most doctors.

The admitting note reads:

> "Patient admitted to O.R. (operating room) at 9:30 Dr. Vidrine present - examination made by Dr. Vidrine (shows wound under ribs rt. side, clothes and body with blood.)
>
> "Pulse Vol - very weak & fast - fully conscious - very nervous - given Caff. (caffeine) and Sod. (sodium) benzoate two cc by hypo. Dr.

Cook present.

"Put to bed in 314 and 9:45 foot of bed elevated, Morphine grs. 1/6 (H) for pain. Asks for Ice continuously - Dr. Cecil Lorio present - External Heat, Pt. in cold sweat.

"After consultation - to O.R. at 11:20 P.M. Pulse weak and fast. Still asks for ice."

The caffeine administered was an injectible type that was used as a stimulant. Perhaps a good strong cup of coffee would have accomplished the same thing but physicians did not want to administer anything orally.

Dr. Loria has interpreted Long's thirst as a symptom of shock and this is probably correct. This is further borne out by the rapid pulse and Long's apparent nervousness.

Following Long's return from the operating room, this entry was made in the same hand that wrote the original admitting notice:

"Dr. Vidrine, C.A. Lorio, Cecil and Dr. Cook. Put to bed in 325 at 12:46 - foot of bed elevated-"

The notes are seriously deficient in that they are unsigned and they do not record vital signs of pulse, respiratory rate, body temperature and blood pressure. Physicians in attendance have since provided information about the patient's rapid pulse rate and a graphic chart that is part of the hospital record traces, through a line graph, the steady increases in temperature, pulse and respiration rates. This is, like most of the other records, anonymous and is not a satisfactory substitute for surgeons' notes.

When Long's vital signs reached the point where physicians became concerned, the decision to operate was made. In the words of the ever-present Seymour Weiss, the decision was made "by all of us," meaning physicians and politicians alike.

This shows how difficult it is to fix responsibility for what later happened to Long. Many were involved but none seemed to be truly responsible. Seymour Weiss' statement gives us a good insight into the pressures that were felt by operating physicians. Any physician has a natural concern for the welfare and survival of a patient but few are forced to function under the supervision—and probably direction—of powerful agents and allies of the patient.

How much bullying and intimidation—overt or not—colored the atmosphere in the operating room cannot be measured. I prefer to believe that it was considerable. But regardless of the degree, it certainly did nothing to help the surgeons. I also choose to believe that this climate was probably responsible for several of the errors in judgment and procedure that were made that night. Others may not agree.

One of the early mistakes involved in Long's care was in not adequately evaluating the wound on Long's back, the so-called "wound of exit." It has been noted earlier that the wound was so small that it could easily escape detection. Vidrine correctly surmised at first that it was a penetrating wound. However, so deceiving was the small blue puncture that some in the operating room who examined the wound believed that it was superficial, perhaps nothing more than a bruise.

Another early error was in not having Long x-rayed. This would have disclosed the existence of a bullet or bullets in Long's body and, as it turns out, could possibly have saved his life, although this is debatable.

It is possible that the pressure to establish a single assassin, a single firearm and a single bullet convinced Vidrine to take a few shortcuts and depart from basic surgical procedure.

Long was given his first blood transfusion while he was being prepped for the operation, once again in keeping with proper surgical technique.

In surgery, when Vidrine opened the abdomen, he and Doctors Cook and Cecil Lorio noticed that the right side of the transverse colon had been punctured in two places. This organ is that section of the bowel that crosses the abdomen, becoming the descending colon as it carries body waste to the rectum. Fecal spillage and blood (Dr. Vidrine reported "considerable hemorrhage" while Dr. Loria said "very little blood was found") were cleaned from the area. The perforations were sutured.

Then Vidrine addressed the possible wound to the kidney, indicated by the falling blood pressure, accelerating pulse and projected course of the bullet.

He could have checked the kidney in any of three ways. He could have turned the patient over onto his stomach and made an incision through the back, which would have exposed the entire kidney to view. This, however, posed certain risks. Long had undergone shock as a result of the shooting and he had undergone additional shock because of the abdominal surgery. Further surgery might have been fatal.

Or he could have made an incision through the peritoneal wall, that tissue which separates the abdominal space from the renal space—colon on one side and kidneys on the other.

A third choice would have been to simply examine the kidney without further surgery. Organs in the peritoneal, or abdominal, space are arranged in layers and they can be moved and shifted to varying degrees in order to view others beneath them. This choice would have allowed them time to observe the kidney before deciding whether or not to operate further.

Vidrine and the operating team decided to take this third course.

When the incision was made in the abdomen, the first compartment contained the small intestine, the liver and other organs. By moving the small intestine it was possible to see the transverse colon and note the damage done by the bullet—a single wound that perforated the organ in two places: where the bullet entered and where it left. This was repaired as described above.

There was also a hematoma, or blood clot, about the size of a half dollar, on the mesentery, a supporting tissue that connects the small intestine with the posterior wall of the abdominal cavity. On the other side of this back wall is the kidney. Although hidden by the transverse colon and its attachment, it was possible for the doctors to move the colon from side to side, just enough for the surgeon to inspect one area or another. However, it was not possible to lift it out of the way entirely because the tissue attaching it to the posterior abdominal wall is relatively short.

It was during this procedure that Vidrine uncovered a .38 caliber bullet in the peritoneum. The experience had to have been unnerving. Having diagnosed the injury as being caused by a single projectile that entered and left the body, he was altogether unprepared for this development. He would have to think fast to come up with an explanation.

He had two choices.

With a bullet in the peritoneal space, there was no way that the penetrating wounds in the stomach and back could have been caused by a single bullet. He could determine that there was another bullet somewhere, or he could determine that one of the wounds was not really a penetrating wound.

If he opted for another bullet, then what happens to the "one man, one gun, one bullet" hypothesis? What happens to the assembled goons and henchmen when the surgeon scuttles the theory that will keep the Long machine in power following the January elections? What happens to Vidrine? If the Greeks killed the bearers of bad news, what would the Long group do to this expendable rural surgeon?

The second choice, to conclude that the wound to the back was not really a penetrating wound, was not fraught with these political pitfalls. After all, the wound had not been so carefully examined as to preclude it being, in reality, a superficial wound. One of those who observed it told me it looked more like a bruise or small trauma. Vidrine did a rowback. He revised his diagnosis and concluded that, in reality, there was a single wound—a wound of entry. The bullet came to rest in the peritoneal space and never did really nick the kidney. It caused the blood clot on the mesentery but never penetrated the abdominal wall.

This is where the literally fatal mistake was made. Despite the fact that a bullet had been found and the diagnosis revised, if the physicians were suspicious that Long's kidney had been damaged and the patient lay on the operating table with his abdomen open, an incision in this right posterior abdominal or peritoneal wall over the renal bulge would have exposed the kidney. If it was noted that the kidney was damaged and the surgeons were certain that the patient had a functioning left kidney, the right kidney should have been removed. In those days, repair of the kidney was beyond the surgeon's skills.

Some have explained the surgeons' decision not to operate further by the problems involved in removing the kidney from the back but I am told that this complicated route was unnecessary. According to those practicing at the time, the anterior, or frontal, approach was satisfactory and, under the circumstances, the route of choice for removal of the kidney.

Vidrine (and others) made the decision not to operate and it was wrong. But none of us understand all of the constraints that affected the choice.

When Long's surgery was completed, Vidrine and Clarence Lorio checked the wound in the back more thoroughly and Vidrine received another shock, causing him to make still another diagnosis, which he would keep to himself until the day he died. It was clear that the back wound was a penetrating one and surely another bullet remained in Long's body. Again we encounter a decided lack of professionalism and a breach of ethics on the part of Vidrine and the others who had stumbled upon a major discovery and concealed it.

This diagnosis would later prompt Clarence Lorio to scurry to the mortuary where Long's lifeless body was sent Tuesday morning and, under the watchful eye of the undertaker and his principal assistant, he would extract the second bullet, a .45 caliber slug which I believe came from the gun of Joe Messina or Elliott Coleman.

In surgery, the physicians studied the outline of the right kidney. Inspecting the anterior contour of the organ, they palpated it, applying hand and fingers to the posterior abdominal wall to detect characteristics and conditions of the underlying kidney. In feeling the kidney they could detect no sign of injury to that surface.

Nor was there any sign of bleeding. The kidney appeared intact and stabilized, the pulse was steady and the pressure was good. You might ask, "But wasn't it obvious that there was a hemorrhage? What did they expect to do about it?"

Well, the answer to the first question is, "Yes and no." It was true that the pulse was rapid and the pressure was down before surgery but this could have been due to shock of trauma to the abdominal wall. Then again, if it was a hemorrhage, wasn't there considerable blood in the peritoneal space that could have accounted for this hemorrhage? And wasn't it true that the "black eye" or hematoma had clotted? And wasn't it true that the preliminary kidney examination had disclosed no apparent damage to that organ?

As a practical matter, Long's stable condition could easily have been a result of the shock of the abdominal wound or surgery. The lowered blood pressure would have slowed the flow of blood to the point where the bleeding would slow or even stop. However, as the shock of surgery wore off and the pressure went up, given the infusion and additional blood through the transfusions, the bleeding could and, in fact, did start again.

The operative record shows the following entries:
"Name: Huey P. Long

Room or Ward No: 325
Surgeon: Dr. Vidrine
Anesthetists: Dr. McKeown
Assistants: Dr. Cook - Dr. C.A. Lorio, C.
Lorio

Anesthesia: N^2O started at 10:51 p.m.
ended 12:14 a.m. Pulse during anesthesia 104-114
Operation began: 11:22 p.m. Ended
12:25 a.m.
What was done: Perforation - 2 -
transfer (transverse) colon."

This operative report is one of the few documents actually signed but
unfortunately the signature is illegible. Presumably it is that of Vidrine.

When Long was returned to his hospital bed, physicians were optimistic. Their bulletins indicated this. He was catheterized and there was no blood in
the kidney.

His condition between midnight and 2:40 a.m. Monday morning is a
mystery since those records are not included in the reports I received from the
hospital. At 2:40 a.m., Long's systolic blood pressure was 96, a drop from the
104 measured at about 11:00 p.m. the previous night. The diastolic measurement
was not shown at the 2:40 a.m. check. However, the pulse was 140, up from 114
the night before.

Blood pressure and pulse would continue to fluctuate Monday morning.
At 6:00 a.m. the pressure read 82/63 and the pulse was a frightening 154. In addition, a blood count taken indicated the presence of an infection in Long's body
and the fact that he was losing blood.

But ever the optimist, at 6:00 a.m., Long's secretary, Earle Christenberry, announced, "He has improved more in the last 15 minutes than during all
of last night." At 8:30 a.m., the hospital reported that Long was gaining strength.

Dr. Russell Stone, one of the physicians summoned by Long, estimated
the Senator's chances at 50-50.

Throughout the morning, intravenous injections were made of glucose,
sucrose and saline solutions and adrenalin. Morphine was administered for pain.
At 6:40 a.m. the records show that Long was catheterized.

At noon, Long was reported by the newspapers to be passing blood.
According to Dr. Edgar Hull, he observed the blood but it was attributed to
trauma caused by the catheter. However, at that time a second transfusion was
performed, using blood supplied by bodyguard Joe Bates. Because of the infusion, pressure rose from 105/78 to 115/80. However, the pulse had risen to 140
and, according to the graphic chart, the temperature continued to rise, probably
indicating that the physicians were losing their fight to contain the infection.

But then, around mid-afternoon, everything fell apart. The renal wounds and vessels opened. The patient's blood pressure fell several times and was almost too faint to count. It measured 92/82 and the pulse quickened to 170. At 3:00 p.m. an oxygen tent was moved into the sick room.

At 6:30 p.m. blood pressure dropped again, down to 92/65 and the pulse continued at between 160-170. The hospital chart noted at 6:46, "General appearance of patient is less favorable."

At 7:00 p.m. attendants told newsmen that Long was undergoing a "serious sinking spell." At 8:15 p.m. his pulse was reported to be "very thready" and another transfusion was made. Blood pressure increased to 114/84 but pulse still measured 170 and temperature contined to rise.

However, at 8:30 p.m. Doctor Vidrine told reporters, "Senator Long is holding his own."

At 10:30 p.m. the hospital's head nurse was reported to be telling friends of the senator, "There is little hope." At 10:45 p.m. physicians typed blood from bodyguards and state officials preparatory to attempting another transfusion at midnight.

Shortly after midnight Long became delirious, imagining that photographers were in the room. His respiration was shallow and forced and physicians removed the oxygen tent because of Long's restlessness. At 12:30 a.m. it was noted that he was "resting fairly well" although his condition was noted as being weaker. His pressure was 100/79, his pulse 170 and his temperature was 104-4/5 degrees, taken under the armpit. At 1:00 a.m. the pressure had dropped to 92/64.

At about 1:30 a.m. Dr. T. Jorda Kahle, summoned from New Orleans, injected a long needle into the retroperitoneal spaces surrounding the kidneys and drew out, in the words of Dr. Loria, "pure blood."

(Despite the fact that Drs. Hull and Loria clashed over whether Long was bleeding from the kidneys or not, it turns out that they were both right. When the catheter was inserted Monday, there was no bleeding into the urinary passage. When the perirenal spaces were aspirated Tuesday, massive bleeding around the kidney was observed.)

There are no hospital records after 1:00 a.m. but news reports tell us that shortly after 2:00 a.m., a physician rushed a policeman to a drug store with a prescription for ephedrine, a medication which constricts blood vessels to improve circulation. At 2:25 a.m. a fifth transfusion was attempted but not completed.

At 3:00 a.m. Dr. Sanderson made official what many had suspected: "Senator Long is dying."

At 4:10 a.m. he passed away.

Was the surgery bungled?

I do not believe so. Retrospectively, it might seem that it would have been wiser to excise the kidney, but do we know that Long would have survived that operation? If it had been done and Long had perished, perhaps Vidrine would have been criticized for not taking the other course.

It seems to me that this account of the surgery and late findings point to the dilemma that faced the physicians. I can understand that it would have been impolitic for a politician to say what I have said with an important election in the offing. Possibly it would have even been unwise to reveal these details when a citizenry was still dazed and shocked over the passing of the Kingfish, but this is hardly the normal course of action for ethical physicians.

But were those who were privy to these details justified in withholding this vital information for half a century?

Not in my book. And thus we have one of the enduring tragedies associated with the death of Huey Long.

Again, I am not absolving Dr. Arthur Vidrine of some responsibility for the death of Huey Long. But I am asking the reader to understand the circumstances that existed on that September night. I am also reminding the reader that there were other, perhaps even more competent surgeons in the operating room than Vidrine. And, finally, I am asking the reader to consider the possibility that Vidrine was not really in charge. It is possible that he was wary of "too much surgery" which could, in itself, bring criticism upon him and the same kind of blame he would be forced to live with until his dying day.

There is another, greater tragedy in the continuation of the "one man, one gun, one bullet" myth and that tragedy is covered in the account that follows.

Part Two: All the Kingfish's Men

Nor do I believe that Carl Austin Weiss shot Huey Long.

There are, in essence, three versions of the shooting of Huey Long from which we can choose. One can believe that the senator was willfully shot by Carl Weiss or that he was willfully shot by someone else present in the hallway that night. A third choice is that he was shot accidentally.

The Weiss family and Walter Winchell reject outright the first theory. They place Carl Weiss in the role of a supplicant, a petitioner pleading with Huey Long to cease his attacks upon Yvonne Pavy Weiss, her family and other innocent victims of Long's politics. In this version he is clearly a martyr.

We can all understand why the family of Carl Weiss would want us to believe this story. To have to live with the knowledge that he was guilty of this terrible crime was a burden the family was reluctant to bear. Hence, this fanciful account.

I cannot accept this version. It does not square with demonstrated facts. Weiss was capable of strong feelings. He hated Huey Long with a bitterness that threatened to overflow. He went into the capitol that night armed, for no other reason than to confront Long. In his disordered state of mind, he was perfectly capable of killing Long. But I don't think he did, and I don't think he even attempted to.

But those who put together the second version, having Carl Weiss coldly approaching Long and pulling the trigger, had as much reason to fabricate their story as did the Weiss family to concoct theirs.

Every single individual who testified as an eyewitness to the shooting had an axe to grind, a reason to alter the truth. The bodyguards existed for one reason: to see that Long was not done in by an assassin or an assailant. They failed their assignment in the clumsiest fashion.

John Fournet was a creature of the Long machine. He was chosen as speaker of the House by Long himself and was selected to run for lieutenant governor by Long. When Huey's control over the state supreme court was threatened by the death of a pro-Long justice running for re-election, Long contrived a new election which seated Fournet, despite a crystal clear law which called for the certifying of the lone opponent who had qualified against the dead jurist.

Fournet had hopes of campaigning for the governorship and it would have been disastrous to his chances if the shooting were pinned on anyone except Carl Weiss.

So when we study the testimony of the eyewitnesses, let us keep in mind that they had very good reasons to shade the facts.

Does this mean they lied? No, not lying. Instead, there was a great deal of mendacity involved in the eyewitness testimony; "mendacity" meaning "characterized by deception or falsehood which is not intended to mislead."

Most of those who testified gave their honest recollections of what happened. They testified to what they thought they saw. Let us suppose that there is a group milling around in a crowd dense enough to block the full vision of everyone. We see someone draw a gun. A shot is heard. Someone shouts, "I'm shot!" Do we conclude that the person who drew the weapon shot the person who shouted? No. There could have been another gun, perhaps several guns, drawn by others in the crowd.

But let's look at it another way. Coleman Vidrine's father gave him a .38 caliber bullet which he said came out of Huey. Merle Welsh said he saw Dr. Clarence Lorio take a bullet from Long's body in the mortuary. Mr. J. B. Broussard said that Dr. Arthur Vidrine told him that Huey Long was shot twice. The Special Agent in Charge of the FBI in New Orleans wired J. Edgar Hoover that Long was shot twice. And others have given information that contradicts the "one man, one gun, one bullet" hypothesis.

Are all these people lying? Let us assume that one side or the other is lying and that these two views are so divergent that they cannot be reconciled and we must conclude that someone is just simply not telling the truth. How do we determine which side is twisting facts?

One simple way is to determine which of the two sides has a reason to tell something other than the truth. Using this measurement, we must conclude that disassociated persons, acting independently and having no communication with each other, are far more believable and credible than their opposite number who refused to testify for eight days following the shooting, who were all briefed by the head of Huey's Criminal Bureau of Investigation and who constantly altered their testimony.

I believe that Weiss never got close enough to place his gun against Long's body and fire. This would be contrary to the history and nature of Long and his "Cossacks." No one ever got that close without the bodyguards allowing them to do so. It is hard to believe they relaxed on that night—of all nights—after having been warned that an attempt would be made on Long's life. I believe that Murphy Roden, trained to react immediately, fired at Weiss at close range and the bullet struck Long, possibly even passing through Weiss' body before hitting Long.

The morning after the shooting, the New Orleans *Item* dispatched staff artist John Chase to the state capitol to recreate the shooting. The head of the Criminal Bureau of Investigation had promised to smash any cameras (and possibly cameramen) attempting to photograph the scene but Chase remembers that the newspaper management was willing to risk his pencil being smashed. Most of Chase's information came from Chick Frampton, also an employee of the *Item,* and the artist was able to recreate the scene, placing the participants in the positions they were the previous evening.

In Chase's drawing, Weiss is standing between Long and Roden as Roden fires his .38 caliber pistol. In this environment, it is highly possible that a shot from Roden hit Long. Some have said that a .38 caliber bullet fired at close range would have gone completely through the body and this could be correct. It is likely that the bullet found its intended target and struck Weiss, passing through the body and, having spent much of its energy, penetrated and remained in Long's abdomen. Other reconstructions of the shooting show approximately the same positions, although this hardly proves anything since they all seem to have been copied from Chase's drawing.

This accounts for the first bullet taken from Long's body, the .38 caliber projectile removed at the hospital by Dr. Vidrine.

I believe the other bodyguards responded almost as quickly and fired at Weiss as Roden was emptying his magazine into him. They panicked. One of the bullets, fired by either Joe Messina or Elliott Coleman, struck Roden's wrist watch and ricocheted, hitting the fleeing Kingfish in the back. This was the .45 caliber bullet taken from Long's body in the funeral parlor. Once again, this was a spent projectile, having lost much of its momentum and it is highly possible that its force was insufficient to carry it through the body. Instead, it came to rest in the renal area.

I think this is the way it really was. Part of the proof of this theory is contained in the Linney Hypothesis. The balance can be deductively organized from the testimony of eyewitnesses.

In the preceding pages, I offered many questions that cast doubt upon the "official" record of the shooting and death of Huey Long. It might be well to restate some of these now.

1. In the face of what seems to be certain knowledge that an attempt would be made to kill Long, how was it possible for an assassin to get close enough to shoot him at point-blank range?

2. If Weiss intended to kill Long, why did he not shoot when Long entered the Governor's office alone, his bodyguards 15 feet away, rather than wait for the Kingfish to be surrounded by them?

3. What accounts for the conflicting testimony of the bodyguards and Judge Fournet? Elliott Coleman claims to have struck someone. Another bodyguard supports him, yet Fournet and Roden do not mention this happening.

4. Both state and city police conducted investigations into the shooting. The gun was taken from the scene of the shooting by Baton Rouge detectives. It was last recorded to be in the possession of the state police. Now it has disappeared and neither city nor state police have any record of it. Where is the gun?

5. Why were hospital records stripped?

6. Why is there no record of an investigation, or even the inquest conducted by the coroner, in anyone's files? All that survives of the entire incident, in the way of official documents, are two death certificates, one for Weiss and one for Long.

Why? Why? Why? We could continue asking "why" at every step of the way of this perplexing event. The questions abound. There are no answers.

I believe the story that has come from Douglas Linney is the real story of the shooting of Huey Long. It answers all questions raised by the theory I have propounded and the evidence I have gathered.

Throughout this manuscript I have examined the various theories seeking to explain that others might have been involved in the shooting of Huey Long. As mentioned before, many believe that Roosevelt and the New Deal were responsible. Others consider that Long's bodyguards and his followers might have been in on a plot. Some have blamed organized crime.

I have offered evidence about the possible involvement of these "suspects" as I have uncovered it but the presentation has not been to level blame as much as to serve as a vehicle to describe characters and situations that had profound influences on Long.

I do not believe any of these groups or individuals were involved in any way in Long's death. Carl Weiss is not linked with any of them. He had no ties to the Roosevelt administration, except for the staff of Congressman J. Y. Sanders, Jr. and perhaps Sanders himself. He had no communication or contact with the Long organization and he certainly had no involvement with organized crime.

It is my feeling that Long would eventually have been assassinated, if not on September 8, 1935, then perhaps on October 8, 1935. And if not in 1935, then perhaps in 1936, and so on. To a large extent, he created the climate that resulted in his demise.

He struck out so savagely at his critics and enemies that he planted in many of them the desire for revenge. By his constant references to his assassination and the efforts to convince others that there were active plots to kill him, he gave his enemies an idea for realizing that revenge.

Some have speculated that Long dwelt upon his violent death to provide an aura of mystery and romance that would help him politically. I was told by one individual that perhaps Carl Weiss was set up for the killing by being enticed over to the capitol that night. The frameup got out of hand and Long himself was shot.

This is hard to believe.

But I do believe that Long broadcast a message of violence that would undoubtedly be seized upon by sick minds somewhere along the way who would undertake to act upon it. By his excessive concern for his safety and by his encouragement of his ill-trained cadre of bodyguards to indulge in violence and carry weapons, he probably had as much to do with his own death as anyone. He inflamed tempers to the flash point, resulting in the explosion that happened that Sunday night in Baton Rouge.

In this respect, we can conclude that Huey Long killed Huey Long as much as anybody did. In effect, he was his own assassin.

I do not offer this manuscript as any definitive treatment of the subject. I am prepared to concede that it might have happened "another way" and my mind is open to any evidence that will point in this direction.

I simply say that it did not happen the way the "official" explanation would have us believe and I offer this as an alternative. It may or may not stand the test of time. But, for the present, it represents a believable and plausible explanation of Long's shooting and death.

For the present, at least, I believe that it must stand. I believe also that the "official" theory must now be relegated to that graveyard of hoaxes, frauds and fairy tales into which history inevitably consigns that which is not true.

Chapter Notes

Chapter 1 Notes

1. *Assassination and Political Violence, A Report to the National Commission on the Causes and Prevention of Violence,* U.S. Government Printing Office, October, 1969, pp. 27-29.

2. *The Nation,* CXLI, September 18, 1935.

3. Murray Clark Havens, Carl Leiden, Karl M. Schmitt: *The Politics of Assassination* (Prentice-Hall, New Jersey, 1970), p. 75.

4. Lauren Paine: *The Assassins' World* (Taplinger Publishing Company, New York 1975), pp. 23-24.

5. New Orleans *Times-Picayune:* "Psychiatrists Profile Would-Be Assassins," April 1, 1981.

6. Dr. Thomas E. Weiss interview.

7. Ms. Freddie Harris interview.

8. W.W. McDougall interview.

9. *Newsday,* September 8, 1985.

10. New Orleans *Times-Picayune:* "Hermann Deutsch Reminisces," September 2, 1968.

11. Baton Rouge *State-Times,* September 9, 1985.

12. David H. Zinman: *The Day Huey Long Was Shot* (Ivan Obolensky, New York 1963), p. 250; Alan Michie and Frank Rhylick: *Dixie Demagogues* (The Vanguard Press, New York 1939), p. 116.

13. *Life* magazine, June 26, 1939.

14. Elmer L. Irey and William J. Slocum: *The Tax Dodgers* (Greenberg: Publisher, New York 1948), p. 100.

15. Confidential source.

16. Judge John Parker interview.

17. T. Harry Williams: *Huey Long* (Alfred A. Knopf, New York 1969), p. 872.

18. Williams: "Louisiana Mystery—an Essay Review'' (*Louisiana History,* the Journal of the Louisiana Historical Association VI, Summer, 1965), p. 287.

Chapter 2 Notes

1. Forrest Davis: *Huey Long, A Candid Biography* (Dodge Publishing Company, New

York 1935), pp. 21-22.

2. Raymond Gram Swing: *Forerunners of American Fascism* (Books for Libraries Press, New York 1935), p. 94.

3. George F. Will: Baton Rouge *Morning Advocate,* November 4, 1979.

4. John Salmond: *A Southern Rebel: The Life and Times of Aubrey Willis Williams* (University of North Carolina Press, North Carolina 1983), p. 46.

5. R.G. Tugwell: *The Brains Trust* (The Viking Press, New York 1968), pp. 433-434; James A. Farley: *Behind the Ballots* (Harcourt, Brace & Company, New York 1943), p. 240.

6. Thomas O. Harris: *The Kingfish, Huey P. Long, Dictator* (Claitor's Publishing Division, Louisiana 1968), p. 267.

7. Jesse McLain interview.

8. FBI papers.

Chapter 3 Notes

1. Merle Welsh interview.

2. Dr. Thomas E. Weiss interview.

3. Unless otherwise noted, all of the testimony cited in this account of the inquest is based on clippings from the E.A. Conway scrapbook on file with the Louisiana State Library in Baton Rouge.

4. Baton Rouge *State-Times,* September 14, 1935.

5. Melinda Delage interview.

6. Modest Messina interview.

7. Hermann Deutsch: *The Huey Long Murder Case* (Doubleday, New York 1963), pp. 93-94.

8. Zinman: *The Day Huey Long Was Shot,* p. 119.

9. Deutsch: *The Huey Long Murder Case,* p. 95.

10. Ibid.

11. Zinman: *The Day Huey Long Was Shot,* pp. 217-218.

12. Deutsch: *The Huey Long Murder Case,* p. 94.

13. Ibid, p. 95.

Chapter 4 Notes

1. Huey P. Long: *Every Man A King* (National Book Company, Louisiana 1933), p. 1.

2. *Louisiana, A Guide to the State* (Hastings House Publishers, New York 1971), pp. 374-75.

3. Davis: *Huey Long, A Candid Biography,* p. 45.

4. Long: *Every Man A King,* p. 2.

5. James R. Green: *Grass-Roots Socialism, Radical Movements in the Southwest 1895-1943* (LSU Press, Louisiana 1948), p. 405.

6. Benjamin Stohlberg: *The Nation,* September 25, 1935; Davis: *Huey Long, A Candid Biography,* pp. 48-49.

7. Harris: *The Kingfish,* p. 13.

8. John P. Dyer: *TULANE, The Biography of a University* (Harper & Row, New York 1966), p. 179.

9. Carleton Beals: *The Story of Huey P. Long* (Greenwood Press, Connecticut 1971), pp. 34-35.

10. Harris: *The Kingfish,* pp. 222-223.

11. Long: *Every Man A King,* pp. 25-28.

12. Harris: *The Kingfish,* pp. 42-43; New Orleans *Times-Picayune,* June 25, 1928.

13. Long: *Every Man A King,* p. 31.

14. Ibid, pp. 37-39.

15. Ibid, p. 42.

16. Baton Rouge *State-Times,* September 23, 1923.

17. Beals: *The Story of Huey P. Long,* pp. 42-43.

18. Peter Collier and David Horowitz: *The Rockefellers* (New American Library, New York 1977), p. 55.

19. Long: *Every Man A King,* pp. 48-50.

20. Ibid, p. 77.

21. New Orleans *Times-Picayune,* January 13, 1924.

22. Stella O'Conner: *Louisiana Historical Quarterly,* Vol. 31, No. 1, January 1948, p.88.

23. Hermann Deutsch: *The Kingdom of the Kingfish,* a series of articles in the New Orleans *Item* July 19-September 20, 1939. This item is undated but the number of the article is XXIV. I have turned this material over to the Louisiana State Library in Baton Rouge and it can be found in the Louisiana Collection.

24. Ibid, XXV.

25. Impeachment Proceedings, I, pp. 29-32; *Kingdom of the Kingfish,* XXV.

26. Ibid.

27. Davis: *Huey Long, A Candid Biography,* p. 109.

28. Ibid, p. 171.

29. *New York Times,* September 11, 1935.

30. Beals: *The Story of Huey P. Long,* p. 368.

31. Harris: *The Kingfish,* p. 124.

32. Julius Long: "What I Know About My Brother," *Real America,* September, 1933.

33. Ibid.

34. New Orleans *Times-Picayune,* February 8, 1933.

35. John Wilds: *Afternoon Story* (LSU Press, Louisiana 1976), p. 236.

36. Ibid.

37. Harris: *The Kingfish,* pp. 243-244; *New York Times,* September 5, 1935.

38. Beals: *The Story of Huey P. Long,* p. 369.

39. *New York Times,* March 27, 1935.

40. Williams: *Huey Long,* p. 826.

41. Baton Rouge *State-Times,* July 28, 1971.

42. New Orleans *Times-Picayune,* December 23, 1981.

43. *Wall Street Journal,* October 22, 1984.

44. Joe Darby, New Orleans *Times-Picayune:* "An Assassination Plot?"; Baton Rouge *State-Times:* interview with John Fournet, September 11, 1935.

45. Williams: *Huey Long,* p. 876.

46. Harvey G. Fields: *A True History of the Life, Works, Assassination and Death of Huey Pierce Long* (probably privately printed 1945), p. 55.

Chapter 5 Notes

1. Jim Gillis interview.

2. Baton Rouge *State-Times,* September 9, 1985; Baton Rouge *Morning Advocate,* September 10, 1985.

3. Dr. William Norris interview.

4. Deutsch: *Kingdom of the Kingfish,* No. 48.

5. Davis: *Huey Long, A Candid Biography,* p. 228.

6. Harris: *The Kingfish,* p. 108.

7. Long: *Every Man A King*, p. 107.

8. Donald W. Whisenhunt: "Huey Long and the Texas Cotton Acreage Control Law of 1931," *Louisiana Studies*, Northwestern Louisiana University, Natchitoches, La., Vol. XIII, No. 1, Spring, 1974.

9. Matthew James Schott: Doctoral Dissertation, Vanderbilt University, Nashville, Tenn., August 1969, p. 492.

10. Gerald Hugh Pettit interview.

11. Jim Gillis interview.

12. Beals: *The Story of Huey P. Long*, p. 282.

13. Harris: *The Kingfish*, pp. 161-164.

14. Deutsch: *Kingdom of the Kingfish*, No. 48.

15. Raymond Moley: *Masters of Politics* (Funk and Wagnalls Co., New York 1949), p. 229.

16. Deutsch: *Kingdom of the Kingfish*, No. 43; Williams: *Huey Long*, p. 721.

17. David E. Koskoff: *Joseph P. Kennedy, A Life and Times* (Prentice-Hall, Inc., New Jersey 1974), footnote p. 531.

18. Deutsch: *Kingdom of the Kingfish*, No. 45.

19. Williams: *Huey Long*, p. 791.

Chapter 6 Notes

1. FBI papers.

2. *Congressional Record*, August 9, 1935, pp. 12789-12791.

3. Adela Rogers St. Johns: *The Honeycomb* (Doubleday, New York 1969), pp. 383-385.

4. FBI papers.

5. Finis Farr: *FDR* (Arlington House, New York 1950), pp. 265- 266.

6. *New York Times*, April 1, 1935.

7. Beals: *The Story of Huey P. Long*, pp. 10-11.

8. Raymond Moley: *After Seven Years* (Harper, New York 1939), p. 305.

9. T. Harry Williams: Inaugural Lecture, University of Oxford, 1967.

10. Swing: *Forerunners of American Fascism*, pp. 82-84.

11. Elliott Roosevelt: *FDR, His Personal Letters* (Duell, Sloan and Pearce, New York 1950), p. 9.

12. James A. Farley: *Jim Farley's Story* (Whittlesey House, New York 1975), p. 183.

13. Elliott Roosevelt and James Brough: *A Rendezvous with Destiny* (New York 1975), p. 83.

14. Ibid, p. 102.

15. Michael R. Beschloss: *Kennedy and Roosevelt* (W.W. Norton and Co., New York 1980), p. 97.

16. Williams: Inaugural Lecture, University of Oxford, p. 3.

17. Arthur M. Schlesinger, Jr.: *The Crisis of the Old Order, 1919-1933* (Houghton Mifflin, Massachusetts 1957), p. 418; Roosevelt and Brough: *Rendezvous with Destiny*, p. 83.

18. *New York Times*, January 26, 1932.

19. Ibid, April 26, 1932.

20. *Congressional Record*, Senate, January 4, 1934, p. 58.

21. Beals: *The Story of Huey P. Long*, p. 11.

22. Farley: *Behind the Ballots*, pp. 116-117.

23. Ibid, p. 171.

24. *Congressional Record*, Senate, March 5, 1935, p. 2952.

25. Farley: *Behind the Ballots*, p. 242.

236

26. Arthur Schlesinger: *The Politics of Upheaval* (Houghton Mifflin, Massachusetts 1957), pp. 55-57.

27. Irey and Slocum: *The Tax Dodgers,* pp. 89-90.

28. FBI papers; Memphis *Commercial Appeal,* January 23, 1933.

29. William "Fishbait" Miller: *Fishbait, the Memoirs of the Congressional Doorkeeper* (Warner Books, New York 1977), pp. 28-29.

30. Irey and Slocum: *The Tax Dodgers,* pp. 92-93.

31. Matthew James Schott: Doctoral Thesis, pp. 491-492.

32. Davis: *Huey Long, A Candid Biography,* p. 245.

33. *Congressional Record,* Senate, January 7, 1935, p. 156.

34. Irey and Slocum: *Coronet Magazine,* January, 1948, p. 51.

35. Frank Wilson: *Collier's,* May 17, 1947; FBI papers.

36. Matthew Josephson: *Infidel in the Temple* (Alfred A. Knopf, New York 1967), p. 337; Roosevelt and Brough: *Rendezvous with Destiny,* pp. 120-121.

Chapter 7 Notes

1. *New York Times,* February 10, 1935.

2. Williams: *Huey Long,* p. 459.

3. Deutsch: *Kingdom of the Kingfish,* IX.

4. *Congressional Record,* Senate, June 12, 1935, p. 9138.

5. Dr. Ashton Robins interview.

6. Julius Long: "What I Know About My Brother," *Real America,* September, 1933.

7. St. Johns: *The Honeycomb,* p. 393.

8. J.S. Goff interview.

9. Baton Rouge *State-Times,* September 9, 1935.

10. Williams: *Huey Long,* p. 880.

11. Unless otherwise noted, this version of the Sands Point incident is drawn from the following sources: Nassau (Long Island) *Daily Review,* August 29, 30 and 31, 1933, August 11, 1934 and February 10, 1937; *New York Times,* August 29, 1933, September 1, 3, 6, 7 and October 17, 1933; Baton Rouge *Morning Advocate,* August 30 and 31 and September 1 and 3, 1933.

12. Miller: *Fishbait, Memoirs of the Congressional Doorkeeper,* p. 29.

13. Williams: *Huey Long,* pp. 651-652.

14. Leonard Katz: *Uncle Frank* (Pocket Books, New York 1975), p. 97.

15. Hank Messick: *Lansky* (G.P. Putnam's Sons, New York 1971), pp. 81-82.

16. Jay Robert Nash: *Bloodletters and Badmen* (Warner Paperback Library, New York 1975), p. 99.

17. Deed 2719, pp. 556 and 566, May 18, 1944, Clerk's Office, County of Nassau, New York.

18. FBI papers.

19. U.S. Congress, Senate Special Committee to Investigate Commerce, 81st Congress, 2nd Session and 82nd Congress, 1st Session (Washington, D.C., 1951), Part VII, pp. 910-973.

20. FBI papers.

21. Hamilton Basso: *The New Republic,* January 1, 1935.

22. Katz: *Uncle Frank,* p. 95.

Chapter 8 Notes

1. *New York Times,* January 27, 1935.

2. Ibid, January 5, 1935.

3. Ibid, January 17, 1935.

4. Ibid.

5. Ibid, February 1, 1935; FBI papers.

6. Williams: *Huey Long,* pp. 825-826.

7. Deutsch: *Kingdom of the Kingfish,* No. 47; FBI papers; New Orleans *Item,* January 27, 1935.

8. *New York Times,* February 10, 1935.

9. *New York Times,* February 1, 1935.

10. Harris: *The Kingfish,* p. 205.

11. Jimmy Robinson interview.

12. Williams: *Huey Long,* p. 827.

13. FBI papers.

14. *New York Times,* February 10, 1935.

15. Hodding Carter: *Review of Reviews,* "Louisiana Limelighter," March, 1935.

16. Will Irwin: *Liberty Magazine,* "The Empire of the Kingfish," April 6, 1935.

17. Williams: *Huey Long,* p. 858.

18. Confidential interview.

19. Jimmy Robinson interview.

20. *Congressional Record,* Senate, p. 12786, August 9, 1935.

21. J.S. Goff interview.

22. Carlos Spaht interview; confidential interview.

Chapter 9 Notes

1. New Orleans *Times-Picayune,* January 5, 1936.

2. Ibid, September 10, 1935, "Long increased guard recently."

3. Messick: *Lansky,* p. 84.

4. FBI papers.

5. Ibid.

6. Harnett T. Kane: *Louisiana Hayride* (Pelican Publishing Co., Louisiana 1971), pp. 154-155.

7. FBI papers.

8. Edward F. Haas: *deLesseps S. Morrison and the Image of Reform* (LSU Press, Louisiana 1974), p. 13.

9. Kane: *Louisiana Hayride,* p. 33.

10. FBI papers.

11. F. Edward Hebert: *Last of the Titans,* (University of Southwestern Louisiana, Louisiana 1976), pp. 112-113.

12. Roosevelt and Brough: *Rendezvous with Destiny,* p. 166.

13. FBI papers.

14. Long: *Every Man A King,* pp. 146-147.

15. FBI papers.

16. New Orleans *Times-Picayune,* June 4, 1970.

17. Ibid, February 8, 10 and 18 and November 30, 1933.

18. FBI papers.

19. Hamilton Basso: *New Republic,* January 1, 1936.

20. This citation and all of the material contained in the balance of this chapter, unless otherwise attributed, are derived from the FBI papers.

21. W.W. McDougall interview.

Chapter 10 Notes

1. Joe Vitrano interview.

2. John Alan Simon: "He Always Walked in Front," interview with James P. O'Connor, New Orleans *Times-Picayune,* September 7, 1975.

3. Shirley Benton: "She Recalls Tragic Night Long Was Shot," interview with Doris Carnes, Baton Rouge *Sunday Advocate,* March 11, 1979.

4. O'Connor interview with Simon.

5. Joe Darby: "Former Chief Justice Witnessed Fatal Shooting," interview with John Fournet, New Orleans *Times-Picayune,* September 7, 1975.

6. Dr. Frank Loria: "Senator Long's Assassination," *Louisiana Historical Quarterly,* Spring, 1971 (Pelican Publishing Company, Louisiana), p. 13.

7. Dyer: *TULANE, The Biography of a University,* pp. 216-219.

8. Deutsch: *The Huey Long Murder Case,* p. 109.

9. O'Connor interview with Simon.

10. Drs. Reichard Kahle and Edgar Hull interviews.

11. Deutsch: *The Huey Long Murder Case,* pp. 117-118.

12. Melinda Delage interview.

13. Deutsch: *The Huey Long Murder Case,* p. 113.

14. Melinda Delage interview.

15. New Orleans *Item,* September 9, 1935; personal recollections.

Chapter 11 Notes

1. Dr. Frank Loria: "Historical Aspects of Penetrating Wounds of the Abdomen," *International Abstracts of Surgery,* December, 1948, pp. 546- 547.

2. Ibid.

3. Dr. Arthur Vidrine Scrapbook, LSU Medical School Library, New Orleans.

4. Loria: "Historical Aspects of Penetrating Wounds of the Abdomen," p. 531.

5. Theoda Carriere interview.

6. Deutsch: *The Huey Long Murder Case,* p. 114.

7. Melinda Delage interview.

8. Dr. Ashton Robins interview.

9. Loria: "Historical Aspects of Penetrating Wounds of the Abdomen," p. 531.

10. Fournet interview with Darby.

11. New Orleans *Item,* September 9, 1935.

12. *Literary Digest,* September 14, 1935.

13. FBI papers.

14. Zinman: *The Day Huey Long Was Shot,* p. 151.

15. Confidential interview.

16. Melinda Delage interview.

17. Barrow Norwood interview.

18. Francis Landry interview.

19. Dudley Stewart interview.

20. From T. Harry Williams papers on file at LSU.

21. Leon Coleman Vidrine interview.

Chapter 12 Notes

1. Williams: *Huey Long,* p. 919.

2. New Orleans *Item:* "Chronology of Life Fight," September 10, 1935.
3. New Orleans *Item:* "Doctors Give Another Blood Transfusion," September 9, 1935.
4. Personal recollection; confidential source.
5. Dr. Ashton Robins interview.
6. *LSU Medical Alumni Quarterly,* Fall 1983, No. 4; Dr. Edgar Hull interview.
7. Loria: "Historical Aspects of Penetrating Wounds of the Abdomen," pp. 546-547.
8. Drs. Thomas E. Weiss and Reichard Kahle interviews.
9. New Orleans *Times-Picayune,* September 10, 1935.
10. Fournet interview with Joe Darby.
11. Loria: "Historical Aspects of Penetrating Wounds of the Abdomen," p. 547.
12. New Orleans *Item,* "Chronology of Life Fight," September 10, 1935.
13. New Orleans *Item,* "Doctors Give Another Blood Transfusion," September 9, 1935.
14. Baton Rouge *State-Times,* September 9, 1935.
15. Ed Price interview.
16. New Orleans *Item:* "Oxygen Tent Is Used," September 10, 1935.
17. Ibid, September 9, 1935.
18. New Orleans *Times-Picayune,* September 10, 1935.
19. Redfield Bryan interview.
20. Theoda Carriere interview.
21. Baton Rouge *Morning Advocate,* September 7, 1975, "James Noe Remembers;" New Orleans *Item,* September 10, 1935, "Earl Long, Oxygen Tent Is Used;" New Orleans *Item,* September 13, 1935, "Eulogy on Long Is Delivered by Gerald K. Smith;" Baton Rouge *Morning Advocate* extra, September 10, 1935, "Senator Long Dies at 4:10 A.M.;" New Orleans *Item,* September 10, 1935, "Long's Last Words Told by Physician;" New Orleans *Item,* September 10, 1935, "Body To Lie In State;" Baton Rouge *State-Times,* September 14, 1935, "Dr. Gerald Smith Opens Drive;" New Orleans *Item,* September 10, 1935, "Long May Be Buried at the Capitol."
22. FBI papers.

Chapter 13 Notes

1. Deutsch: *The Huey Long Murder Case,* p. 124.
2. Dr. Edgar Hull interview.
3. Loria: "Historical Aspects of Penetrating Wounds of the Abdomen," p. 548.
4. Dr. Edgar Hull papers.
5. Letter to the author from Dr. Ray Lamonica, April 25, 1984.
6. Merle Welsh interview.
7. O.C. Unbehagen and Mrs. Julius Unbehagen interviews.
8. Ellen Bryan Moore interview.
9. *Time Magazine,* September 23, 1935; Baton Rouge *State-Times,* September 10, 1935, "Funeral Plans for Late Huey P. Long;" Castro Carazo interview.
10. Beals: *The Story of Huey P. Long,* pp. 291-292.
11. New Orleans *Times-Picyune,* September 13, 1935.
12. Ibid, September 12, 1935, "Senator Long's Body Lies in State;" September 13, 1935, "50 Men, Women Faint;" New Orleans *Item,* September 12, 1935, "Crowd Breaks Through Ropes;" New York *World Telegram* (?), September 12, 1935.

Chapter 14 Notes

1. Undated and unattributed article by Mercedes Garig, "Dr. Carl Austin Weiss as Pictured by Former Teacher" (probably Baton Rouge *Morning Advocate*).

2. William H. Vahey, Jr.: *Washington Post Magazine,* September 29, 1935.

3. Garig article.

4. Ibid.

5. Letter from Carl Weiss to Dr. John J. Archinard, January 6, 1931.

6. Dr. Edgar Hull: "The Last Hours of Huey P. Long: An eyewitness account" (unpublished manuscript).

7. Vahey article.

8. Zinman: *The Day Huey Long Was Shot,* p. 62.

9. Archinard letter.

10. Deutsch: *The Huey Long Murder Case,* p. 70.

11. Archinard letter.

12. Vahey article.

13. Ibid.

14. Archinard letter.

15. Letter from Carl Weiss to Dr. T.K. Golden, February 1933, quoted by Vahey.

16. Zinman: *The Day Huey Long Was Shot,* pp. 66-67.

17. Garig article.

18. Dorothy Morgan interview.

19. Pavy family interview. A number of family members participated in this interview and it is not possible to identify individual speakers.

20. Carlos Spaht interview.

21. Ibid.

22. Baton Rouge *State-Times,* September 13, 1935, "Wife of Slain Dr. Weiss Says..."

23. Redfield Bryan interview.

24. Hermann Deutsch: New Orleans *Times-Picayune,* September 2, 1968, "More Light Is Shed on Huey Long Case."

25. New Orleans *Item,* September 9, 1935, "Weiss Wept Over Long Dictatorship."

26. Pavy family interview.

27. New Orleans *Item,* September 13, 1935, "Sunday One of Happiest Days."

28. Confidential interview.

Chapter 15 Notes

1. Dr. Thomas E. Weiss interview.

2. Dr. Ashton Robins interview.

3. Unless otherwise noted, press sources used in this chapter were drawn from the E.A. Conway scrapbook on file at the Louisiana State Library in Baton Rouge.

4. Dr. Carl Weiss, Jr. interview.

5. Pavy family interview.

6. Dr. Dudley Stewart interview.

7. Pavy family interview.

8. Dorothy Morgan interview.

9. Henry Larcade interview.

10. Patsy Odom LeBlanc interview.

11. Deutsch: *The Huey Long Murder Case,* p. 79.

12. Deutsch: *Kingdom of the Kingfish,* No. 51.

13. John Fournet interview with Joe Darby, New Orleans *Times-Picayune:* "An Assassination Plot? Fournet Says Yes," September 7, 1975.

14. Joe Vitrano interview.

15. Ibid.

16. New Orleans *Item,* September 9, 1935, "Guards Feared Some Trouble."

Chapter 16 Notes

1. *The New Republic,* Vol. LXXXIV, No. 1085, September 18, 1935.
2. Undated and unattributed Walter Winchell column, probably New York *Daily News,* Monday, October (?), 1935.
3. Williams: *Huey Long,* p. 915.
4. Fournet interview with Darby.
5. Roy Wilkins: "Huey Long Says—An Interview with La's Kingfish," *Crisis,* XLII, February, 1935.
6. Personal recollection; Deutsch: *The Huey Long Murder Case,* p. 164.
7. Ruth Mae McDermott interview.
8. From the files of the Louisiana Department of Corrections, made available by Secretary John King.
9. John Kingston Fineran: *The Career of a Tinpot Napoleon* (privately published in New Orleans, undated), p. 47.
10. Brunswick Scholars interview.

Bibliographical
Notes

Appearing in print for the first time in this volume are documents obtained from the Federal Bureau of Investigation under the Freedom of Information Act. The file is composed of inter-office memoranda, correspondence to and from the Bureau, newspaper clippings, telegrams and, in several cases, correspondence between the Bureau and the White House.

I purchased something numbering close to 2,000 separate pages, which are part of a larger file going beyond 1939. I was advised by Bureau personnel that there was little beyond the file I purchased that related to Huey Long and that most of what was in the file consisted of newspaper clippings concerning the scandals that followed in the wake of Huey's death. In many cases there are multiple copies of the same stories as they appeared in different journals.

My dealings with this federal agency and its personnel were pleasant. They cooperated with me in every way and I express my appreciation to Mr. Allen H. McCreight, Chief of the Freedom of Information-Privacy Acts Branch of the FBI.

It is no reflection upon Mr. McCreight and his staff if I comment that there are obviously many gaps in the files that were supplied me. Some of the correspondence, for example, refers to other correspondence and memos that were not supplied me. My offhand conclusion is that J. Edgar Hoover, with his distaste for making public any embarrassing information, had some of the material removed.

While there is very little in the FBI files prior to 1935, what remains is revealing and gives us an insight into the operations of J. Edgar Hoover and the Bureau. The material also provides documentation for the assumption that the Roosevelt administration was watching Louisiana very closely, perhaps seeking a pretext to take pre-emptive action against Huey Long's Louisiana.

These documents have been donated to the Department of Archives and Manuscripts of the LSU Middleton Library and may be inspected there. It was one of Dr. T. Harry Williams' wishes that LSU obtain these papers. A contact by the university to the FBI elicited the information that I had already purchased a set and the FBI suggested to LSU that perhaps I might donate these papers. Dr. Steve Bensman, Social Sciences Bibliographer of the Middleton Library, contacted me and I readily agreed to donate the papers.

During the course of writing this book, I was impressed that there still remained many

243

people who had observed Huey Long personally and that many of these had information to contribute about his life and death that had never been made public. Some refused to talk, so great is the repressive aura that still surrounds this moment in history. Others were willing to talk and even gave me leads to follow.

Several gave me interviews but requested confidentiality. I have honored their wishes.

With the exception of confidential interviews, transcripts of all of my recorded conversations and interviews, along with the medical records of Our Lady of the Lake Sanitarium and those individual pages from the *Congressional Record* which mention Long from the period of 1932-35, have been given to the Louisiana State Library, in partial settlement of the debt I owe them for their gracious cooperation in preparing this manuscript.

Here follow the names of those I have interviewed or contacted in the course of preparing this work.

Freddie Adolph, Shirley Arrighi, Pat Bonnano, Tom Burbank, Castro Carazo, Doris Carnes, W.W. Carnes, Theoda Carriere, Anthony Catanzaro, John Chase, Earle Christenberry, Ray Cresson, Dr. David Culbert, Waverly Davidson, Jimmie H. Davis, Joseph Dazzio, John DeArmond, Melinda Delage, Murphy Dreher, Herman Engelhardt, Robert E. Downey, Lucille Falgout, Chris Faser, Rose Feingold, Verna Floyd, Dr. Reed Fontenot, Jim Gillis, Ashton Glassel, J.S. Goff, Ernie Gremillion, Dan Griffin, Lieutenant Peter Hand, Sam Hanna, Bert Hatten, Ms. Freddie Harris, Dr. Edgar Hull, Harold Huckaby and Hazel James.

Also Elaine Ventress Johnson, Norman Johnson, Dr. Reichard Kahle, W.M. Knoblach, Aaron M. Kohn, Roland Kizer, Dr. Ray Lamonica, Francis Landry, Dr. Hypolite Landry, William E. Landry, Henry Larcade, Francis M. LaSalle, Anna Lee, Eddie LeBlanc, Patsy Odom LeBlanc, Sheriff Elmer Litchfield, Ted Liuzza, Dr. Clarence A. Lorio Jr., Colonel Wiley McCormick, Ruth Mae McDermott, Jesse McLain, Modest Messina, Judge Cecil Morgan, Dorothy Morgan, Annie Lou Murphy, Dr. William Norris, J. Barrow Norwood, Mercedes Norwood, George Odom, J. Huntington Odom, Fred C. O'Rourke, Fred Parker, Judge John Parker, The Pavy family: Mrs. Albert Boudreaux (nee Ida Pavy), Marie, Coy and Veazey Pavy, Gerald Hugh Pettit, Sargent Pitcher, Ed Price, Kathryn Prokop, John "Red" Rice, Murphy Roden, Dr. Ashton Robins, Jimmy Robinson, Homer Russell, Mrs. Frank Schriever, Brunswick Sholars, Carlos Spaht, Dr. Dudley Stewart, John Thistlethwaite, O.C. Unbehagen, Mrs. Julius Unbehagen, Captain L. Coleman Vidrine, Dr. Ramson Vidrine, Joseph Vitrano, Dr. Carl A. Weiss, Jr., Dr. Thomas E. Weiss, Merle Welsh, Dr. Chester Williams and David Zinman.

Books

As has been noted in the text, there was no lack of editorial coverage of Huey Long. Only a freshman senator, he sometimes edged out such media notables as Franklin Roosevelt and Charles Lindbergh. I sought out the biographies and other treatments that dealt specifically with Long. I also haunted libraries and bookshops, consulting indexes of books written during the '20s and '30s that referred to him in passing while dealing with other personalities and subjects.

I owe special thanks to authors Hermann Deutsch and David Zinman, who wrote works dealing exclusively with Long's shooting and death. I am also indebted to the late Dr. T. Harry Williams, whose biography is the definitive cradle-to-grave treatment of the Kingfish. I met Harry when I was press secretary to Louisiana Governor Jimmie H. Davis and I was able to put him in touch with several of his sources. It is unfortunate that Dr. Williams' work ends as abruptly as it does, giving a lick and a promise to the shooting and death of Huey Long, relying principally on other material to describe these events. We can only wonder what his conclusions would have been had he chosen to concentrate his considerable talents upon the subject of Long's shooting and death.

Following is a partial listing of books consulted by me in preparing this manuscript.

Albani, Joseph L. *The American Mafia,* Appleton-Century-Crofts (New York 1971).

Allen, Frederick Lewis. *Since Yesterday: The 1930s in America*, Harper & Row (New York 1940).

Aronson, Harvey. *The Killing of Joey Gallo*, New American Library (New York 1973).

Beals, Carleton. *The Story of Huey P. Long*, Greenwood Press (Connecticut 1935).

Bennett, David H. *Demagogues in the Depression*, Rutgers University (New Jersey 1969).

Beschloss, Michael R. *Kennedy and Roosevelt*, W.W. Norton (New York 1980).

Briley, Richard III. *Death of the Kingfish*, Triangle Publishing Co. (Texas 1960).

Brinkley, Alan. *Voices of Protest*, Alfred A. Knopf (New York 1982).

Garrett, Charles. *The LaGuardia Years*, Rutgers University Press (New Jersey 1961).

Graham, Hugh Davis. *Huey Long*, Prentice-Hall, Inc. (New Jersey 1970).

Green, James R. *Grass Roots Socialism: Radical Movements in the Southwest 1895-1943*, LSU Press (Louisiana 1978).

Haas, Edward F. *deLesseps S. Morrison and the Image of Reform*, LSU Press (Louisiana 1974).

Harris, Thomas O. *The Kingfish*, Claitor's (Louisiana 1968).

Hebert, F. Edward, with John McMillan. *Last of the Titans*, University of Southwestern Louisiana (Louisiana 1976).

Ickes, Harold L. *The Secret Diary of Harold L. Ickes*, Simon and Schuster (New York 1953).

Irey, Elmer L. and William J. Slocum. *The Tax Dodgers*, Greenberg: Publisher (New York 1948).

Israel, Lee. *Kilgallen, A Biography of Dorothy Kilgallen*, Delacorte (New York 1979).

Josephson, Matthew. *Infidel in the Temple*, Alfred A. Knopf (New York 1967).

Kane, Harnett T. *Louisiana Hayride*, Pelican (Louisiana 1971).

Katz, Leonard. *Uncle Frank*, Pocket Books (New York 1975).

Kefauver Committee Report on Organized Crime.

Kirkham, James F. et al. *Assassination and Political Violence*, Vol. 8, U.S. Government Printing Office (Washington 1969).

Klorer, John D. *The New Louisiana*, Franklin Printing Co. (Louisiana, undated, probably circa 1938).

Koskoff, David E. *Joseph P. Kennedy: A Life and Times*, Prentice-Hall (New Jersey 1974).

Leuchtenburg, William E. *Franklin D. Roosevelt and the New Deal*, Harper & Row (New York 1963).

Logue, Cal M. and Howard Dorgan. *The Oratory of Southern Demagogues*, LSU Press (Louisiana 1981).

Long, Huey P. *Every Man a King*, National Book Co. (Louisiana 1933).

Long, Huey P. *My First Days in the White House*, The Telegraph Press (Pennsylvania 1935).

Long, Huey P. *Share Our Wealth*, Solar Age Press (West Virginia 1980). I do not vouch for the authenticity of this booklet. The publisher states, "All the body of this pamphlet is just as Huey Long wrote it." The front cover maintains, "Back in print after being 'lost' for 44 years." This may or may not be true, but it is worth reading for those who have an interest in Huey. This item, along with many of my other sources, has been given to the Louisiana State Library in Baton Rouge.

Luthin, Reinhard H. *American Demagogues: Twentieth Century*, Beacon Press (Massachusetts 1954).

Maas, Peter. *The Valachi Papers*, Bantam Books (New York 1969).

Martin, Ralph G. *Cissy: The Extraordinary Life of Eleanor Medill Patterson*, Simon and Schuster (New York 1979).

Meltzner, Milton. *Brother, Can You Spare a Dime?*, New American Library (New York 1969).

Messick, Hank. *John Edgar Hoover*, David McKay Co. (New York 1972).

Messick, Hank. *Lansky*, G.P. Putnam's Sons (New York 1971).

Messick, Hank. *Secret File*, G.P. Putnam's Sons (New York 1969).

Michie, Alan A. and Frank Rhylick. *Dixie Demagogues*, Vanguard (New York 1939).

Miller, William "Fishbait." *Fishbait, The Memoirs of the Congressional Doorkeeper*, Warner (New York 1977).

Moley, Raymond. *After Seven Years*, Harper & Row (New York 1939).

Moley, Raymond. *The First New Deal*, Harcourt, Brace & World (New York 1949).

Moquin, Wayne. *The American Way of Crime*, Praeger Publishers (New York 1976).

Nash, Jay Robert. *Bloodletters and Badmen*, Books 2 and 3, Warner (New York 1975).

Phillips, Cabell. *From the Crash to the Blitz 1929-1939*, MacMillan (London 1942).

Roller, David C. and Robert W. Twyman. *The Encyclopedia of Southern History*, LSU Press (Louisiana 1979).

Roosevelt, Elliott. *FDR, His Personal Letters*, Duell, Sloan and Pearce (New York 1950).

Roosevelt, Elliott and James Brough. *A Rendezvous with Destiny*, Putnam (New York 1975).

Rosen, Elliott A. *Roosevelt and the Brains Trust*, Columbia University Press (New York 1977).

St. Johns, Adela Rogers. *The Honeycomb*, Doubleday (New York 1969).

Salmond, John. *A Southern Rebel*, University of North Carolina Press (North Carolina 1983).

Schlesinger, Arthur M. Jr. *Crisis of the Old Order*, Houghton Mifflin (Massachusetts 1956).

Schlesinger, Arthur M. Jr. *The Politics of Upheaval*, Houghton Mifflin (Massachusetts 1960).

Sherill, Robert. *Gothic Politics in the Deep South*, Ballantine (New York 1969).

Smith, Gene. *The Shattered Dream*, William Morrow (New York 1970).

Smith, Webster. *The Kingfish: A Biography of Huey P. Long*, G.P. Putnam's Sons (New York 1933).

Swanberg, W.A. *Luce and His Empire*, Dell (New York 1972).

Swing, Raymond Gram. *Forerunners of American Fascism*, Books for Libraries Press (New York 1935).

Thomas, Gordon and Max Morgan-Witts. *The Day the Bubble Burst*, Penguin (England 1979).

Tindall, George B. *The Emergence of the New South 1913-1945*, LSU Press (Louisiana 1967).

Tugwell, Rexford G. *The Brains Trust*, Viking Press (New York 1968).

Turner, William W. *Hoover's FBI*, Dell (New York 1971).

Wilds, John. *Afternoon Story: The History of the New Orleans States-Item*, LSU Press (Louisiana 1976).

Williams, T. Harry. *Huey Long*, Alfred A. Knopf, 1969.

Williams, T. Harry. *Romance & Realism in Southern Politics*, LSU Press (Louisiana, 1966).

Wilson, Donald V. *Public Social Services in Louisiana*, Louisiana Conference of Social Welfare (Louisiana 1943).

Wolf, George, with Joseph Dimona. *Frank Costello, Prime Minister of the Underworld*, Bantam Books (New York 1973).

Zeiger, Henry A. *Frank Costello*, Berkley (New York 1974).

Zinman, David H. *The Day Huey Long Was Shot*, Ivan Obolensky (New York 1963).

Periodicals, Collections and Other Sources

I used the *Reader's Guide to Periodical Literature* from the year 1928 forward for sources of articles about Huey Long. This valuable tool is available in most libraries, although the sources listed might not be on file. I was fortunate to have the unreserved cooperation of the staff of the Louisiana State Library in Baton Rouge and was given full access to their excellent collection of Huey Long material.

I had copies made of all references to Huey Long in the *Congressional Record* proceedings of the U.S. Senate from 1930 until 1935. I also consulted the *New York Times* index for Long citations and had these copied. Both these collections have been donated to the Louisiana State Library. I made selected checks of the microfilm files in the State Library of the New Orleans *Times-Picayune* and the Baton Rouge *Morning Advocate*.

A complete listing of magazines and miscellaneous newspaper sources would be too voluminous to appear here. I will resist the temptation to grade or qualify them but I feel compelled to comment on the works of one author. Hermann Deutsch, author of a very readable book on Long's shooting which is mentioned elsewhere in this bibliography and throughout the text, was perhaps the most prolific of the Long watchers. His series of articles appearing in the *Saturday Evening Post* during the fall of 1935 is satisfying reading. His series of newspaper articles appearing in the New Orleans *Item* from July 19 to September 10, 1939 is as clear and as lively an account as was ever written about Long's entire political career. Since Deutsch covered the state capitol, his writings have the added flavor of an eyewitness.

I would advise any readers seeking to broaden their knowledge of magazine articles to begin, as I did, with the *Reader's Guide* and take it from there.

The Louisiana State Library also has several scrapbooks on file, notably the E.A. Conway scrapbook, which gives a picture of the varying ways that Long's shooting was treated by the various news media, since stories are placed side by side.

I availed myself of several master's and doctor's papers, among which were a dissertation submitted to Vanderbilt University by Matthew James Schott entitled, "John M. Parker of Louisiana and the Varieties of American Progressivism" and a no-nonsense accounting of the campaigns of Huey Long from 1918-1928 by Betty Marie Field in partial fulfillment of the requirements for a master of arts degree.

A rewarding source of raw material can be found in the Historic New Orleans Collection, a nice group of folks to work with. There is some solid historical background material on Dr. Arthur Vidrine in the medical library of Louisiana State University in New Orleans.

Index

250